Dead End Gene Pool

Dead End Gene Pool

· A MEMOIR ·

WENDY BURDEN

GOTHAM BOOKS

GOTHAM BOOKS
Published by Penguin Group (USA) Inc.
375 Hudson Street, New York, New York 10014, U.S.A.
Penguin Group (Canada), 90 Eglinton Avenue East, Suite 700, Toronto, Ontario
M4P 2Y3, Canada (a division of Pearson Penguin Canada Inc.); Penguin Books Ltd,
80 Strand, London WC2R oRL, England; Penguin Ireland, 25 St Stephen's Green,
Dublin 2, Ireland (a division of Penguin Books Ltd); Penguin Group (Australia),
250 Camberwell Road, Camberwell, Victoria 3124, Australia (a division of Pearson
Australia Group Pty Ltd); Penguin Books India Pvt Ltd, 11 Community Centre,
Panchsheel Park, New Delhi—110 017, India; Penguin Group (NZ), 67 Apollo
Drive, Rosedale, North Shore 0632, New Zealand (a division of Pearson New
Zealand Ltd); Penguin Books (South Africa) (Pty) Ltd, 24 Sturdee Avenue,
Rosebank, Johannesburg 2196, South Africa

Penguin Books Ltd, Registered Offices: 80 Strand, London WC2R oRL, England

Published by Gotham Books, a member of Penguin Group (USA) Inc.

First printing, April 2010
10 9 8 7 6 5 4 3 2

Gotham Books and the skyscraper logo are trademarks of Penguin Group (USA) Inc.

LIBRARY OF CONGRESS CATALOGING-IN-PUBLICATION DATA

Burden, Wendy.
    Dead end gene pool : a memoir / Wendy Burden.—1st ed.
        p.   cm.
    ISBN 978-1-592-40526-8 (hardcover)
    1. Burden, Wendy—Childhood and youth. 2. Burden family. I. Title.
    CT275.B785218A3   2010
    929'.20973—dc22   2009028953

Printed in the United States of America
Set in Janson Text
Designed by Victoria Hartman

While the author has made every effort to provide accurate telephone numbers and
Internet addresses at the time of publication, neither the publisher nor the author as-
sumes any responsibility for errors, or for changes that occur after publication. Further,
the publisher does not have any control over and does not assume any responsibility for
author or third-party Web sites or their content.

For my mother, goddamn it.

· CONTENTS ·

Prologue

IT'S A TESTAMENT to his libido, if not his character, that Cornelius Vanderbilt died of syphilis instead of apoplexy.

In 1794, a few miles from where his powdered bones eternally lie, within the eight-foot-thick walls of the largest tomb ever built in America, the origin of my family's fortune was born into what would prove to be a very material world. As the sixth of nine children, Cornelius was expected to pull his weight. At eleven he had dropped out of school, and at sixteen he was piloting his own small ferryboat. At nineteen he married his cousin Sophia Johnson (an act of consanguinity that arguably heralded the start of our genetic troubles) and set about fathering the first of thirteen children. By twenty-one the Vanderbilt name was on several schooners, and by thirty-five Cornelius had earned the sobriquet of Commodore and controlled a network of steamboat routes that traveled up and down the East Coast. At seventy he had the wherewithal to switch from steamships to railroads. And at seventy-five he eloped to Canada to marry a thirty-one-year-old woman named Frank.

Many colorful adjectives have been used to describe my great-times-four-grandfather: egomaniacal, unethical, coarse, brilliant, vulgar, ingenious, pigheaded, underbred, ruthless. Only one is necessary: rich. And not just a little rich; at the time of his death—in the midst of a blizzard, which caused the glass roof of Grand Central Terminal to collapse, even as its creator lay rasping his final, philandering breath—the full market value of the Commodore was in the neighborhood of 167 billion bucks.

Call it syphilitic dementia; in his will the Commodore disinherited all of his offspring—save one. William H. Vanderbilt, already in possession of the world's largest muttonchops, was ceded control of his father's fortune. To show his appreciation, he repaid his father with the monumental morgue he now resides in, a replica of the French twelfth-century church of Saint-Gilles-du-Gard in Arles, designed by the favorite architect of the Vanderbilts, Richard Morris Hunt. William H. had his father's corpse exhumed and transferred posthaste, post-construction, and interred beneath an elaborate stone relief carving of the Creation.

Eight years later, William H. was no doubt surprised at his own removal to the family vault. He now lies across the apse from his father, reposing in a kindred niche, beneath a depiction of Paradise. And whereas the Commodore died the richest person in America, his son managed to double his inheritance in the corporeal time he had left, and he died the richest person In The World.

Thankfully, William H. was more egalitarian than his father. Instead of stiffing his children, he divided his wealth (however misogynistically) between his four sons and four daughters, one of the latter, Florence, being my great-great-grandmother.

The sisters, Margaret, Emily, Florence, and Eliza, all married, and spent the remainder of their lives outbuilding one another. If a sister built a summer cottage with forty rooms, the next had to build one with forty-two. In 1877, the year her grandfather, the Commodore, died, Florence married a financier named Hamilton McKay Twombly. The groom came with his own money, and proved to be no slouch at making lots more of it. He invested all of their assets in mining ventures and transportation, and multiplied them. Florence went on to be the wealthiest of her siblings, as well as the longest lived, and she was without a doubt the biggest spender of them all. Which would explain why we, her descendants, carry the malignant code for extravagance in our genomes.

The Twomblys had four children: Alice, Florence, Ruth, and Hamilton. The family lived the simple life of the wildly rich; they wintered in New York City, in their town house, the last great private home to be built on Fifth Avenue, and when not traveling in Europe, they summered in Newport, in a fifty-room cottage on Cliff Walk, overlooking the sea.

It wasn't enough. Hamilton Twombly wanted something within commuting distance of the city. So in 1890 he purchased twelve hundred acres in Morris County, New Jersey, and enlisted the architectural services of McKim, Mead and White. Six hundred laborers were shipped over from Italy, and it took them six years to construct a 110-room rose brick and limestone Georgian house that was a faithful reproduction of Christopher Wren's west wing of Hampton Court palace. (Emulating the houses of King Henry VIII was not considered a frivolity at the turn of the century.) Thomas Edison, a neighbor and friend, designed the massive electrical generator and heating plant needed to run the estate. Stabling was built to house fifty horses, as were carriage houses and garages, a dozen greenhouses and an orangerie. Frederick Law Olmsted rearranged a hundred and fifty acres of the wild New Jersey rolling hills, and forests of oak and beech, into a series of formal gardens, terraces, and parkland. The remaining 750 acres were designated for the working farm and the dairy operation of several hundred prized Guernsey cattle, the largest such private breeding farm in the country.

The Twomblys named their labor of love "Florham," a combination of their two first names. It was close enough to the city that you could see the skyline of New York from the east terrace, and for four months out of the year, during the spring and fall social seasons, they lived, and entertained, there.

The opulence of the newly rich was at its zenith in the late 1800s, and no one did it better than my great-great-grandparents. They stuffed their houses full of "important" furnishings: Queen Anne, Georgian, Chippendale, Hepplewhite, Sheraton, and Regency furniture; seventeenth-century Barberini tapestries, paintings by Rubens and Vandyke; eighteenth-century colored mezzotints; antique Chinese and Persian rugs; Meissen, and K'ang and Ming Dynasty, porcelains; bronzes and miniatures, and gold and enamel snuffboxes; and Louis XV gilded chandeliers the size of the *Hindenburg*. They lured the highest echelon of workers imaginable, like Queen Victoria's head gardener. They had nonstop weekend house parties, and dances and lunches and teas and balls. In just two generations what had begun as a meritocracy had turned into a lifestyle that could rival that of European royalty. It was all so wonderfully arriviste, so very *American*.

Rarely do things go as planned: Alice, the eldest Twombly child, died of pneumonia when she was sixteen. Hamilton, the youngest, drowned a few years later, when he was a counselor at a camp for poor boys.

My great-great-grandfather was inconsolable over the loss of his only son. He suffered a nervous breakdown. It eventually leeched into his kidneys, and he died—a brokenhearted, if extremely wealthy, man.

Grandma Twombly, as she was now known, went on to thrive for another forty years. Tiny and birdlike, autocratic, elegant, frosty, and brittle, she worked like a party animal for her title of the Vanderbilt Hostess. As the undisputed head of old-guard New York society, she entertained lavishly, with the help of her famous French chef and her staff of two hundred, in an imperial style that few could match.

And when she finally died, at the age of ninety-eight, from

injuries sustained during a tumble in the living room–like con-fines of her Rolls-Royce limousine, it was said (by those who cared) that New York Society died with her.

Out of the four Twombly children, two daughters remained: Florence, my great-grandmother, and her younger sister, Ruth.

Ruth was never to marry. After her father's death, she as-sumed management of her mother's empire, and she excelled at running it. When her mother died, she continued to occupy the houses, and devoted the rest of her time to charitable pursuits in the City, and three-martini caviar-foie-gras lunches at Delmon-ico's and the Pavillon. A practical girl, she had rung the wine merchant the day she'd heard the Volstead Act was coming, and had stocked her capacious cellars with enough drink to last a hundred years. (We're still drinking it.)

Florence, on the other hand, did marry. Which vastly bene-fitted my father's side of the family, where we will remain, be-cause even though this book is about my father *and* my mother, the truth of the matter is my mother's family didn't have a lot of money, and my father's family did, and rich people behaving badly are far more interesting than the not so rich behaving badly.

Across and north of the river from the Vanderbilt mauso-leum, in a pastoral necropolis known as the Albany Rural Cem-etery, within the less imposing ramifications of the Burden family vault, another great-etc.-grandfather reposes away. Born within a few years of the Commodore, Henry Burden was an inventor who emigrated from Scotland and settled in Troy, New York. There he took on a job of managing the local nail and iron factory, and with the same raw talent and unerring work ethic as the Commodore (but a much nicer personality), he rose through the ranks to become proprietor of a massive foundry. The Bur-den Iron Works was famous for the world's tallest, most power-ful waterwheel, and for the world's first horseshoe-making machine, which was capable of spitting shoes out at the rate of one per second, allowing Henry, in the entrepreneurial spirit of his adopted country, to sell them (at great profit) to both armies during the Civil War.

The sons of Henry Burden worked in the ever-expanding family business. His grandsons all followed suit—except for William Armistead Moale Burden, my great-grandfather; he was destined for a far more spectacular, if spectacularly shorter, life.

William did everything right from the get-go. He went to Groton, then to Harvard, where he was captain of the football team, class president, first marshal, and president of the Hasty Pudding Club. Throughout, he even remained a devout Christian. In 1900, after only three years, he graduated cum laude, and embarked on a trip around the world, during which he was photographed repeatedly (and becomingly, for of course he was also handsome) astride everything from camels to elephants and in front of every edifice referenced in Baedeker's. Upon his return to New York he was elected a member of the New York Stock Exchange and became a partner in the banking firm of J. D. Smith and Company. And then he married my great-grandmother, Florence Twombly.

Florence must have sensed it was high time to clean up the waters of the gene pool. The family had been practically self-pollinating, what with all those cousins marrying cousins. And William in turn must have known it was time to evolve financially. The Burden fortune was known for its ups and downs, but mostly its downs, having been tossed about by several generations of ne'er-do-wells and inopportune matches.

My great-grandparents were married on April 12, 1904, in a ceremony at St. Thomas Church, in New York. *The New York Times* devoted several columns to describing what it called a "full force turnout by New York society." After a false start (a baby girl who died in infancy and was never again mentioned), William quickly sired two sons: my grandfather, William Armistead Moale Burden II, and my uncle Shirley Carter Burden. And then he died.

A *New York Times* article dated February 3, 1909, explained:

W.A.M. BURDEN DIES
OF STRANGE MALADY

Chronic Recurrent Fever the Only Name Physicians Can Give It—— No Remedy.

If one has to die of a malady, it might as well be strange.

My grandparents met at a cocktail party in London in 1928. William A. M. Burden II was fresh out of Harvard and was on leg number four of his Grand World Tour. Margaret Livingston Partridge was in Europe for the season. My grandfather was bowled over by her beauty. For their first date, he picked her up at her hotel in a supercharged four-and-a-half-liter Bentley convertible. He remembered her as being unsuitably, if stunningly, dressed in high heels and an impressively grand picture hat. Which he also recalled she had difficulty holding on to during their fourth 110 mph lap around the Brooklands Raceway, which he only noticed because while she was cowering under the dashboard, the flapping brim of her hat was obstructing the temperature gauge.

Peggy Partridge was the autumn leaf and only child of respectable, if bohemian, artist parents. Her mother was a fashionable poet and a follower of the occult. Her father, William Ordway Partridge, was also a poet, as well as a novelist and a critic, but he was famous for his portrait sculpture, such as the equestrian statue of General Grant in Brooklyn and the beautiful Pietà in St. Patrick's Cathedral, which has been handled and stroked so many times, Jesus is beginning to look conceptual.

My grandparents were married at St. Thomas Church in New York City in February of 1931. After a four-month honeymoon to just about everywhere, they settled into a cozy duplex apartment at Number 10 Gracie Square with their French chef, their English butler, and their frequently intoxicated Scottish valet. My grandfather went to work on Wall Street, and my grandmother took classes at the Art Students League on Fifty-seventh Street, where she spent her days drawing naked people in charcoal.

Right away, of course, a son was born. Then another, and another, and another. My father, the eldest, was christened (un-surprisingly) William A. M. Burden III. He did everything he was expected to. He went to the Buckley School in New York, and then to Milton Academy, and then to Harvard. Along the way he met a girl named Leslie Hamilton. They fell in love and were married when both were in college. Their future was bright and scholarly.

In September of 1951 Ruth Vanderbilt Twombly died while vacationing abroad. A week later my brother was born. And it was a good thing his father gave him a Y chromosome when he was a zygote, because otherwise he would have been stuck with the name of Ruth, instead of entering the world as—you guessed it—William A. M. Burden IV.

None of Aunt Ruth's heirs wanted anything to do with the three Brobdingnagian abodes and all their museum-quality contents; not her sister, Florence; her nephews, William and Shirley; or her great-nephew, my father. In 1955, the year I was to be born, Florham was put on the market, the Newport cottage was bequeathed to a Catholic college for girls, and the house in the city was sold. In an apocryphal four-day sale, Parke-Bernet auctioned off all of the contents of all three.

If that's not an omen, you tell me what is.

Thirty-one Moons

"YOUR ATTENTION, PLEASE—whoops!" The head stewardess, a beehived blonde, dropped her microphone. While she grappled for it on the floor of the DC-4's galley, the resultant screech and the disclosure of her pneumatic bust ensured all eyes were directed her way. "Ladies and Gentlemen," she began again, "we have a little problem. In a short while, the captain will ask all of you to . . . ah . . . to assume the crash position as illustrated in the safety information located in the seat pocket in front of you—excuse me . . . ah please, your attention again—PLEASE!"

The words *crash position* had thrown a switch. People began twisting in their seats, trying to figure out why such a measure was deemed necessary when the plane had not changed altitude for the last half hour and was, in fact, chugging nicely along. "Huh?" became "What's happening?" which then turned to "Just what the HELL is going on?" Finally the stewardess lost it and yelled, "QUI—ET!" which was the cue for the captain to assume control from the flight deck.

"Now, ladies and gents," he began, "there's nothing for y'all to get worked up about. This is a standard safety procedure we instigate whenever there is the little ol' bittiest chance of an incident acurrin'." His voice was creamy, with just the right amount of manly authority. But no one was buying that sky commander crap if the plane was going down.

A roar swelled up. Women cried out, babies squalled, and businessmen grabbed at the sleeves of the stewardesses, pleading for information and emergency cocktails.

"Oh, great," I muttered, folding my arms, "we're gonna miss *My Favorite Martian*."

"Well, if the plane crashes, maybe we won't have to go to school tomorrow?" my brother said helpfully.

"There's no way the plane's crashing, stupid. You gonna drink the rest of that Coke?"

❧

My brother Will and I were en route from Washington, DC, to New York's LaGuardia Airport to visit our grandparents. In spite of our youth—I was seven and Will eight—we were traveling alone, as we'd been doing for as long as I could remember. Our grandfather's secretary, Miss Pou (satisfyingly pronounced *pew*, as in *pee-yoo*), had been forced to book us seats in the midsection of the cabin. The humiliating rear, that quarantine semicircle reserved for losers and the grandchildren of safety-conscious men who sat on the boards of TWA and Pan Am, had already been taken by a group of dark, glittering Indian women and their children. Will and I were thrilled not to be back there and, up until this recent announcement, had been deliberately out of control—which is understandable when you've consumed five Coca-Colas in under an hour.

I couldn't decide whether to cry or hit my brother. I'd been in a horrible mood ever since that morning when I'd noticed our tickets were printed out as "Master William A. M. Burden IV and companion." Being a girl meant squat in my father's family. Honestly, you'd think I'd been born to Chinese peasants. So there hadn't been any of us for a couple of generations; you'd have thought everyone would be delighted. I liked to think that my grandmother was, but her efforts were curtailed by my grandfather. It was obvious that he would have preferred me to have Will's quieter disposition—and vice versa. He was forever telling me to stop talking and let my brother speak, and wanting only Will with him in the photo when my grandmother pulled out her Brownie.

My mother's advice was to (quote) shut up and put up. Leslie Lepington Hamilton Burden (and eventually Beer and Tobey) was not one to coddle her children with parental guidance. She'd lectured me one evening while I was lying on her bed making snow angels on the striped Mexican bedspread.

"The sooner you figure out how to deal with being a female in your father's family, the better." I'd admired her covertly as she'd cinched a wide calfskin belt over her narrow black sheath, yanking it into an extra hole with a slight grunt. Her waist was smaller than mine and she made sure I knew it.

"I'll figure it out, I guess," I'd grumbled. My mother's way of dealing sure wasn't going to be mine. On the rare times I got to see her around my grandparents, she was weirdly unlike herself and acted as sweetly subservient and dumb as Snow White. It was so *fake*.

"If I were you, Toots—"

"Don't call me Toots!" I said. I hated the nickname she used interchangeably on my brother and me. It was like some stupid moll-speak. But she had her own little language, a kind of lexicon she substituted for the vocabulary of humor she lacked; adages and names and twisting up of words that I guess she thought were funny. I found it unfunny and embarrassing. And I was already missing her. These days, it seemed I only spent time with my mother when she was getting ready to leave. My brother and I had recently come to view her as a glamorous lodger who rented the master bedroom suite.

"Why do we have to visit Gaga and Granddaddy so much, anyway?" I whined. "I feel like I *live* on Eastern Airlines." Dusty Springfield sang from the phonograph in the corner and I waggled my legs in time to "Wishin' and Hopin'." Ever since our father had abruptly died the year before, Will and I had become virtual commuters shuttling back and forth from our home in Washington to those of our grandparents in New York, Maine, and Florida.

"Oh, don't be so bratty," my mother replied, blacking in her eyebrows with a red Maybelline pencil. "There are lots of little girls who'd give up growing tits for a chance to hang out on Fifth Avenue and be waited on by servants. Hand me my lipstick?" She passed the frosted tube across her mouth and smacked a Kleenex to set it. Fabergé Nude Pink was her lifelong color of choice, a pastel shade that brings to mind Sun Belt drag queens and leather-faced Junior Leaguers. She would die wearing it.

"Anyhoo," my mother said, giving a blast of Final Net to her French twist, "you know your grandparents have insisted on this visitation schedule ever since your father turned up his toes. And so have their goddamn lawyers." She walked across the room and stood over me then, a tanned blond bombshell in a cocktail dress, fishnets, and stilettos, reeking of Diorissimo. When she leaned down, I was afraid she was going to kiss me or something, but instead she remarked with disbelief, "That can't be a pimple on your chin already!" I clamped my *CREEPY* comic book down over my head as the doorbell chimed.

Then she and Dusty sang their way down the stairs, leaving me to search my reflection in the mirror for the dreaded signs of preprepubescent acne.

❧

It never occurred to our mother when she left us at the airport that we might not be returned in the same condition. The notion that our chaste little bodies could be taken aside and fingered by unfamiliar hands didn't cross her mind. Nor did thoughts of Tunisian white slavery, the narcotic courier trade, Lower East Side sweatshops, or abduction by green pedophiles in silver pods. Or maybe they did.

She would leave us at the departure gate, Will in a blazer and clip-on bow tie, me in a scratchy plaid jumper from Best & Co., and then stride off. In the beginning, I pretended she was only going to the restroom, and that the line there was so long that by the time she rushed back, we'd already boarded. I imagined her lingering until the plane departed, blowing kisses and waving to our tiny portholes as the props whined us out to a speck in the sky. I pictured her driving home in her humpy red Volvo to an empty and joyless house where, in despondency, she'd spend the weekend organizing our rooms and planning vacations to Disneyland until she picked us up on Sunday night. But I got over that pretty quick.

Truth be known, our mother delivered us to any person wearing any semblance of a uniform standing anywhere near the gate, and left without waiting for the plane to board. From the "Standing Only" spot she had parked in, she could make it downtown to Trader Vic's in less time than it takes to put on a pair of sheer black stockings and get the seams straight.

In the early 1950s everyone married early, and my parents had been no exception. My mother had been a nineteen-year-old anthropology major at Radcliffe, and my father had been twenty-one, and a junior at Harvard. Now, a decade later, she was a young widow, and was she ever making the most of it.

"Surprise!" she would say to us at breakfast on the mornings after her returns. She'd take her hands from behind her back and plunk down some huge, hairy arachnid suspended in an alcohol-filled jar.

"Wow," we would slur through our Froot Loops, "you went to Haiti again."

"Look what else I brought you!" she'd say, holding out batik swimwear you'd rather get rat-bite fever than be seen in.

"Thanks," my brother and I would say as we grabbed our book bags and headed out the door like we were worried about missing the bus.

The presents our mother brought were our only clue as to where she'd been. Ice plants meant California. Live alligators in shoe boxes meant Miami and the Roey Plaza Hotel. Dead ones on handbags meant Tijuana. So did jumping beans. Gardenias were routine; they came from an evening of scorpions at the Outrigger Bar at Trader Vic's. We would open the fridge to get out the orange juice and find them, bruised and dog-tired from floating around in rum and dodging the straws of my mother and her date. You could see the little stab marks all over them.

For the sake of convenience, I'd learned to do a passable forgery of my mother's signature by second grade. The teachers mostly let it slide (it was a liberal primary school for the children of Washington diplomats), but when I okayed four Ds and an F in a parental note, they reeled me in.

"I'm truly sorry about your daddy," my homeroom teacher said, addressing me across her desk with compassion. "And I know your mommy is frequently out of town, no doubt dealing with her own . . . *grief.*" She adjusted her glasses. "That must be very difficult for you and your brother."

I nodded and gave a little sniff for good measure. Ha. Was she kidding? It was completely cool to have a dead father. I was the class celebrity. And I loved it when my mother was away. I hung out in the basement with my governess, Henrietta, lying on her double bed, inhaling secondhand smoke and watching *Ted Mack's Amateur Hour* or *The Ed Sullivan Show*—she with a tumbler of whiskey, and I with a bag of Wise potato chips. One thing my mother knew how to do was pick out a good governess.

Henrietta and I had a running joke about my mother's schedule.

"So when's Mommy coming home?" I'd say.

"When she's darker than Sambo, lassie," Henrietta would say back, laughing and choking on her own phlegm. Lighting a fresh Winston off the glowing butt of the last, she'd reach over and tousle my hair. "A wee more dip with those crisps, lassie?" We absolutely understood each other.

Over the PA system, the captain came on again. "I'm sure y'all have noticed we've been circling. We're trying to use up some a that big ol' tank a gas before we come on in." He proceeded to tell us that there was a little ol' problem with getting the landing wheels to go down. That got everyone thinking. Now all you could hear was the vibration of the propellers slicing evenly through the dark, and the muffled terror of people mentally preparing to die. Only the Indians in the back appeared unconcerned; what did they care—they'd be back.

My brother had gotten the window seat, despite my efforts to scratch and bite my way into it first, and since the captain's announcement, he'd been springing up and down, calling out numbers. Every time I told him to shut up, he said he was counting the moons.

"Fifteen . . . sheesh! I can't believe how many there are," Will said to his tiny oval aperture. He had his nose flat against its own reflection. The cabin lights had been dimmed for landing (or whatever), and an eerie column of light from the reading lamp bounced off my brother's crew cut.

"George is gonna be mad we're late," Will said to the glass.

"He's probably hoping the plane'll crash and we'll be dead, so he won't have to drive us anymore." I was trying to sound tough, even though my heart was starting to make weird little jumps in my chest.

Will turned from the window. "You think we have time for one last Coke?"

⊘≈⊘

At LaGuardia (or West Palm Beach, the gateway to our grandparents' house in Hobe Sound; or Bangor, ditto for the summer house in Maine), we were always met by George, our grandparents' marzipan-pink, chrome-domed, unsmiling German chauffeur. He treated my brother and me like medical waste, propelling us through baggage claim by the back of our collars with a gloved vise-grip, out to the waiting Cadillac limousine. In magnanimous moments I reasoned that because George had never married, he was unable to appreciate children, let alone share our enthusiasm for acrobatics in the back of his car. Chaperoning us was clearly beneath his dignity, but he couldn't afford to lose this job because George was a Nazi escaping justice. I knew he was a Nazi because one of my uncles was into Hitler. Uncle Ham–Uncle Ham (we called him that because he said everything twice—like "Hitler was a good man! A good man!") was my father's younger brother. He liked to neutralize the effects of his Thorazine, which he took for an as yet undiscovered but clearly out there mental condition, with coffee, Coca-Cola, chocolate bars, NoDoz, and four packs of Parliaments a day. This made him more than a little chatty, even to a kid. Over the course of a weekend with Uncle Ham–Uncle Ham, you could, through osmosis, learn enough about the Third Reich to write a dissertation on the Nuremberg Rallies.

A Jewish friend of mine from summer camp had told me that German people liked to cover their lamps with lamp shades made from the skin of Jews gassed at Auschwitz. She was three years older than me, and I believed her.

You think my grandfather's shofur has some? I'd written her by return post. (No way could I spell *chauffeur.*)

Duh, she had written back, and had gone on to graphically describe all kinds of atrocities on several sheets of Snoopy stationery, the visualization of which had kept me awake at night for a month.

I'd asked Uncle Ham–Uncle Ham if he thought George had human-skin lamp shades in his apartment, and he had laughed and nodded his head vigorously.

"You mean the green ones with the circles and squares on them?"

"That's right! That's right!" he had chortled, blowing smoke out through his nose while guzzling a highball of straight Coke.

"But that's *gross*!"

"Yes! Yes! The color was unfortunate! Unfortunate!"

After that revelation, I resolved to behave as badly as possible on George's watch, and I warned my friends that if anything fishy were to happen to me, like my skin got removed for redecoration purposes, to tell the police the chauffeur did it.

The stewardesses were demonstrating the crash position. Miss Bossy Beehive stopped and clucked her tongue at me. "*Sweet*heart, where is that seat belt? I know this is all terribly exciting, but I want your belt securely fastened. Now, show me the position you need to be in—in case we CRASH. No, sugar pie, all the way down . . ." With a hook like Cassius Clay, she slammed my head down so hard I got a carpet burn from my dress. She turned to my brother, saying, "Buckle up, little man!" Strafing me with her concrete bosom, she leaned over and nipped in his waist so hard, his rib cage shot out over the metal fastener. She nodded to herself and moved on.

"What d'you think it'll be like?" I heard Will mumble in a nasal voice. His head was turned on his lap away from me.

"What?"

"To die." He turned toward me, one eye on the retreating back of the stewardess.

"Messy, I guess."

Will sat up and grinned. "I think it's going to be pretty cool. I think we'll make a gigantic fireball and everyone will see it, from California even, and we'll get our names in the papers. Maybe they'll even name a ride at Disneyland after us."

It didn't sound so bad the way he envisioned it. In fact, it did sound sort of cool. Dammit, he would probably get to die first.

❧

Number One Son got everything before me. Even psycho-analysis.

On Saturday mornings Will went to see Dr. Berman. He had started going after our father died. According to my grandfather, it was necessary for the son to talk to someone but not the daughter. When Will returned from his appointment, I sniffed him all over like a dog checking out a mate who's been to the vet. "So?" I would demand. "Did he ask you any weird questions? Did he stick needles in you? Did you have to take down your pants?"

"Naw. We just played games," Will said.

"Well what kind of games, idiot? Cards? Mouse Trap? Stratego? Does he have Creepy Crawlers?" After jigsaw puzzles, I was obsessed with Creepy Crawlers. It was a control freak's dream set with a baking unit that could leave scars worthy of an acetylene torch. You put this liquid Plasti-Goop into molds carved with half reliefs of things like cockroaches and stinkbugs and silverfish, and scorpions and millipedes and bats, scratching the stuff into the antennae and spindly bug legs with a needle. Then you baked them in the cooker right there on the flammable shag carpeting of your bedroom floor.

"I don't know—just games!" Will didn't recognize his hour with Dr. Berman as the spotlit, center-of-attention shower of love I knew it to be.

I was burning up with curiosity; I needed to *know* what I was missing. But inevitably, my weekly joust for the dirt ended with no answers, and Will punching me in the stomach and declaring, "Dr. Berman says you're acting out 'cause you're jealous." No shit.

⁂

Anyway, that stewardess was wrong. I did not find the present situation exciting. Tragic would describe it more appropriately, because I was going to miss my eighth birthday party.

My birthday was the single day out of the year when my mother behaved like a mother. In fact, she behaved like she was running for Mother of the Year, though that didn't make up for the 364 other days when she either embarrassed me, ignored me, or was geographically elsewhere. I summoned a birthday hostess image of the Merry Widow: she was wearing her signature black stretch pants, Beatle booties, and favorite swirly Pucci blouse. Her skin was as toasty golden brown as a pretzel, her shoulder-length lemon-colored hair side-parted like a starlet's, and she held out a layer cake of heroic color and proportion, and questionable flavor. She was fond of maple or tutti-frutti cake mixes, which she enhanced according to whim, with whatever was on hand, like adding to the batter tinfoil-wrapped charms that you broke your new molars on. She wasn't great with presents either. She was the kind of person who told you on the gift card outside exactly what was on the inside. However, she made up for it with her contagious enthusiasm. And her decorations and games were truly inspired. No insipid Pin the Tail on the Donkey for us; it was a real donkey and a real horse tail that you had to slap on the animal's butt with masking tape. Or, in the case of my brother's most recent birthday party, a thumbtack, which caused the donkey to place his hind feet on the ribs of Brian O'Donahue and send him flying backwards into the library bookcase.

She really was the best. All the kids in my class were so jealous of me.

Overwhelmed, I began to cry, which put me close to drowning in my mayday position.

"Twenty-three . . . Hey, look down there on the ground! They've put Crazy Foam all over the place!" my brother squealed. He was having a blast.

"Shut up, dumbbell," I hissed, and bit his elbow for good measure.

I stared at him with self-indulgent hatred as the airplane droned steadfastly in its orbit over Queens. Will was only a year and a half older than me, but my grandparents treated him like he was off to college. This past Christmas, instead of a pony, which was what I'd begged for, Santa had brought me an Hermès scarf printed with Lipizzaner horses, a fawn-colored cashmere Hermès cardigan with velvet appliquéd horse heads, and a topaz bracelet in a velvet box from Tiffany's. Nothing you crow about to your second-grade classmates when school reconvenes. My brother, in addition to a television, an electric typewriter, Davy Crockett pajamas, a four-lane slot-car racetrack, and Rock'em Sock'em Robots, had gotten the pony. After all the presents had been unwrapped, I had raged at my mother, who was making a rare Yuletide appearance on a stopover between Palm Springs and Tenerife. We were in one of the guest bedrooms of my grandparents' apartment in New York. My mother was in a pink striped bikini, stretched out on the carpet in a contorted pose beneath a couple of carefully positioned sunlamps.

"Why does stupid Will get a pony when *I'm* the one who takes all the riding lessons?" I'd sobbed from the bed where once again I had flung myself.

My mother had done her best to comfort me. She totally got the horse-love thing. Speaking in a monotone without moving, so that her eye protectors wouldn't shift, she said, "I'm sorry, Toots, I know how you feel, but your grandparents gave him the horse. Don't look at me."

"Why didn't you stop them? You should have told them he hates horses!"

"Oh, get over it. They decided he should have a horse. End of story." She was done comforting. "And listen, if I were you, I'd get over potato chips too. Oink, oink."

I put my hands up to my chipmunk cheeks. As if she could see this, my mother smoothed her own hands over her own nutmeg-colored, flat-as-a-cow-pie abdomen. She flexed her painted toes a few times to ease the strain of the peculiar tanning position she was in.

"Hey. Sometimes that's just how the cookie crumbles."

I got up to leave. I had a mind to go finish the bag of Cheetos I'd hidden in the help's pantry.

"I know where your stash is, Toots," she said as I was doing my best Indian walk out the door. "And hey, tell Adolph, or Albert—whatever the new butler's name is—tell him to bring Mummy another daiquiri, would you? There's a good girl."

The following afternoon I attempted to snuff out my brother by shoving him out of the limo into midtown Manhattan day-after-Christmas-sale-mania traffic. He had swung out like a cartoon character, holding on to the handle of the huge door with the tenacity of a booger, while it yawned out over the whizzing tarmac of Fifty-seventh Street. We'd traveled that way for several blocks until George braked to avoid mowing down a police officer.

Yeah, I got in trouble, but it was worth it.

❧

"What d'you think the Crazy Foam's for anyway?" Will said to me now. I sat up and unbuckled myself, after checking to make sure the stewardess wasn't looking. "Let me see," I said, shouldering him out of the way.

"I'll tell you what the foam's for." The passenger across from us put out his hand and laid it on the armrest of my vacated seat. He was so tall it was no effort for him to lean across the aisle. Will and I, crowded into the window seat, stared at the huge boney paw, the veins raised and the knuckles lumpy, and then at his long pale face. The man's tortoiseshell reading glasses were pushed up onto his forehead like they were surfing a wave of mangy caterpillars.

"The foam," he said, "is to cushion the plane's fuselage when we land on the runway without the aid of wheels. The pilot will attempt to slide the aircraft down the asphalt runway without it, and us, igniting into a ball of fire."

"Oh" was my response. That, and a little spurt of pee into my Carter's.

"Coooolll," breathed my brother, turning back to the window. "There's another! That makes thirty-one. I gotta tell my science teacher about this."

Engrossed in his moon tabulation, Will was oblivious to what the rest of us knew to be happening. I felt a swell of affection for him, like he was a dumb puppy or something, and I pressed close beside him at the window. I looked out into the apocalyptic night. As we glided slowly over the airport, I could see emergency vehicles clustering below, their red and white lights like the beating hearts of cornered mice. They were alarmingly visible even from our height of ten thousand feet.

I had never known real fear before. No person, no thing had really frightened me. When my brother had led me downstairs to the policemen in our living room, on the night our father's body was found, I hadn't been afraid, just confused. But something about those flashing lights below terrified me, because they validated the certitude of death in a way my father's could not. This was real, because this was for me.

Popeye

ON THE EVENING of the day my father died, I was in my bedroom on the second floor swinging a red leather dog leash around my head, trying to graze the overhead light with the brass clip. This was a forbidden pastime for me, and I had a jagged red scar on my shoulder to prove it, but there I was, moth to the flame, at it again. This was how my brother found me when he threw the door open.

"Get out!"

Will just stood there, all quiet and serious, like someone had drained the kid out of him.

"Okay, what?" I said, dropping my weapon.

"Daddy's dead."

"Oh, is *that* all," I fake-laughed.

We stood there, eyeballing each other. Then he spun around and started walking back down the hall. I followed him, silently, to the stairs, and down to the landing, where we paused to listen. There was a murmur of deep voices, but none that I knew. I could just see into the living room below, but all I caught was the back end of Obadiah, our basset hound, his tail clamped hard between his quivering hind legs.

I followed Will down the rest of the stairs, my hand dragging squeakily on the waxed banister, my nightgown catching under my bare feet. Our mother was perched on a chair near the empty fireplace. She didn't see us, even though we were practically in front of her. Her face was composed, but it was very red. I knew that look; it was her version of crying. On either side of her stood two tall policemen in dark blue uniforms. Obadiah was sitting at our mother's feet, staring up at her, registering far more readable emotion in his soupy eyes and drooping expression than his mistress. Will and I just stood there, facing them.

Something about everyone's body language told us to keep our distance. No one said anything to us. No one explained why there were a couple of DC cops standing with their hats in their hands in the room we used for company and for Christmas. The only reason we were down there was because my brother had overheard my mother get the phone call.

When Will didn't turn and pinch me and say *See?* in a bratty way that would have validated my stubborn mistrust, I began to think our father might really be dead after all.

I don't remember how I got back upstairs, or into bed, but that night I dreamt I was standing next to a boxing ring. Brutus and Popeye were the contestants, and Brutus was really letting Popeye have it—fists were flying, hooks and jabs and uppercuts and below-the-belt punches and everything else they did in fights in the cartoons. Finally a right hook sent Popeye to the floor in a crumpled heap. Clearly, there wasn't any spinach around. The referee counted it out, and Brutus was declared the winner. Popeye struggled to his feet and staggered over to where I was standing by the ropes. On the way, he morphed into my father. Swaying before me, he said, "I'm all right, Wendy, really I am," over and over. His eyes were two crosses, and that's how I knew, on my six-year-old terms, he was dead.

In the morning the policemen were gone, and our mother was nowhere to be found. With minimal conversation, Henrietta got us up, and my brother and I went to school as if nothing was wrong. I was dying for some kind of recognition. Something momentous had happened to me and, unbelievably, nobody wanted to notice.

By third period I couldn't stand it any longer. I raised my hand. Miss Clark ignored me. I waved and wiggled and flapped my arm until she had no choice but to acknowledge me.

"Yes?" she said, looking at me like I was a scary thing in the road she had to go around. The children twittered around me in the hopes of a comeuppance.

I stood up. "My father died last night," I announced.

My classmates sniggered and looked at me like I was telling the mother of all attention-getting fibs.

Miss Clark called for silence and then, with excruciating kindness, said, "We know, dear. Now, please sit down."

That shut everyone up. Not only was the homeroom teacher wigged out, but also "death" was an abstract notion. Especially the death of a father. In fairy tales the mother was the one who always got killed: Bambi's mother, Cinderella's and Snow White's. (*The Lion King* was eons away.)

On the playground later, a boy I had a crush on asked me how it had happened. I had no idea, but, acutely aware of my nascent celebrity, I told him my father was brutally murdered by a man with a black beard.

I don't remember anything after that, even though I am able to recall all of Anne Francis's outfits in *Honey West* and the exact pattern of moles on the back of Ward Tattenall's head from when I sat behind him in third grade. Will and I were not allowed to go to the funeral, and nobody talked about what had happened. It was like the daddy slate had been wiped clean. We had hardly known him when he was alive, he was such a remote parent, but you'd think in death he'd at least be talked about.

Up until my inadvertent catapult to fame, I had been a quiet, well-behaved, myopic kid with unruly red hair and good grades. I got pushed around on the playground, and my brother regularly made me eat Milk-Bones to keep me in line. If I refused, he punched me in the stomach. Well, sayonara to all that. Nobody was going to ignore *me* again. I became the precocious loud-mouthed showman that teachers shrink from in bad visions. D+ was my call letter, inattention my consort.

Consequently, I got to know the principal, Mrs. Johansen, a whole lot better. The blue upholstered chair in front of her desk became as familiar to my butt as the toilet I shared at home with my brother.

"What are you in for this time?" she would remark, shoving a mountain of folders off the chair so I could sit down.

"I dunno," I'd say and shrug, knowing full well it was for something like eating handfuls of mud at recess and charging morons twenty-five cents to watch me do it. Or pooping in my underwear on purpose. Or hoarding all the red and blue squeaky pens in art class and then scribbling all over Louise Close's rainbow masterpiece. After an amount of time Mrs. Johansen knew my teachers would deem sufficiently punishing, during which I sat contentedly munching on Euphrates crackers, of which she was inordinately fond, I would be escorted back to my classroom.

Afternoons I ran with a neighborhood gang of older kids, eight- and nine-year-old Wonder Bread–white boys. I was the only girl and proud of it. Our territory was three square upper-middle-class blocks of mellow old Washington houses with leafy yards and new cars parked in the driveways. We communicated with a call that was somewhere between the cry of a howler monkey and the Bedrock quittin' time whistle.

My gang status was secured the afternoon I got into a cat-fight with a girl who had recently moved into the neighborhood. Her house was the biggest and fanciest one around, and it was set up high over an elm tree–lined sidewalk that looked like an illustration for shifting tectonic plates, what with all the roots snaking under it. The turbulent concrete wreaked havoc with my Sting-Ray's training wheels and made my roller skates go from twenty to zero without warning. I felt the new girl was to blame for all that, plus she was so ugly that two separate dogs had bitten her in the face on two separate occasions. And dogs know.

I can't remember who made the initial overture, but we agreed to settle it at the alligator graveyard in my backyard. Behind our house, a long grassy triangle ran down a steep hill to a stand of three tall maples. At their base was a collection of tiny pebble-marked graves containing the curled-up corpses of a dozen baby alligators. I had spent a lot of time organizing the little cemetery, and I kept it raked and ordered, and solemnly decorated with pansies from my mother's straggly flower bed up the hill. The most recent inductee had arrived from Miami with my name on its box, and only three legs. It had quickly succumbed to crippledom, though Will's alligator was still alive (of course), so it had to endure bath time twice each night in 120-degree water, with Mr. Bubbles, to compensate for its continued good health. It would be in the ground in another week.

The ugly girl and I went at each other in the flattened dirt, name calling and swinging misses and clawing the air. The boys ringed us, yelling and egging us on, and I felt like an Indian princess warrior. We were getting absolutely nowhere, when suddenly my opponent grabbed my hair and pulled out a massive chunk. I couldn't believe my scalp had betrayed me like that. We both stood there in disbelief, she with a nine-inch-long ponytail in her thin fist, me with a reddening bald spot over my brow. Now I was mad. My hair was just starting to be a big deal to me, and I had spent the night before trying to deconstruct the mystery of Spoolies. I lunged for her, grabbing her sleeveless cotton shirt and ripping it off her sunken torso, revealing inverted nipples and a strawberry birthmark that looked like the head of one of the dogs that had bitten her.

The ugly girl ran home mortified, and I was cheered by the boys, including some of the ten-year-olds. Even after I was forced to apologize to the ugly girl and her mother, who was always dressed in a fancy ruffled dressing gown, no matter what the time of day, I had the sharp, delicious taste of victory on my tongue.

For weeks I glowed. I finally *mattered*.

That revelatory feeling even carried me through the birth of my brother Edward, a few months later, and my unceremonious demotion from the status of youngest child. The question of whether my mother even knew she was harboring a two-inch embryo when she received the call from the city morgue remains a mystery.

❧

We stayed on in the house on Forty-second Street for another year. The week before we moved, I was up in the attic after school one afternoon, languidly poking around in some cardboard boxes. When my father's youngest brother, Ordway, used to stay with us on weekend leave from boarding school, he always brought a hoard of *Playboy* magazines, and I was trying to find his leftover stash. I was pretty sure they were well hidden after the last time I had uncovered them (and planted one in my brother's room, open to Miss December), but I kept up the search.

Over by the south-facing window there were some cardboard file boxes sealed up with tape and string. Tape and string means one thing to a busybody: *Open me.*

The first box was boring: just a bunch of files, checkbooks, and gun magazines. The second box was all gun magazines, and so I almost didn't open the third, but I did. On top of a pile of manila folders, positioned squarely in the center, was a newspaper clipping. The headline, in heavy italics read:

WILLIAM BURDEN 3D IS RULED A SUICIDE

Washington, Feb 28–A certificate of suicide was issued today in the death yesterday of William A. M. Burden 3d. He
was found shot in the head in his automobile . . .

I sat back on my heels and tried to absorb this piece of information. I knew what suicide meant, but because it said *shot in the
head*, it sounded like someone else had done the shooting.

I skimmed the rest, anxious I might be caught, because surely
this was way worse than looking at centerfolds. My eye focused
on the end: *a son, William, 7, and a daughter, Wendy, 6.*

The very last word was my name! And ha ha ha, I wasn't six
anymore, I was seven and a half. I threw the clipping back in the
box, slammed down the flaps, resticking the tape as best I could,
and raced for the stairs. I had to tell someone my name was in
the papers!

Gaga in the Jungle

THE FORMER MARGARET Livingston Partridge was listed in the Social Register of 1963 as Mrs. William A. M. Burden II, mother of three surviving sons and two grandchildren, member of several prominent clubs, and chatelaine of four impeccably located residences, as well as one yacht. The long list of her charitable and social affiliations conjured up a woman of ceaseless energy, but in truth, my grandmother was never happier than when recumbent.

Before she faced her day in the ruthless jungle of Manhattan, my grandmother had her breakfast served to her in bed. At seven the butler carried in the newspapers and a tray table set with starched, floral Porthault linens, white Limoges china, and a silver Hermès thermos of Colombian coffee. The menu never varied: three stewed prunes and a bowl of All-Bran. As the butler retreated, he powered up the big RCA television across from the bed and tuned it to *The Today Show.*

At seven-thirty a maid collected the twin toy poodles to walk them around the block, and my grandmother began her day.

The chef appeared first, notebook in hand. He was received in bed.

"*Bonjour*, Madame."

"*Bonjour*, Chef.

"*Aujourd'hui*, Madame, I 'ave some nice haricots verts from the con-tree."

"Lovely."

"An some feegs from California."

"Very nice."

"Pear-aps tonight some 'alibut, *oui*?"

"Marvelous. We'll be six, and Monsieur will choose the wine."

"Of course, *merci*, Madame."

Monsieur, who liked to be referred to as the Honorable William A. M. Burden II, but whom everybody called Bill, and his wife called Popsie, had risen much earlier and breakfasted, as always, on scrambled eggs with truffles. And he had already worked out the next two weeks of meals with the chef before departing for work.

Angelle, the lady's maid, presented herself as the chef departed. She was a sweet, dimwitted soul who was married to Adolphe, the butler. Informed as to Madame's choice of the day's wardrobe—morning, afternoon, and evening—Angelle bustled away to select, press, steam, and polish.

Finally, the gaunt Swiss housekeeper entered.

"Good morning, Mrs. Burden," said Ann Rose in a voice that sounded like she was introducing *Tales from the Crypt*. She consulted the schedule she had typed out in quadruplicate. "You have a fitting for the Givenchy ball gown in half an hour, and then your usual hair appointment at the Sherry-Netherland. Lunch is at Grenouille with the directors' wives. The car will then take you to Bergdorf's to look for a pocketbook and shoes for the two new Mainbocher suits you ordered. You have an appointment back here with the decorator to replace the carpet in the Hobe Sound pool house; then tea with the head of the co-op committee to discuss updating the doormen's uniforms; then cocktails at the Modern; and then back home for dinner with your guests."

"Right-o," said my grandmother cheerfully, as she penciled in 28 Down in the *Times* crossword. Like my mother, my grandmother had her own funny roster of words and expressions, and anyone else saying them would have sounded mental. She said things like *isn't she cunning* for isn't she cute, or *jazzy* and *snappy* for good-looking. If you were having a good time, you were *gay*. My brother and I called her Gaga because that's the name she herself came up with when Will was born, not knowing that before long it would prove to be a self-fulfilling prophecy.

❧

My brothers and I spent at least two weekends a month with our grandparents, something that had been instigated, at their demand, after our father died. During the school year most weekends were spent in New York, sometimes at their country estate forty minutes away in Mount Kisco, but usually in the city, at their apartment on Sixty-third Street and Fifth Avenue. My grandmother especially lingered in bed on Sunday mornings, and when I was really small, I would fetch a picture book from the hallway shelves and climb in with her. I'd wedge myself between her warm quilted side and the bumpy spines of the poodles, the frills of her bed jacket tickling my cheek as she brought *Babar* or *Norman the Doorman* to life in her funny old-fashioned accent. Every New Yorker has a version of the city that they love best, and that remains mine—when it was all about going to FAO Schwarz and the zoo, and looking in the windows at Tiffany's; and the smell of my grandmother's Chanel No. 5, and the sun filtering through long Belgian linen curtains while we read books and the sea of yellow checker cabs honked pleasantly below.

My grandfather was a busy man. In addition to heading up the family venture capital company that bore his name, he was an expert aviation consultant to the government, a director of the Council on Foreign Relations, and on the boards of a dozen relevant companies. He was a thoroughly modern man: he collected modern art, he lived in a modern apartment, he weekended and summered in modern houses, and, to his profound satisfaction, he was president of the Museum of Modern Art.

Accordingly, my grandparents' apartment looked as if it had been professionally decorated by Dr. Seuss. Against the starkness of the huge rooms, long stripped of their prewar moldings and parquet, the walls bone white and the floors alabaster, art provided animation. Calder mobiles spun from the ceilings. Naked African sculptures posed in corners next to fluid marbles by Arp. What seemed like acres of wall space were hung with abstracts by Klee, Kline, Mondrian, and Miró; and figurative works by Léger, Bacon, Picasso, Matisse, and Seurat. A monolithic Brancusi bronze loomed over a black thirty-foot pond set into the pale marble concourse that ran the length of the apartment. A school of anemic goldfish lapped the pond's three-inch depths, regularly driven to suicide by the absence of plastic pirate treasure and aqua-colored gravel.

I sort of liked the place. That is, until I discovered Charles Addams.

On this particular spring morning my grandmother was still recumbent. She was reading aloud to her late son's final contribution to the world: my baby brother. At a year old, Edward was happy for anyone's attention.

I was sulking, having been publicly rebuked at dinner the previous evening for divulging my plans to pursue a career in mortuary science. I was seated Indian style in the long booklined hallway that led from my grandparents' suite to the back staircase. *Dear Dead Days*, an Addams compendium of deliciously macabre photographs, lay open across my knees. I count the Addams Family books among the most influential literary and philosophical forces in my life. For one thing, they were an early admission to the intellect of the adult world without having to read more than a sentence or two per page, the most demanding words being *blunt instrument* or *cyanide*, and the sentences rarely more complex than *"Careful of poison ivy, Lois."* Plus, they made death seem like fun. I'd fortuitously come upon the Addams due to erratic cataloging, *Nightcrawlers* having been reshelved next to my favorite gross-out book, *Life's Epic of Man.*

I scooted over to look up *embalming* in the encyclopedia.

The embalmer washes the body with germicidal soap and replaces the blood with embalming fluid. I snapped the volume shut as I heard someone creep up behind me. It was only Selma. She was about a hundred years old, and it was all she could do to squeeze the orange juice in the morning and exchange the plates on the dining table at lunch and dinner (replacing the cold service plate with a hot soup plate, replacing that with a hot dinner plate, replacing that with a dessert plate and finger bowl, then removing the used finger bowl, then the dessert plate and finally setting down the coffee cup and saucer). Selma could have witnessed me carving up my two brothers for all I cared; her sanity had been seriously in question ever since she'd seen the Virgin Mary outlined in potatoes and carrots. "Right there in me own stew she was, plain as the nose on your face, bless us and save us!"

Selma proceeded on her way, and I bent back to the book.

Embalmers may reshape and reconstruct disfigured or maimed bodies using materials such as clay, cotton, plaster of Paris, and wax. Wow. Talk about arts and crafts.

I had been in this morbid phase for about six months now, though I'm not sure anyone had noticed. On weekends, when I didn't have to wear a school uniform, I dressed in black button-down cardigans and did my hair in two braids like my soul sister, Wednesday Addams. Gone were the leaping horses I used to doodle on everything; now I drew little memento mori: skulls on the telephone pad, scythes in my school notebooks, dark ravens across my grandfather's *Wall Street Journal* and *Economic*

Review. On Santa's knee at Macy's I had requested an embalming table, a pony, and a subscription to *American Cemetery.*

To reiterate, last night's dinner had not gone well. My brother Will and I were not usually allowed to eat with the grown-ups, but an exception had been made because a godparent was there. Between the *potage St. Germain* and the *pigeonneau à la diable,* there was a lull in the conversation. Personally, I can't stand a quiet dinner table. "Hey, did you know," I addressed the elderly dyspeptic on my left, "that up to five hundred different kinds of plankton can be found in the juice that comes out of drowned people's lungs?" (I had an emerging talent for regurgitating text.)

"Do have some more of the chicken, dearie," my grandmother quickly said. "You're wasting away!"

"No thank you," I said. Show me an eight-year-old who likes pigeon.

The godfather directed his attention to my brother. "Young William," he called to him across the chrysanthemums and candles and Steuben glass animals crowding the table, "I'll wager you want to become a financier like your grandfather when you grow up, eh?" My brother stared at him for a moment and then resumed picking at his dinner roll, body language that cued my grandmother to slide her jeweled evening slipper out to the buzzer concealed beneath the table. This she stomped on for a good five seconds. *DRINNGG!* The electrical jangling ping-ponged around the dining room, ricocheting off an abstract sculpture of a naked lady and onto a cubist portrait of someone's three-eyed mistress before skittering aurally across the long, dark green marble table.

"Well *I'm* considering a career in mortuary science," I confided to Will's godfather. His dewlaps shuddered in disgust.

"With an emphasis on restorative art," I added.

DRINNGGG!! went the buzzer again. Adolphe burst through the door, with Selma and the equally rheumatic Anna trailing in his wake. My grandmother started, surprised (albeit pleasantly) by the appearance of her staff. She believed the communication between dining room and pantry to be telepathic.

I switched to the dowager on my right. "When I'm in junior high, which I know is not for five years, I can get in on the ground floor with a summer job waxing the hearses and—"

"That's enough!" my grandfather shouted.

I'd then been excused, and glad of it.

⁓⁓

The book my grandmother was reading to my brother was Ludwig Bemelmans's *Fifi*. Less popular than *Madeline* (and infinitely more entertaining), it's a mildly racist tale of a naughty poodle, told in rhyme and child-scary pictures. Lady Fimple Fample is a stout, no-nonsense English woman of middle age who is on her way to visit the dentist in Zanzibar. Fifi, her slathering, beribboned white poodle, escapes to chase a cat (meaning leopard) when the plane stops to refuel. The formidable Lady Fimple Fample sets out to rescue her dog, navigating the jungle in sensible tweeds and long pointy-toed brogues, whacking at the dense undergrowth with her walking stick. The natives who plan to boil up Fifi for supper are scantily clad, with bones in their noses and hair. The women have the apple-breasted figures of supermodels, though genetic mutation has left them without nipples; and they are clearly devious.

When my grandmother had first read me the book, I'd been concerned that Fifi was entering the stockpot without adequate preparation.

"How come the natives they don't skin her? I mean, what about all that dog hair?" I had asked. But my grandmother had only farted—*brfffttt!* That was as verbal as she got when she chose to pass something by. (My grandmother was enormously flatulent. I know older people tend to be gassy, but she topped the charts. She blasted her way in and out of rooms, down hallways, getting up from or into an armchair, and when she laughed. You would hear a *brrffft brrffft brrffft* with each step she took. Or a rhythmic squeak. Sometimes, it went *ah-hrrrt ah-hrrrt ah-hrrrt* in a trumpet toot, especially at night.)

I sat on the edge of the pink George Jetson chair at my grandmother's makeup station and stared at my face in the big table-top mirror as my grandmother pointed out the pictures to Edward. The face that stared back bore the kind of icky pinky flush that goes with red hair. Way too healthy for an Addams. I searched around for something to tone it down to a sickly pallor, sorting through the feminine paraphernalia that took up about six linear feet of the long desk running beneath the windows. My rummaging shook the forest of spiraling jewelry trees grouped around the mirror; the pairs of earrings perched on the coils like garish songbirds of the genuses Schlumberger, Verdura, and (the common) Ciro, and I paused to rearrange them in order according to species, size, and color.

After she dressed, my grandmother sat down before this mirror each morning to apply foundation, darken her brows, put on lipstick (Revlon's Cherries in the Snow), and smudge rouge into her cheeks. She'd untangle a fresh hairnet from a tissue envelope and stretch it carefully over her Clairol Ash Blonde hairdo, humming while she worked. (She hummed as much as she farted.) Then she'd select a pair of ear clips, a necklace—always pearls—and one of the heavy gold-and-enamel bracelets that were stacked on a little velvet pole. A suitable wristwatch and gloves completed the toilette. Thus armed and adorned, her grit enriched with a prophylactic nip or two, my grandmother would stride forth into the concrete jungle to negotiate the Avenues, or the chatter and howl of charity luncheons, or the exotic labyrinth of ground-floor shopping at Bergdorf's.

"Gaga," I said, twisting around to face the bed, "don't you think Granddaddy was a lit-tle hard on me last night?" A small frown creased my grandmother's brow as she tried to remember what had happened between the hours of six and ten. The children had been at dinner, yes. Popsie had led an erudite discussion, as usual. Dessert had been . . . had been . . . oh, yes—a marvelous *coeur à la crème*! "I don't think so, dearie," she said to me with a smile, and resumed reading to Edward, who was now sucking noisily on a poodle ear (and would, within the hour, require two stitches).

"Gaga," I interrupted again, "do you plan to be embalmed with herbs and spices like they used in the olden days, or good old formaldehyde?"

My grandmother responded with a *boouuffft*. Words like *embalm* or *suicide* found no harbor in her little gray cells. This could have been a by-product of her faith; her father, the celebrated sculptor, and mother, esoteric poetess, had raised their only child to be a Christian Scientist. My grandmother claimed a firm belief in the human spirit's ability to assuage the body's physical ills, though you would never have guessed this from the *Valley of the Dolls* hoard of sedatives and amphetamines in her medicine cabinet.

As the vacuous Fifi chased after a kitty that grew in size and spots, I rifled idly through the wide birch drawers beneath my grandmother's desk. Most of them contained seemingly random overstock: dozens of detachable Turnbull and Asser collars, all with embroidered initials and dates, boxed up, brand-new Tag Heuer stopwatches, and piles of foreign stamps on envelope corners awaiting cuttelage and placement in my grandmother's stamp collection. There were rolls of penny stamps, sealed boxes of 14k gold Cross pens, and a prodigious assortment of magnifying glasses. In one drawer there must have been forty years' worth of prescription eyeglasses that had never been worn. In another, enough cellophane-wrapped packages of Bicycle playing cards to supply all the summer camps along the Eastern Seaboard. Tucked beneath them were at least twenty unworn full-length kidskin gloves for white-tie dinners, and a holiday collection of miniature sweaters and booties for the poodles. There were newspaper clippings and spent diaries, an assortment of Bibles—leather, paper, vinyl, miniature, micro, large print, French, Italian, illustrated, and Braille—and wondrously fanatical pamphlets that warned of disasters and afflictions, ranging from the Apocalypse and masturbation to anti-Darwinism.

The drawers on either side of my grandparents' bed were reserved for their sleeping masks. To facilitate the after-lunch snooze, and to conk out at night, both had to be in a blackout void. Seconal helped, as did curtain liners the weight and density of X-ray-shielding lead aprons, but the masks were crucial. They were little pillowy things shaped like welding goggles; basic black, red plaid for the country, and cobalt blue faux Chinese brocade for festive occasions.

(One night my brother and I stole into our grandparents' bedroom because we wanted to see what people looked like when they snored. We just about died laughing because they looked like a couple of sleeping bandits.)

From time to time the family photos displayed along the desk were refreshed, and on this particular day there were some new additions. There was my brother on his goddamn pony. I removed it from the silver frame and slipped the photograph down my waistband to be mutilated at a more opportune time. And my uncle Ordway in a police car, not sitting in the back like any self-respecting undergraduate would have been in 1964, but in the driver's seat. Who the hell would go to Harvard and join the campus riot police?

I put down the Max Factor pancake I was applying to get a closer look at a new color enlargement. My grandmother posed amid a flock of stony African natives, towering over them, a statuesque blue-eyed ageing beauty in a chic dove-colored suit and workaday double-stranded natural pearls. The striped feathers of waving headdresses barely reached her square chin. The men had tough matte-skinned faces of a color so black it was navy. Their broad noses had flared nostrils, and there were raised, tattooed scars across their sharp cheekbones. The man on my grandmother's left, presumably the chief, was wearing a sort of bonnet made from dark fur trimmed with a border of white cowrie shells. He held a red beaded spear close to his bare chest. My grandmother held her crocodile pocketbook close to hers. In contrast to the men's unease, she was smiling away, a smudge of lipstick on her front teeth, like she'd just spent quality time at Bonwit Teller. You could practically smell the Dubonnet on her breath.

"Unrgdfoo!" said Edward.

"Aarrrrrr," snarled the poodle with the wet ear, and it plopped down off the bed to go urinate in a corner of the pink-carpeted bathroom.

My grandmother had come to my favorite part. Fifi was about to be boiled alive by the natives. As Lady Fimple Fample handed over a few nose bones she kept in her pocketbook expressly for such rescues, I asked about the photograph.

"Oh, well *that*, dearie," she said, removing an eye mask that had somehow fallen onto her head, "that was when Popsie and I were in the Congo."

I found that pretty exotic, and told her so.

"Not as exotic as the worms they found in Daddy's tummy when we returned home," she said, laying the book aside and settling back on the enormous floral pillows. "That picture was taken the day I met the king of the Bakubas."

I prostrated myself beside her on the bed. "Sounds like the king of the elephants," I said, because there was Babar, wearing his kelly green suit, on the cover of a book Edward was gnawing on.

"The jungle was marvelous, but Jiminy Cricket—the transportation!"

My grandmother, not exactly a *North to the Orient* kind of

girl, was routinely tested just riding in a taxi from East Sixty-third Street to the Met. She was a modern woman only when it came to self-medication—in that field she was a pioneer. Nearly every form of surface travel worried her, although she quite liked first-class Pullman sleeper cars and five-star corner cabins on the Cunard line. When the mood for adventure struck, she took gentle drives in the country (disregarding all road signs) in her ultramarine Studebaker. She found plenty of excitement just window-shopping along Madison Avenue with her skittering animals attached to leashes the weight of fishing line. If you'd seen her, humming and farting and smiling at everybody along her way, you'd have thought she had the IQ of a pull toy.

It was ironic that my grandmother had married a man besotted with the internal combustion engine. To paraphrase the member profile for *Burden, William A. M.*, in the 1939 *Town and Country* social directory, romance, for my grandfather, was centered in the engine of a car or a boat or an airplane. Following that premonitory first date, and since their marriage in 1931, my grandmother had been compelled to grit her big teeth and partner her husband around the world in all manner of motor-driven vessels, from the *Graf Zeppelin* to the Concorde. For her bravery, she was rewarded with enough jewelry and haute couture to wear into the afterlife.

When I was little, I thought that was how people showed their affection for one another—by buying lots and lots of *stuff*. I had little thought to spare for my grandparents' love life. Believe me, if I had thought about it, it would have grossed me out. It wouldn't be until very much later, when one was dead and the other on her way out, that I would get to know, through the written word, the sweetness and intensity of their courtship, and the depth of love they had for each other.

During the Eisenhower administration, my grandfather was ambassador to Belgium. You would have thought he was royalty brought back from exile by the manner in which he conveyed wife, butler, chef, chauffeur, and Cadillac limousine with blacked-out chrome; an extensive art collection; and fifty cases of Cheval Blanc (plus four of Mr. & Mrs. T's Bloody Mary Mix) to the American embassy in Brussels.

Soon after his appointment began, my grandfather flew down to the Belgian Congo, home to seventy hostile tribes on the cusp of liberation, to inspect some of the provinces. He brought his wife along for diplomacy. A visit was planned to the king of the Bakubas, one of the last traditional tribal rulers in Africa. On a steamy African morning, my grandparents prepared to board the single-engine Piper Cub that would transport them deep into the jungle. The pilot was a Texan missionary who held scheduled clinics in the villages, inoculating everything he could corner and attending to victims of various sanguinary rites. In addition to a picnic lunch that featured cold chicken and a nice Côtes du Rhône, my grandmother had taken the precaution of slipping a flask of sherry into her pocketbook.

"And thank goodness I had, dearie," she said. "A girl needs fortification for thermal descents and Lord knows what in the jungle!"

According to my grandmother, as they loaded the tiny plane, my grandfather began to puke his guts out. "Ah, the African Complaint," said the doctor. "I'm afraid you must be beside a toilet today." He had my hurling grandfather bundled off to the guesthouse they had stayed in overnight. Presumably the doctor was happy to spend the day flying around alone with an attractive (if mature) blonde who smelled of French cologne instead of jungle B.O. or fetid body seepage.

"As we were taxiing to the end of the grass strip," my grandmother said, "I thought of poor Popsie retching away . . . "

The thought of taking off in a gnat over man-eating treetops made me want to retch too.

"Of course I was terrified," she confided, patting my knee, "but I had a bag of peppermints to give to the native children and I didn't want to disappoint them. Besides, I had my Bible (miniature and condensed) and it always gives me resolution."

At the first village, a collection of grass huts in a forest clearing, the natives swarmed the Piper as it came to a stop on the dirt runway.

"They pressed their dark faces against the windows," said my grandmother, "sturdy little men with fur belts and spears, and goggle-eyed pygmy ladies with their heads shaved and, honestly, no clothes!"

"Are you sure?" I eyed my grandmother with skepticism. I had a suspicion there'd been an in-flight cocktail service.

"They were naked as the day they were born—well, except for a few very pretty beads."

Waiting at the clinic was a twelve-year-old who'd been delivering twins for three days. The doctor needed to rush her to a hospital, so my grandmother was left behind on the dirt, spiritually contained within a magic circle the doctor scratched around her with a borrowed spear. His parting words were "Don't move a muscle till I get back."

"So there I sat, waiting and waiting," my grandmother said. "Mercy, but I became anxious with all those natives staring at me, and me staring right back at them. I had my new Polaroid camera, so I thought it would be diverting to take some snaps and pass them around. Unfortunately, the camera wouldn't cooperate, and I'm afraid each picture came out blank. I thought the chief was going to make a fricassee out of me!"

My grandmother poured some more coffee and shook out two tiny saccharine tablets from a bottle. She continued her story after a couple of sips. "The women were all staring at me with these silent babies strapped to their backs, so I said to one, 'That's a lovely bracelet, dearie.' " If nothing else, my grandmother was known for her manners. "And it was. Why it might have been the inspiration behind that snappy little Cartier cuff Popsie gave me for our twenty-third."

She paused to remove Edward's hand from the canine pudenda it was groping.

"So what happened next?" I said, tracing the letters A-U-T-O-P-S-Y along the edge of the half-finished crossword. I was picturing the Addams cartoon of a missionary couple simmering in a stockpot. Both are wearing pith helmets and khaki shirts, and they are roped together back-to-back. The husband is admonishing his wife for her remarks about how cute the natives surrounding the cauldron are, calling them knee-high to a grasshopper—which of course they actually are. I imagined my grandmother sitting calmly in a similar kettle, checking her lipstick with a compact and patting the curls around her head, oblivious to the rising temperature of the soup.

She repositioned Edward on the pillows and the indignant dog at the foot of the bed. "I handed each of them a peppermint Life Saver."

"*YAP!*" squealed Edward. "*YAP! YAP!*"

"One Life Saver?" I asked.

"Why, that was more than plenty."

This didn't surprise me. My grandmother was a complete, if completely innocent, cheapskate. I hated riding in taxis with her because she always stiffed the driver. As soon as I was mature enough to grasp the concepts of both guilt and money, when I was about four, I began to supplement her miserly gratuities once she was out of the cab. At first it was Monopoly money, which didn't make me any more popular with the drivers than my grandmother, but I slept better at night.

"Anyway," she continued, "the natives weren't terribly appreciative, because they popped the mints in their mouths and then stuck their dark little hands out for more. They were upset when I couldn't produce any."

Six hours later, my grandmother was still sitting in the magic circle, shivering in the chic linen Mainbocher suit that had seemed so appropriate that morning. Her flask was empty and she was down to her last two Pep-O-Mint Life Savers (and nobody was getting them but her). The natives were leaping back and forth across the line in the dirt, brandishing sticks and bones and shaking their booties to tempt the Bwana magic.

"And when the doctor *finally* returned," said my grandmother, "I positively skedaddled for that plane! And for once, I must admit, I had faith in the concept of flight."

They were late arriving in Bakuba and had to spend the night. The king received them in his straw palace, to which they were delivered by the head tribesman.

"Was he naked?" I asked.

"Certainly, dearie, and so was the king. But he was too fat to get up. He received us from the floor, where he lay on a leopard skin, surrounded by all his councilors."

"I bet you never saw so many naked guys in your life," I said, sniggering at the thought of my modish grandmother taking the time to dress in exactly the right outfit only to face a barrage of natives in the raw. I was proud of her, and pushed my face closer into her cozy-smelling bed jacket.

My grandmother glanced at her watch now and hurriedly concluded her Congo tale. "Poor Popsie, he really was quite miffed to not meet the king."

She threw off the bedclothes and was pushing her feet into her slippers when the phone rang. After a few terse words, she handed the heavy black receiver to me. It was my mother calling on a crackling line from Acapulco.

"Listen, you," she shouted, "I got a wire from your grandfather's secretary talking about some kind of nitwit behavior. If you don't stop harassing the servants, you're going to be in deep shit. What the hell did you do to that poor ignorant maid, anyway?"

"Nothing." The great thing about the phone is no one can read your guilt.

"Well *nothing* somehow had the old bird serving your grandfather lunch with piss all over the backside of her uniform."

"It was Will's idea," I protested. Actually, it had been Wednesday's. She had subliminally suggested I put Saran Wrap under the toilet seat in the help's bathroom. Poor Selma had taken a pee in between serving the vichyssoise and the crab soufflé.

"And what the hell did you do to the poodles?"

"Nothing."

"*Nothing* doesn't require a trip to the goddamn vet. Listen, Toots, I've had it up to *here*. No more riding lessons and I'm cutting your allowance and throwing out your troll collection. End of story." Click.

So what. Most of my trolls had been metaphorically disemboweled or were undergoing various stages of mutant transformation. But the riding lesson thing hurt.

"Madame—?" Angelle padded into the room. "Madame 'as a fitting in 'alf an hour?" She lowered her head and backed out of the room.

"Right-o," my grandmother called out and sprang for the bathroom with a vigor she normally reserved for playing the net in doubles.

The poodles trotted arthritically off to investigate the preparation of the help's lunch, always served promptly at eleven-thirty, and Edward managed to clamber down and crawl after them, out the door and down the long, red-carpeted hallway.

I remained alone on the big bed, surrounded by picture books and the mounting rhythm of the traffic below, suddenly missing my grandmother. I stayed for a while, hatching petulant plots of revenge against my unjust family while I systematically covered the photograph of my brother and his pony with a pattern of angry little skulls.

Terrapin Soup

AFTER THEIR MOTHER died, my great-grandmother, whom we called Gran, had been happy to have her sister, Ruth, occupy the three Twombly houses. When Ruth died, Gran sold the block-long town house on Fifth Avenue and donated the fifty-room cottage in Newport to a Catholic school for girls. Florham remained unsold for several years and was boarded up. Just when it seemed the beautiful thousand-acre estate would get carved up into suburbia, providence arrived in the form of higher education, and Fairleigh Dickinson University purchased the property.

On an April morning a few years later, my grandparents, my brother Will, Gran, and I drove out to Florham for a tour of the new campus. We had an Asprey picnic hamper in the trunk of the limousine and George the Nazi at the wheel. Edward, being the unreliable age of two, had been left at the apartment, in the capable hands of four maids, one nanny, the laundress and her niece, and Ann Rose. The back of the limo was bigger than my bedroom at home. Sitting in it made me feel like a ring in a jewelry box because it was all padded in soft, dove gray felted wool and suede, and there were pleated pockets and snug little compartments all over the place. There was even a matching gray sheared-mink lap rug to pull across your knees, just like the puffs you were supposed to cover your diamond bracelets with in the real thing.

The grown-ups were on the deep seat in the rear, and Will and I perched on the two forward-facing jump seats that pulled down from the driver's partition and were only fun to ride in if you didn't have to. We were playing the highway memory game.

"I packed my grandmother's trunk and in it I put an apple, a body bag, a Cadillac, a decapitation machine, an eggbeater, a funeral home, a gamma ray, a hearse, an Indy car, a jellyfish that was poisonous, a kangaroo, Lurch, malted milk balls, a necromaniac, an orangutan . . . *and* . . . the sawed-in-half body of a pygmy," I said in a triumphant rush.

"No fair!" protested Will. "*Sawed-in-half* doesn't start with a P."

"Okay, half a pygmy then."

"I'm not sure I'd like even a whole pygmy in my trunk, dearie," my grandmother remarked.

"You're cheating and I don't want to play anymore," Will said and turned away from me to face his window. I kicked him, he kicked me back, and then my grandfather got involved. "He said he doesn't want to play, now *will* you, for five minutes, just be quiet!"

George allowed himself the smallest of smiles, and I clamped my arms around myself like I was in a straitjacket and glowered out my window at the New Jersey Turnpike. I hadn't wanted to come on this dumb trip to Ancestorland in the first place. There were few things less appealing than a long car ride to look at an old house with a bunch of old people. I'd already done my annual duty with my mother's grim, colonial kin in Massachusetts, a handful of decrepit spinster third cousins and widower historians, all as concerned and up-to-date with the goings on of the Colonial Dames and the Sons of the American Revolution as if the Redcoats had just been sighted cresting Bunker Hill, even as they sat drinking sherry in front of the fire and the turkey rested on the sideboard.

My father's past had permeated my childhood, living as much as I did with his parents, but I found my mother's family esoteric and impenetrable. Each Thanksgiving, we visited her childhood home, a small, spotless house on Dudley Lane, across from the cemetery in Milton. Her widower father, whom everyone called the Colonel, was an intimidating, reflective man who looked like a partridge and wore waistcoats and watches on chains, and pince-nez glasses. He wrote books about the French and Indian Wars, carved beautiful wooden birds, and collected and rebuilt clocks and watches for fun. In the summers he moved up to Lake Champlain to oversee the running of Fort Ticonderoga. He scared the academic hell out of me, and from the moment I crossed the threshold of his beeswax-scented little history-house, I didn't open my mouth other than to squeak a couple of times at the Macy's Thanksgiving Day parade, which we were allowed to watch "*quietly!*" on the small black-and-white television in the spare bedroom. Despite the repository of curios that the Colonel's house was, I would no more have gone through a drawer in it than I would have eaten horse meat.

❧

My great-grandmother tapped the toe of my shoe with her cane. "Mr. Frick's son once brought a pygmy back from Africa," she said. "Donan, my mother's chef, never batted an eye, and cooked him all of his favorite meals." She knew I was into the Addams.

"What did he eat, Gran?" I asked. I was hoping she'd say missionaries, but she smiled and said, "Rice and vegetables and potatoes, and I believe broiled steak, but no missionaries." God I loved her for that.

Gran was cozy in a dignified, Victorian way. Whereas my grandfather had the rounded physiognomy of a blue-eyed owl, his mother had creased eyes and a crumply sort of face that managed to look austerely bluestocking, yet warm and amused. She was tall and functionally bosomy, and she wore her snowy hair set in soft waves, and little velvet headband-hats, and the kind of pumps from the forties that made everyone's ankles look puffy, although hers really were. Gran's husband had died of leukemia shortly after they were married, so she mostly wore plain black or navy. When she got dressed up for someone's anniversary dinner or black-tie birthday, she'd simply pin on one of her gigantic Schlumberger brooches and she was good to go.

My other great-grandmother, Nina, was a dud as far as I was concerned. She might have been riveting in her prime, like when she was living in Paris and was publishing poetry, into séances and smoke interpretation and listening to distant tambourines, but now she was ancient and looked like one of those humanized chimpanzees you see on postcards. She wore flowery tea dresses, tiny hats with veils, and ropes of pearls, and to this day I can't remember a single word she said. One of my least favorite photographs on the desk in my grandmother's bedroom was of me as a hairless, fat baby, sitting in Nina's lap. She's holding me like I'm a two-minute egg that jumped out of its egg cup, which is exactly what I look like.

Nina lived in the apartment building next door to my grandparents, but Gran lived directly underneath us, on the fifth floor. My grandfather had built a spiral staircase to connect the two floors, and hung a big red and black Calder mobile over the top of it. You could almost always find Gran in her football-field living room overlooking Central Park, sitting in a wing-backed chair near the window, knitting sweaters for the blind. She knit the same boxy pattern for as many years as I knew her, and always in the same tiny size, using rough blue yarn that was as charmless as the Atlantic in winter. Not that the color mattered. Upstairs, my grandmother knit the identical pattern with the same yarn, and for a while there I thought blind people only came in one size.

It was appropriate that Gran's sister, Ruth, died of alcoholism. She was completely wild. The two of them were close, despite being as different as wax and string. Gran, the elder by several years, had never looked at another man after her husband died. Ruth had never looked at a man, period. Referred to as "a handsome outdoor girl," which back then was a quaint way of saying she was a lesbian, Ruth had lived her life in hedonistic opposition to her sister's abstemious one. And she had died that way, too—magnificently, if painfully, of full-blown cirrhosis of the liver, while vacationing at the Ritz in Paris.

With the help of a butler, a footman, a French chauffeur named Lucien, a cook, several maids, and a governess, Gran had raised her two sons on her own. Like Gran and Ruth, the two boys could not have been more different. My grandfather studied at Harvard, graduated cum laude in 1927, and went to work on Wall Street as an analyst of the nascent aviation industry. In 1949 he founded the private investment firm of William A. M. Burden and Company. As ambitious as he was civic-minded, he was eager to make his mark on the world, particularly because he didn't believe in the afterlife. He was on the boards of everything from CBS and Lockheed, to Columbia University, New York Hospital, and the Smithsonian. He collected affiliations and memberships the way I would go on to collect *CREEPY* comics. A 1953 profile of him in *The New Yorker* concluded with: "If you ever wonder what the Brook, the Racquet & Tennis, the River, the Links, the Grolier, and the Century can possibly have in common, the answer is Burden." By 1964 my grandfather had added the Knickerbocker, the Somerset, the Chevy Chase, the Metropolitan, the Cosmos, 1925 F Street, the Capitol Hill, the Jupiter Island and the Harbor clubs, Buck's and White's in London, and the Travellers and the Jockey Club in Paris, as well as Ye Ancient and Honorable Society of Chief Sorcerers and Apprentices, whatever that was.

My grandfather and his brother, who, for unknown reasons, was named Shirley, remained the closest of siblings throughout their lives (both remarkably long, as both were remarkably alcoholic). Uncle Shirley never went to college. Instead, he went to Hollywood. He had married Flobelle Fairbanks, Douglas Fairbanks' niece, and a member of Hollywood royalty, and they lived in the oldest part of sunny, delicious Beverly Hills. We had gone there for Christmas the year before my father died, and from the moment we entered the rambling Spanish-style mansion, I craved from the depths of my five-year-old soul to be a part of that domain. Everything about the place, the things we did, and the way we were treated was tantalizingly foreign. Uncle Shirley was warm, riotously funny, and endearingly irreverent, despite his conversion to Catholicism. Instead of a coffee table display of aviation officials and Republican presidents, film stars and Hollywood producers grinned from the silver frames in Uncle Shirley and Aunt Flobe's living room. Their shelves and walls were crowded with black-and-white candids of their grandchildren, climbing over their parents, in the arms and on the laps and kissing the wrinkly faces of their adoring relatives; tumbling around in the grass in Connecticut, playing with their innumerable toys and pets and bikes; on the trampoline, in the pool, on ponies, on sailboats, and on skis. There must have been a thousand pictures of them. Back in New York, I looked with new eyes at our grim, formal lineups, the older generation with the retouched visages of dewy teenagers, my brother Will and I like Stepford children, a six-foot-wide stand of lilies beside us and a world renowned Léger painting behind.

For a year after that trip to California I pretended I'd been a victim of mistaken identity and that any day now the hospital would call and announce that they had made a terrible mistake, that my cousin Lore and I had somehow gotten swapped at birth (despite being born a year apart and on different coasts) and that I actually belonged to the fun, happy branch of the family, not the horrible, girl-hating one.

Surprise, that didn't happen, and here I was, stuck in a car with my direct lineage.

Will was taking impressions of the car door with Silly Putty, and then pulling all the little hairs it had collected from the wool. Nobody was paying any attention because a) he was Will and could do no wrong, and b) Gran was describing all the house parties they'd had at Florham when she was growing up.

"Thirty guests each weekend!" said my grandmother with the tiniest *brfft*. (She was in a car, after all.) "Think of the planning! The staff and the linens and flowers and the *meals*." She snapped open her pocketbook, the black lizard one I thought was so funny because it had two big gold poodles guarding its portals. She removed her lipstick and, without a mirror, applied it to her upper lip, which she then smacked against the lower one, a routinely hit-and-miss endeavor. My grandmother put on lipstick whenever she truly pondered something.

"Mother adored it," chuckled Gran. "Entertaining was her life."

"Well she did have the most superb French chef," said my grandfather with a reverence he usually reserved for Charles de Gaulle or the Cummings Motor Company. "And Donan had five under him in the kitchen, not to mention a half dozen footmen in the pantry as well." He sighed longingly.

"Oh, Bill, nobody has footmen nowadays," chided his mother.

Her son scowled and, with dexterity born of habit, reached across to the bar alcove and poured several fingers of Wild Turkey into a glass without spilling a drop. He tried not to bolt it in front of his teetotaler mother.

My grandfather could never have enough staff. His grandmother Twombly had run her three behemoth houses with the help of two hundred servants, whereas he was forced to make do with a skeleton staff of twenty for his own four. He also could never have enough land. It drove him nuts that his property in Westchester County was only two hundred and fifty acres, whereas Nelson Rockefeller's weekend retreat covered four thousand in Tarrytown.

"Regardless," he said, extracting a gold cigarette case from his pocket and selecting a filterless Chesterfield, "Donan was marvelous, brilliantly marvelous."

My grandfather said "marvelous" the way a character in a Fitzgerald novel would. *Mah-velous.* He said it about a hundred times a day, as if it were the only adjective that could aptly describe the talents of a chef, or the plate of Belon oysters before him, or the Chateau Petrus he was drinking, or how he felt about the overthrow of the Libyan government.

He shook his head at the marvelousness of it all, and fiddled with the cigarette lighter on the door. I rolled my eyes and looked at Will, who rolled his back at me. Unable to make the lighter work, my grandfather began searching his pockets for matches. "Before the first world war," he continued, "one could easily find Escoffier-trained, top chefs like Donan. But then, stupidly, they all went back to France to fight. And naturally they all died. Why the devil aren't there any matches?"

"Imagine the havoc that must have wreaked in the great houses of America," my grandmother observed dryly.

"Peggy, you have no *idea* how difficult it is to procure these fellows nowadays," her husband retorted.

"Why, Popsie, aren't you satisfied with our chef?"

"Yes, yes, of course I am," he replied, patting down the pockets of his Huntsman overcoat for a light. "Only the fellow had no idea the other night that when you serve partridge they must all be from the same hatch. And he seems unable to procure the best terrapin." He took off his round steel-rimmed glasses and polished them with a monogrammed powder blue handkerchief that matched his shirt exactly. I whispered to Will that he looked kind of like a terrapin himself, but Will didn't agree. I resolved never to speak to him again.

"Don't you remember, Momsie," my grandfather continued,

"how marvelous the terrapin was at the luncheon we had for your eightieth at the Pavillon? Donan came out of retirement to prepare it himself. Why in blazes he wouldn't come work for me—"

"Bill, your language! The children."

My grandfather harrumphed, and I snorted into the hand-shirred bodice of my dress.

Blazes? Was that even a swear word? I did a quick mental run-through of all the dirty words I knew, starting with fuck, shit, prick, and butthole, while I doodled tombstones across the front page of the *Daily News*. Will was picking a scab on his knuckle and flicking the pieces my way.

My grandmother leaned toward me and said, "That's a snappy dress you have on, dearie, is it new?" For the outing, I had been coerced into wearing a pale green Belgian party dress that cost as much as a pony.

"No. I got it for Christmas," I said.

"Well it's a lovely color. Did Santa give it to you?"

"No, you did. And I look like a mint."

"A very nice mint, dearie."

Still without a light, my grandfather told his wife to lower the glass partition so he could speak to George. After she'd fumbled with every other button on her seat arm, sending all the windows open and the grit and wind from the turnpike whooshing through the interior, and turning all the reading lights on and off, and the radio on at full volume, he reached angrily across her and did it himself.

"Dammit, George," he spluttered, "I've asked you repeatedly to always provide matches!"

"Yes, Mr. Burden," George said in his Gestapo monotone, glancing into the rearview mirror. I whipped around and grinned at him obnoxiously. George handed me a gold book of matches with MLB, my grandmother's monogram, on the cover.

"Thank you, George," I said. "Can I light it, Granddaddy?" I started to tear off one of the matches.

"No, no, no! Now, give them here and be quiet."

He reached forward and snatched them from my hand. Then he lit his cigarette and sat back, exhaling vigorously. I was used to smoke, but I coughed dramatically because I hated the smell of Chesterfields. I already knew I was going to be a Marlboro girl.

I made a mental note to hide all the matches in the apartment when I got back, and added my grandfather's initials to several tombstones in my drawing.

As Gran's soft old voice continued: —*a marvel . . . whomever came to visit . . . Chicken á la King for Mrs. Prentice . . . Lobster Lafayette . . . Thomas Edison*—my grandfather picked up the mike to the built-in Dictaphone below his seat and rattled off a memo to his secretary.

"Miss Pou, a record of all Vanderbilt houses in Newport and in New York City. Dates and principal residents. On my desk by Monday. And terrapin for lunch in the country this weekend. Must be in season somewhere. Check Australia. Fly them in. Females." He thought a moment and added, "Send six cases of Mr. & Mrs. T's Bloody Mary Mix to all houses. And phone Kyoto about the best chrysanthemums for Mount Kisco greenhouse."

Hmmm, I thought. Weren't chrysanthemums poisonous?

"We're *here*!" piped Will. Gran sat up abruptly as, at last, we turned through a pair of towering, elegantly wrought iron gates. The gravel crunched and popped beneath our tires as we drove past smooth lawns and orchards. My grandmother pointed out the farm in the distance, and the dairy with its shingled silo and beautiful, ivy-covered barns. We blinked at the greenhouses repeating their glare in the sun, and at the imposing glass-and-brick orangerie, and the very adult Playhouse, with its central barroom, and separate wings of tennis courts and swimming pool.

The house was the biggest thing I'd ever seen in my life. The

Nazi swung the car around the circle and stopped in front, and Will and I tumbled out. We started chasing each other around the wide frontal columns, and clambering over the pair of life-sized marble lions guarding the two-storied portico. My grandfather walked up to the massive front door and touched it with a fingertip. "Not as shiny as it used to be," he commented.

His mother struggled up the steps to stand beside him. "No," she admitted, adjusting her hat. "In Mother's time we employed it as a mirror, to check our appearance before we went in to see her. I suppose the university doesn't see the need to keep it that polished anymore."

We were early, so there was no university tour guide waiting to greet us. Gran pushed the door open and we followed her in. We stood for a moment, blinking in the dark coolness of a black-and-white marble hallway that seemed to stretch forever. A massive fireplace faced the entrance, and my brother and I ran to stand inside it.

"Perfect for roasting your victims," I whispered in awe. I imagined bodies on spits being slowly hand cranked by hunchbacks with leprosy.

"Hel-lo . . . hel-lo," called Will up the flue.

"That fireplace is almost twenty feet high. Can you imagine?" said Gran, leaning on her cane. "Father had it copied after the one at Windsor Castle." She turned in a slow circle, remembering. "Mother's Sargent portrait used to hang over there." She pointed to where an aerial map of the buildings and grounds hung crookedly on the wall, and the grown-ups all squinted at it in recollection.

Gran's mother, Florence, was not only the last surviving grandchild of the Commodore, she was the least attractive. In her portrait by John Singer Sargent, the court painter of his day, she is depicted in the ripest of swirling peach tones, all warts and moles removed. Her eyes are as dark and moist as Hostess cupcakes, her mouth chastely sensual. Her figure—in actuality, angular and stick-thin—is as luscious and languid as a Boston cream pie. Seated on the edge of a needlepoint Louis XVI footstool, she is surrounded by icons of her opulent life: a Barberini tapestry (Apollo and Daphne visible in a discreet state of undress), an exquisite ivory fan, a rich Aubusson carpet. It is the portrait of a wealthy fertility goddess, and nothing remotely like the cross, dried-up, dark little bird I'd seen in all the family albums.

"And remember all the Caesars that lined this hallway on their fluted stands?" my grandmother said with a wave of her gloved hand.

"*Pilasters*, Peggy," her husband corrected.

"Let's see," she continued, counting them out on her fingers, "Tiberius, and Caligula—and Claudius and Nero, Augustus and, and—oh, Galba and Titus, and . . . I can't remember the others." *Barfufft!* She subsided, pleased with herself for remembering that many.

Traveling slowly down the hallway, we looked into rooms that had once been the library and the salon, the billiard room and the oak-paneled smoking room. Across from the formal living room was an immense alcove that had held Grandma Twombly's beloved Aeolian pipe organ, an instrument reportedly larger even than the one at Radio City Music Hall. It had gone on the block with everything else, the massive Louis XV gilt chandeliers from the ballroom and the roomfuls of English furniture, the Chinese porcelain, the beautiful paintings, and books, and carpets and tapestries, all of which had contributed to my grandfather's inheritance and allowed him to purchase paintings like Francis Bacon's *Screaming Pope*, which my grandmother had to close her eyes and put a handkerchief to her mouth to walk past.

The grown-ups kept going on and on about how things used to be and what was gone and who had died, and I felt badly for my great-grandmother. As much as I loved the idea of dead people, I couldn't imagine being the only one from my generation left alive. Then my grandfather started reminiscing about Phillip, everyone's favorite footman, and how he would bring them their breakfast in bed—hothouse Marshall strawberries with morning dew on them—although how something grown inside could have dew on it was beyond me.

In the nick of time a university official came hurrying apologetically down the hallway, and Will and I escaped up the marble staircase to the second floor. We counted thirty-six bedrooms, now dull, utilitarian offices, albeit with fancy plasterwork and marble bathrooms en suite with fireplaces. There were still the original brass holders on the doors, where the names of the guests, written out in copperplate, would be inserted for their stay. Up a lesser staircase we found another twenty or so bedrooms, and we ran dizzily in and out of them until we burst in on a large lady in a dusty little office, manning a mimeograph machine that smelt of vanilla. She shooed us out with lavender-stained fingers, but as we retreated, I puffed myself up self-importantly and hollered, "Hey! This is my great-grandmother's house, you know!" Like she cared.

We ate our picnic lunch outside on the wide stone terrace, though it was hardly a picnic since my grandfather insisted a table be brought out. The grown-ups sat at it and ate egg salad sandwiches with the crusts cut off, and cold roast chicken, and Camembert with huge dusty black grapes, the kind you practically need to cut in half and pit like a plum. Will and I straddled the stone balustrade next to them and drank Cokes and gnawed on drumsticks, and when we got bored with eating, we stood up and balanced on the balustrade and tried to jinx each other into falling into the bushes below. After a bottle and a half of Meursault, my grandfather was waxing even more nostalgic for Chef Donan and carrying on about his *marvelous*ness like a tent revivalist.

After lunch that day, I think I knew every dish in Donan's

repertoire. Turns out he was famous not only for his food, but because he was the highest paid chef in the country. In Donan's *New Yorker* profile, he got five pages. My grandfather's was only three.

"Tell me about the breakfast-es you used to have," said Will. Breakfast was his favorite meal. He could eat eggs and pancakes and Little Jones fried sausages all day long. Gran told him how breakfast had been served between seven and eight, either on trays in the guest rooms, or in the breakfast room, and how every morning there had been eggs of every description, and all kinds of fruits from the hothouses, and Donan's famous croissants, which he was credited with introducing to America, and hot muffins and toasts and brioches and biscuits, and cooked or dry cereals, and different cheeses, and chicken hash, and creamed hash and brown hash, and fish balls, and sausages, and bacon, and ham, and any kind of juice you could want, and strong hot coffee, or French chocolate, or China tea. And that was just breakfast.

I only interrupted twice, once to gag at the fish balls, and the other to tell my grandmother there was a bee drowning in her wine, but she ignored me and drank it down on the next gulp. I then had to project potential allergic reactions for her, and spent the next ten minutes worrying that her throat might swell to the point of suffocation and she would die.

"What was Grandma Twombly's favorite?" my grandmother asked, her voice disappointingly normal. God, what a boring last question to be remembered by, I thought.

"Well, Mother adored soufflés," Gran said. "In fact, her very last meal was a chicken soufflé."

That started my grandfather off on a long recourse about egg courses, which I knew would lead to fish courses, and then meat courses, and then caviar and turtles and lobster and pheasant, so I shut my eyes and concentrated on what my own last meal might be. Obviously it would be dependent on what my crime was, as well as how I was going to be martyred. The most important factor to consider was what I'd want the contents of my stomach to be in the hereafter. I wouldn't want to be too gassy for the embalmer, though I knew that was unavoidable, due to the metabolism of my intestinal bacteria. Lobster, maybe? Or would that just sit like a lump in my stomach for months, years even, before the worms broke it down? Perhaps something lighter, like popovers soaked in butter. Or a bacon cheeseburger from the Chevy Chase Club? *That's* it, I thought.

My grandfather, who had now finished a second bottle of wine, was expounding on *Terrapin à la Florham* to Will, who was vacantly pulling all the hairs out of his left eyebrow, one by one. It felt like we had been eating lunch for three days.

"—and every night it was in season, terrapin was served at Grandma Twombly's dinner table. It was superb, brilliantly superb."

Will started in on his other eyebrow.

⤜⤛

It was a forgone conclusion that any outing involving my grandfather and me would end in mishap. An hour later I was lurking behind the limousine, hanging on to one of the twin flags that were attached to the fenders, eavesdropping on the grown-ups. I was straining so hard to hear what was being said about so-and-so's *terminal illness* and *imminent death* (both huge trigger terms for me) that I didn't realize I had the flagpole practically bent in two, and it had not been exactly flexible to begin with.

Just when they were getting to the most interesting part—*and the doctors had to insert a*—and I was almost able to hear what they were saying, I started grasping the flag tighter—*but since she insisted on an open casket*—tighter—*and Campbell's said they wouldn't*—until SNAP!

My grandfather made me sit up front with the Nazi, on the

other side of the bulletproof glass partition. I tried to make conversation with him for a while, but it didn't go well:

"So. Selma tells me you're redecorating the apartment over the garage."

"*Ja.*"

"Anyone I know?"

Between the on-ramp to the Turnpike and the toll booth at the Lincoln Tunnel, I plotted retaliation against my grandfather, my brother, the Nazi, my geography teacher, and the male race in general. When I had mentally sealed their fate with an ingenious plot I'd heard about, where a woman killed her husband by putting nicotine from liquefied cigarettes into his aftershave, which snuffed him in about an hour, I was over it.

I couldn't bear not being a part of the conversation. As we entered the gloom of the tunnel, I took advantage of George's momentary blindness to flip the switch for the partition so I could hear what everybody was saying. I shouldn't have bothered. My grandfather was talking about cheese. I was about to put the window back up when I heard the distinctive sound of his cigarette case clicking shut. Then I heard him ask if Will would do him the honor of lighting his cigarette.

Just as my brother leaned over, proudly intent on his task, I put my arm through the partition and pinched the back of his neck so hard he squealed like a hamster and dropped the flaming match on my grandfather's knee. A tiny smoky hole appeared in the exquisite Savile Row wool. The owner of the knee exploded, and so did Will.

"She pinched me!" he screeched, and lunged through the partition. I was struggling to get the window up as expeditiously as possible, and leaning all over the Nazi to do it, which caused him to swerve and nearly sideswipe a delivery truck. It was all terribly exciting, depending on whose view you saw it from.

When we got back to the apartment, I dove headfirst for the corner seat in the elevator, beating my brother to it and daring, with practically twirling eyeballs, *anyone* to say a word about it. I tore off my prissy dress, stomping up and down on it before stuffing it into a mothball-filled garment bag at the back of the closet. I pulled on a pair of the Y-front boys' underwear my grandmother had actually bought for me, then a pair of jeans and a T-shirt and my PF Flyers.

Rudely awakening them from their slumber beneath a forty-watt-lightbulb sun, I scooped up my brother's three brand-new turtles from their plastic oasis, scurried up the spiral staircase, and made a beeline to the kitchen. It was almost four, and no one was around. I had maybe fifteen minutes before the chef started getting the help's dinner ready. I placed the tiny reptiles on top of the rolled steel worktable, whereupon they instantly retreated into their silver-dollar-sized carapaces. I managed to get down a big soup pot from the overhead rack, and filled it with water. It took me half a dozen matches to get the burner on the big black Garland going, but I did it. I lugged the pot from the sink to the stove, spilling most of it, and then I carefully placed the turtles in the water, using a big spoon the way the chef did when he was poaching eggs. I turned the flame up as high as it would go and sat down on the counter to watch.

At first they didn't do much, just paddled around, but then, as the water started to swirl a bit, they began swimming faster, and then they were *really* swimming faster, bumping into one another, their tiny claws scrabbling against the sides of the pot for a foothold. I hung over the stove and watched as they raced around, their nostrils fibrillating in fear. Tiny bubbles started to form across the bottom of the pot. Almost imperceptibly, the bubbles began to rise, and that's when I burst into tears and grabbed a soup ladle and fished them out. I ran over to the sink and, sobbing into a kitchen towel, tenderly rinsed them under cool tap water.

Later that night, after my bath, I went to visit Gran. Normally I had to go in with someone, in case she was resting or doing whatever it was that old people did when they didn't want to receive, but the door to her apartment was open, so I let myself in. Gran was slumped in her chair, still wearing her dark day clothes, her knitting needles and the cheap blue yarn on her lap. Her face was turned away, and for a while there, I thought she was dead. This alternately horrified and thrilled me since I'd never actually seen a dead person, but when I crept closer, the rise and fall of her chest showed that she was merely sleeping. After I nosed around a little, looking for the chocolates I knew she always had on hand, and rearranging her collection of Battersea enamel boxes in a taxonomic progression of flora to fauna, I settled on the old-fashioned love seat across from her. In the companionable dark, Gran slept on while I ate chocolate, my feet tucked up beneath my nightgown, and kept a vigil over my great-grandmother because, at that moment, she was just about all I wanted to claim as mine.

My Family and Other Domestics

As soon as we figured out that for all intents and purposes we had no parents, Will and I started filling in the gaps with the hired help. At home in Washington, Henrietta and Cassie Diggins assumed virtual parenthood the day our little brother was born, when, following a cursory offering of colostrum, our mother grabbed a couple of bikinis and fled the maternity ward to embark on an open-ended quest for the perfect tan. When she returned three years later, baby Edward was surprised to discover he was not, in fact, the miracle child of a Scottish nanny and an African-American cook.

When we were in Burdenland, which was what our mother called the "goddamn spoiled rotten" world of our grandparents, my brothers and I had at our disposal an extended surrogate family who had known us since we were newborns. The core group, what I liked to consider our immediate family, was based in New York City, and consisted of the chef and his assistant, the butler and his wife, four or five maids, a couple of laundresses, the chauffeur, and the domestic gatekeeper, Ann Rose.

My grandfather may have been avant-garde in his views on culture, but he was strictly Edwardian when it came to his household. In this era of civil rights and bra burnings, he stoically referred to his staff as "the servants." My grandmother would have preferred to call them nothing at all, but she compromised by calling them the "help," for which her husband chided her, saying, "Peggy, don't be absurd. To call the servants the 'help' is insultingly euphemistic."

When it came to hiring, my grandfather referred to a standard formulated during the era of Florham: Butlers were ideally British, and came with a wife. Chefs were French, but could have Swedish or Finnish assistants. Maids were Irish, but ladies' maids were French, unless they were English because they were married to the butler. Coachmen, footmen, and valets were English or Irish; and the order of preference for the chauffeur's nationality was first French, then English, then—as a last resort—German. (Clearly George the Nazi was a last resort.) Head gardeners were absolutely always Scottish, as were the under gardeners, although the latter could on occasion be Italian, but only if they were exceptionally talented. Italian was as dark as anyone got.

The most important person in the household was the chef, and there was fierce competition among my grandfather and his Francophile coterie as to who could attain and then hold on to the hottest one. Requisite criteria included a temper more volatile than Idi Amin's, Swiss or French culinary training begun at the age of two, and documented tenure in the kitchens of de Gaulle, a Rothschild, or, at the very least, Douglas Dillon. Of the dozen or so books my grandfather consumed each week, half of them were on the subject of food or drink. The hallway bookshelves overflowed with the spines of Elizabeth David and Lucullus Beebe, Ali-Bab, Pierre Franey, and A. J. Liebling, and the bedside tables were stacked with wine quarterlies and epicurean almanacs. As he lay pillow-propped in bed at night, waiting for the velvet Seconal hammer, my grandfather did his food reading. He alternated between scribbling pencil notations in a shorthand that only Miss Pou could decipher and pontificating into the mike of a thirty-pound Dictaphone, one of the dozen he had installed, in addition to the one in the car, next to the toilet, the bed, the chair in the library, the indoor swimming pool in Maine, and the tennis court in the country. Within a day, these nocturnal musings (*Curnonsky—Never lunches, but is tolerant of those that do.* Or *Fish are only fresh for a few hours.* Or *Midnight Supper Idea: Thin sandwiches of very rare, or raw, beef, pepper mill, tiny bottles of cold champagne*) would be transposed and typed up in quadruplicate on five-by-seven index cards, to be filed for reference in the kitchens of each house.

If the chef was God, then the butler was Jesus. My grandfather's favorite had been a white-haired Englishman named Day, whom President Eisenhower had seduced from Buckingham Palace, and whom my grandfather had usurped from Ike. Day had retired, and now there was pink-cheeked Adolphe. He should have been English, but he had been with the embassy in Brussels, and despite his being Belgian, my grandfather had liked him so much that he had conveyed him back to New York along with fifty cases of Burgundy. A combination of Alfred Pennyworth (Batman's butler) and Mervyn Bunter (the valet of Lord Peter Wimsey), Adolphe was the epitome of protocol, diplomacy, and discretion, with an appropriate amount of attitude. He may have held my grandfather's underwear for him to step into, but he did it in a morning suit of sartorial perfection, with a ceremonial expression befitting the task. Impeccably turned out as he was—daytime black jacket, gray waistcoat, and pinstripe trousers; evening tailcoat with white gloves and wing collar—Adolphe ensured his master was too, whether in white tie with decorations for a dinner at the White House, a navy Huntsman business suit for the office, or spotless flannel tennis whites for the weekend court. Not a molecule of lint could be found on either man, and this was before the most important invention of the twentieth century: the rolling pet hair remover.

Adolphe, in addition to being butler, valet, and avuncular nanny to Will and Edward and me, had the role of the archetypal family priest who must care for his half-witted sisters. In this case, they were the maids, and they needed explicit guidance from the moment their bunioned feet got out of bed to when they said their Hail Marys in the same spot at the close of the day. They flapped around him like Chicken Littles if the papers were late, or the vacuum cleaner belt broke, or the butter curler went missing.

An old Irish maid has the shelf life of Velveeta. Change in the ranks was rare, and only necessary when one of them staggered repeatedly under the weight of the luncheon dishes, or became so stricken with dementia that she carpet-swept a single square foot of the library for hours on end. Even then, out of a sense of loyalty, they were kept on. Incompetence was never a reason to fire a maid, nor, in Selma's case, was incontinence. Those women knew my brothers and me better than our own mother did, and when I was feeling frustrated in my attempts to have a so-called normal life, I sometimes wished for the predictable routine of the women who occupied the staff wings and basements and attics of my grandparents' houses. Up at six, squeeze the oranges for juice, walk the poodles, choose the linens for lunch and dinner, have a chin wag with Nelly on ten, serve lunch, polish some silver, cup of tea and the *Daily News* crossword at four, serve cocktails, serve dinner, telly for an hour, prayers, and bed by nine. Tuesdays off, Mass on Sunday, a fortnight's holiday in June. They were grounded. They knew what to expect. More importantly, they knew what was expected of them. Nobody expected anything of me, unless you counted my mother expecting me to become thin, blond, and tanned.

There were definite perks to having four or five auntie maids in residence. You never had to make your bed. You could step out of your clothes and leave them puddled right there on the floor, and *poof!* they would disappear and be back in a few hours, magically washed and pressed and folded away in your drawers like you lived in the clothing department of Best & Co. Red-knuckled hands perpetually wiped and dusted, scrubbed and polished, mopped and waxed, and tidied and organized, putting to rights the everyday messes of we, the Goddamn Spoiled Rotten.

Ann Rose, the gatekeeper, was the liaison between front and back, the settler of petty grievances, the soother of egos, and consequently a nervous wreck. She was a mournful, spaghetti-like thing with dark puffs under her sad brown eyes and deep lines on either side of her disappointed mouth. I liked to pretend she was from the Swiss branch of the Addams family, although really she looked more like she came from the clan of Edward Gorey. Sepulchrally dismal, she was the three-dimensional equivalent of woe.

It was difficult not to take Ann Rose for granted. Even the back elevator operator enjoyed more recognition than she did. She had been an au pair dispatched from Zurich the moment the wet nurses had finished with my grandmother's fourth and final son, Uncle Ordway. When, in the tradition of his three older brothers—my father, Uncle Bob, and Uncle Ham–Uncle Ham—Ordway was sent to boarding school, Ann Rose the au pair became Ann Rose the household watchdog, and she spent the remainder of her life in bondage to my grandparents.

Ann Rose was grimly reliable. If she said she'd have the poodles groomed in time for my grandmother's luncheon for Mrs. Astor, you knew the dogs would be posed on the yellow sofa beneath the Monet water lilies in the living room, coiffed and perfumed, when the ladies arrived. And you could always find Ann Rose exactly where you expected her to be, at any given moment, which meant I could ferret around in her office without being disturbed.

Ann Rose's office was my favorite hunting ground. It was also the most accessible, since she went home to her own apartment at night. The office was in the back corner of the apartment, at the end of the long, red-carpeted, book-lined hallway, next to the spiral staircase that led downstairs to the bedroom Will and I shared. Tall wire-glass windows looked through a fire escape onto a quintessential New York view: a brick wall with a scrap of sky visible above it. Floor-to-ceiling shelves bulged with reference books, and iron-colored file cabinets were squeezed shoulder to shoulder in front of them.

The long metal desk that squatted beneath the east-facing window looked as utilitarian as a business envelope, but inside it was a candy store. I considered myself the curator of its eight skinny drawers, and I was forever rearranging the green and red felt-tipped pens, the black china markers, the staples and magnifying glasses and fountain pens and ink cartridges and scissors of a dozen shapes and sizes, and bringing everything to regimental order for Ann Rose—who was forever messing with my arrangements. (How anyone could stand to have their office supplies all higgledy-piggledy was a mystery to me.) A constant source of irritation was the locked drawer on the bottom right-hand side. I could not jimmy or pick my way into it. Nor could I figure out just what could be so important as to be locked up. Nothing in Burdenland was ever locked. Not the wine cellar, or the silver cabinets, or my grandmother's jewelry boxes—even after the time when the window washer stole her rectangular-cut, Color-D, Clarity-SI1 10k Cartier diamond engagement ring, which she got back three hours later because the moron tried to pawn it during his lunch break.

Sometimes I began with a perusal of disfiguring diseases in the medical encyclopedia, but usually I just went straight for the files to catch up on current events. In addition to evaluations from Uncle Ham–Uncle Ham's psychiatrist, Dr. Sharp, and Will's shrink, Dr. Berman, and secret information on the help, like their references, and what my grandfather had ordered from his tailor in London (forty blue shirts and twenty white), and what my grandfather had ordered for my grandmother from Mainbocher and Givenchy and Balmain and Dior and Balenciaga, there were Will's and my report cards, which the schools sent because my grandparents paid the tuition. My mother was forever telling me how Will had scored higher on his IQ test than me, so I needed to keep tabs on the situation and reassure myself I was still smarter than him, even if it was the battle of the D+'s over the Ds. I was terrified of having to repeat a grade the way my brother had, and then having to go to boarding school.

I wanted whatever Will had, but not his school. Glayden was a hippie encampment in the woods of Virginia that catered to children with learning disabilities. These ranged from severe dyslexia, like Will had, to headline mental retardation. My mother had sent me to camp there one summer, with disastrous results. After a few days surrounded by the afflicted, it was impossible for me not to speculate that since I didn't have any learning disabilities, clearly I was there because I was retarded, and this was my family's way of telling me. The nurse said in twenty-six years of working with the mentally ill she'd never seen anyone have such hysterics.

∽∽

Because I loved Christmas so much, despite the constant disappointment of it, I almost always concluded a session in Ann Rose's office with a life-affirming check on the three file cabinets devoted to the seductive paraphernalia of the holidays: the wrapping paper and cards and ribbon and tags and tissue-enclosed stockings.

A kid who can talk herself into believing the Addams Family was inspired by reality can extend faith in the existence of Santa Claus almost indefinitely. Okay, maybe I didn't actually *believe* in Santa Claus—I mean I wasn't stupid enough to think an enormously fat man was going to squeeze down that skinny Philip Johnson fireplace in the living room bearing presents the size of footlockers—but I believed in the eternal optimism and idealism of Christmas, and in the theoretical six degrees of separation as it applied to all grown-ups and Santa Claus.

The first week of December, Ann Rose arranged for the doormen to bring up the world's tallest artificial tree from the basement, along with an even taller ladder, and the butler set about decorating it. (That a couple owning two hundred and fifty acres littered with real Christmas trees would deck the halls with a fake one remains a mystery.) She called the gardener in Mount Kisco and told him the exact number of paper whites needed for the mantels and coffee tables, and he brought in a few hundred, and enough scarlet poinsettias to line the front hall and fill the pair of six-foot-wide circular planters in the living room.

I would tune the McIntosh stereo to WQXR and position myself in one of the living room windows that overlooked Fifth Avenue. With choral music and carols enfolding me, I'd drop the Addams Family act and think about angels and the baby Jesus and stare out, my forehead against the icy glass, at the darkened park, marveling at how the skaters on Wollman Rink made it look like a star exploding in the galaxy.

The Christmas right after Kennedy was killed, Will and I went to our grandparents in New York as usual. Edward came too, and so did Henrietta, and Obadiah the basset hound. My mother even flew up with us and stayed for a tense twenty-four hours before taking off for the Bahamas. Needless to say, my mother snubbed the help. Since they were my chosen family, I compensated by practically making their beds for them when she was around. I'd squeeze the orange juice and carry the breakfast dishes from the table to the pantry for Anna, and I'd walk the poodles for Selma, which the poodles hated because I hated them.

It was considered perfectly safe at that time for children to prowl around the city either by themselves or in the company of toy poodles—and that's what I was doing when I caught sight of

Ann Rose scurrying across Fifty-seventh Street with an armful of shopping bags, bobbing her way toward Tiffany's. Something perverse told me to follow her, and so I ducked into the revolving door, nearly decapitating the dogs, and lingered by the men's watches while she waited for the special elevator in the corner that went to the Schlumberger department on the second floor. She reappeared ten minutes later with a small Tiffany blue shopping bag and then scuttled out the front door and veered left into Bonwit Teller. After purchasing several pairs of gloves, a couple of wallets, and an ugly costume jewelry necklace, she fought her way to the back of the store and into one of the elevators. I had no trouble staying out of sight because the place was crammed with shoppers, but I was clueless as to what floor she was headed to, though by this point I shouldn't have been. I took the next elevator, but almost threw up between Ladies' Sportswear and Ladies' Lingerie because the white-gloved black lady operating it was throwing the lever so hard she was making the thing bounce up and down like a yo-yo. I got out and dragged the poodles down the stairs, and we waited for Ann Rose behind the Max Factor counter on the ground floor.

When she reemerged, she had a couple of long dress boxes under her arms. I could tell one of them was from the children's department because I'd seen my share of them. She was out the door and swimming back upstream through the tourists to FAO Schwarz, where I watched her buy three Steiff animals, a Mouse Trap game, an Easy-Bake Oven, a Wham-O Air Blaster, some Slinkys, a couple of trolls, a G.I. Joe doll, and a Tonka toy jeep. She could hardly move she had so many bags, but I sure wasn't going to help her. I was having that clammy feeling you get when it's just dawning on you that you've discovered something really bad. George the Nazi suddenly appeared with the car, and he bundled her and her thirty-five bags and boxes into the back of the limo, and they headed across Fifty-eighth Street. Back to the North Pole, I thought, with something like pins pricking my eyeballs. The poodles were chattering with frostbite, and so we slogged back up Fifth to Sixty-third, and finally turned under the awning of 820, and I collapsed in the little corner seat in the elevator for the ten-second ride up to the sixth floor.

The light shone late under the door of Ann Rose's office over the next few days, but when I looked around in the mornings before she had come into work, there was no evidence, other than an extra roll of Scotch tape on the desk, a few tiny triangles of snipped curling ribbon, and the telltale drift of gift card glitter. I couldn't figure out who to be angry at. Had I really thought my grandparents ran around town getting the zillions of things that Will and I pleaded for, and that they then sat up into the night wrapping them? Yes. Yes, I had.

I was so incensed by the Betrayal that I nearly blurted it out to my mother when she called the next morning from Nassau to tell me that if "Santa" got me the Easy-Bake Oven I had asked for, I was not, repeat NOT, to place anything in it that was a) alive, b) a troll, or c) an item belonging to either of my brothers. Which was her way of saying it was a done deal.

"Thanks for the tip-off," I said.

"Oh, don't thank me, Toots, thank Santa," my mother replied.

"Oh yeah. Santa. Of *course.* I'll start my thank-you note to him right now."

When I let Will in on my discovery, he had little to say, as usual. We were watching *The Outer Limits,* which always gave me the creeps, right from the moment the Control Voice introduced each broadcast.

There is nothing wrong with your television set . . .

"Guess what," I said.

Do not attempt to adjust the picture . . .

"What?" said Will.

"ANN ROSE IS SANTA!"

"So?"

"So? Whaddaya mean *so*? Listen, it's Ann Rose who goes and buys all the presents and toys and stuff, and then wraps them all up, and then puts them under the tree and in the stockings and everything. *I saw her!*"

My brother turned and gave me a look that said, *You pathetic idealist* (or nine-and-a-half-year-old words to that effect), so I had no recourse but to slap him, and then he punched me in the stomach, and the butler had to come and separate us for an hour. And that was the last time I even uttered the word *Santa* to any-one, until we were unwrapping our presents in the living room in front of the fire, on Christmas Day.

As usual, I had leapt out of bed and thrown open the door to Will's and my bedroom to find the stockings that "Santa" had conveniently delivered to our door (so that the grown-ups could sleep). They were so overstuffed they spilled little presents onto the red carpet like cornucopias. But the customary thrill turned sour as I remembered it was Ann Rose who had purchased and then wrapped, in papers patterned with splashy patterns, and gumdrops and candy canes and snowmen, each of the dozens of presents she had then stuffed into the toes and heels and ankles and calves and knees (that's how big they were) of the eight stockings, for my grandparents, my three uncles, my two broth-ers, and me.

The grown-ups finally emerged and gathered by the fire-place in the living room, my grandparents still in their dressing gowns. Uncle Bob, now the eldest, since my father had died, already had a five o'clock shadow. He had to shave about five times a day in order to not look like a gangster. He resembled the other men in the family in that he was tall and ropey, but his hair, instead of being auburn, was very dark. He had his mother's beauty, if not her clothes sense. For the Christmas festivities he was dressed in his usual bargain basement cloth-ing—an ill-fitting sports jacket and a pair of worn slacks. Uncle Bob was the genetic mutant of the family—he eschewed any and all luxuries, with the exception of birthday and Christmas presents to us, his brother's children. At twenty-nine, he still didn't own a car and lived pretty much like a monk. After graduating from Harvard, Uncle Bob had shocked his family to the core by enlisting in the army. Following a two-year stint, he got a job teaching Greek and physics at a private school in St Louis. Knowing how paltry his son's teaching salary was, my grandfather sent him a check for five thousand dollars every month; and each month Uncle Bob donated the entire amount to the school.

The second-in-line entered the living room like he was being chased by a bee. Uncle Ham–Uncle Ham was clutching a slopping cup of coffee in one hand and a cigarette in a holder in the other. His shirttails were out, and his Yuletide red tie was as askew as a guy with the social skills of a five-year-old could make it. He had been escorted to the apartment that morning by his "companion," one of several that lived with him in forty-eight-hour shifts, because that was just about as long as anyone could take it. The guy never stopped talking. If anyone was around, he chattered incessantly, out of either a fear of silence or his substantial chemical imbalance.

There had been a seismic disturbance in the bloodline when the third Burden son was born. For the longest time my grandfather refused to acknowledge there was anything wrong with young Hamilton. He even sent him to Harvard, though he had to pay about a hundred times the tuition. There was lots of additional tutoring, despite the fact that Hamilton was extremely bright, and could answer virtually any question on politics or history, especially if it had to do with the Third Reich. But after a rumored romantic scandal involving another young man, he was pulled out of his freshman year and done with college, and public life in general.

One evening in Maine, when my uncle had been a little over-served in the caffeine department (as in about fifteen cups of coffee and three Cokes), and he had sprayed the powder room with urine and laughed so hard that snot had flown out of his nose and hit the hors d'oeuvres plate of Brie and Triscuits, my grandmother had pulled me aside and told me that although I may not have noticed, my uncle Hamilton was a little different from other people. Will and I laughed our brains out over that later. *May not have noticed?*

Ordway, the youngest of the three uncles, walked over to the farthest chair and slumped down into it. He was visibly hungover and typically reluctant to be a part of any family activity that involved children. It was clear to Will and me, and probably Edward as well, that he didn't much like us. Ordway had been somewhat of a surprise to his parents. He had the clean good looks of a late edition, but at nineteen, he was already losing his hair and had a weird thing going on with his part.

All the players now present and accounted for, we ripped into the presents. My grandfather sat in the molded plywood-and-steel Eames side chair he always sat in on Christmas morning, with a plate of butter-soaked English muffins and the thermos of coffee he always was served on a small table before him, extracting presents from his ermine-trimmed stocking with his long, slow fingers, just like he always did. My grandmother was on the purple couch, a poodle on each side, doing the same. They both exhibited genuine surprise as they unwrapped their gifts.

"Popsie! Earrings from Verdura! How divine—"

"Why, Peggy, a Charvet tie—how thoughtful!"

My grandmother, however, had not seemed too surprised by the necklace of red and green millipedes I'd made for her with the Creepy Crawlers set I'd gotten for my eighth birthday the week before. Nor did my grandfather swoon with pleasure over the paint-by-numbers horse head on black velvet I'd given him, intending for him to replace the Klee in the hallway with it. Uncle Ham–Uncle Ham got a six-pack of Coca-Cola I'd swiped from the pantry and decorated with incorrectly drawn red and green swastikas and a couple of ponies. At least *he* was thrilled, and exclaimed "Very good! Very good!" in between drags on his cigarette and slugs from his cup of coffee. At one point he sidled up to his father like a working dog trying to ingratiate itself to the herdsman. With his eyes on the buttons of his blazer, for he never looked at anyone directly, he held out the book his father (Ann Rose) had given him. "Why, thank you, Dad! Thank you, Dad!" he said. "Göring was an interesting man! Yes, yes, an interesting man!"

His father brusquely waved him away. I had never seen my grandfather speak to his son, and I never would.

Will had yet to unwrap his Ken doll cadaver, autopsy-ready with *cut here* lines drawn across its abdomen with a red Magic Marker. Edward didn't get anything because what do you get a one-year-old? I was nice to him for an hour, though.

I got the Easy-Bake Oven all right (it practically screamed, *Crematorium!*) and some games and books and Barbies and trolls, as well as the usual fussy clothes in long tissued boxes from Best & Co., the annual Hermès scarf, and cashmere cardigan with appliquéd horse heads. My uncle Bob gave me a pair of flower-shaped ruby and pink sapphire earrings from Firestone and Parsons, which I happened to be staring at in disbelief, when Ann Rose asked who they were from. She had been hovering with pencil and yellow legal pad over Will's and my shoulders in order to properly record who had sent what to whom, so that all could receive an arduous thank-you note in return.

"Well, you oughta know since you picked them out," I said, pitching the earrings into a pile of mangled wrapping paper.

"I think you are mistaken," Ann Rose said, retrieving the dark velvet box and tenderly brushing it off. "Oh, but these are *lovely.*" She didn't bat an eye as she neatly recorded the present that would have made any female other than an eight-year-old cry with pleasure, next to my name.

My grandparents' annual New Year's Day party was an all-out extravaganza that everyone from Upper East Side hoi polloi to Bowery pop artists showed up for. Preparations began the minute after Christmas. Extra help was brought in, and the maids ran around like chickens with their heads cut off. The kitchen and pantries became congested with the steady arrival of deliveries: linens and stemware brought up from storage in the basement, cheese and oysters flown in from France, wooden crates of vegetables, meats and poultry and game, silvery forty-pound salmon, a suckling pig, orchids and chrysanthemums driven in from the country. And there was wine—cases and magnums and jeroboams and Methuselahs of Burgundy and Bordeaux, and two standing lamp-sized Nebuchadnezzars of champagne.

The kitchen was a scene of harnessed insanity. I was allowed to watch, sitting on the tall metal stepstool in a corner, as long as I didn't open my mouth other than to taste whatever the chef demanded of me, even if it was parboiled toenails. French cuisine during the sixties was about as labor-intensive as food can get, and that was reflected in the hubbub of stocks simmering, chickens roasting, sugar caramelizing, cleavers and knives chopping vegetables and mincing herbs and filleting fish and deboning meat, hands kneading flour, and pink-faced voices laughing and cursing and barking orders. Baking sheets with tartlets and barquettes waiting to be baked, or cooled and filled, covered the long central worktable. The chef, Joseph, might spend an entire day piping various mixtures in muslin bags through choking silver tips into tiny circles and squares and oblongs of pastry. I'd ask to taste what looked like mocha frosting, and he'd smile and pipe a star onto my fingertip. Nine times out of ten it was some aquatic bird's mashed up liver, and I'd have swallow it holding my nose.

If I got bored, I played the bones game. I pretended that the leg and rib and neck bones roasting in the oven for stock were not from a cow but from whomever was on my hate list. Usually it was my brother Will boiling away in the stockpot with all the vegetables, on his way to being reduced, through indescribable suffering, to a syrupy essence of just rewards.

On bad days, Will got the duck press. The first time I saw the chef use it I just about had puppies. It was the quintessential Addams Family kitchen appliance. Joseph had explained the reasoning behind the torture machine, remarking that it was not very popular in America. "In my country," he'd said, "we like to have the blood and the insides of the animal in the sauce." Whereupon I'd leaned in next to him, breathing heavily in my rapture. Joseph had given me a rare smile, mistaking my enthusiasm for a burgeoning love of the culinary arts. Ha. I was imagining that those merrily crunching bones and that rosy emulsion trickling out the spout were my brother's macerated brains and skull. I saw myself rising from the dinner table to make a little announcement: "That sauce you're eating with the meat? It's my brother." Mrs. Astor would blanch. Nelson Rockefeller would choke and die. Andy Warhol would ask for seconds. My grandmother would say, "That's nice, dearie, I wondered where that rascal was." *BUUURRRRRUUUFFFFTT!*

When I saw Ann Rose enter the kitchen to speak to the chef, I quickly substituted her head in the duck press for Will's. When she saw me over in the corner and waved, I glared guiltily back at her and then clattered down from the stool, and was through the lineup of white-coated kitchen assistants and out into the help's dining room before anyone could read my evil thoughts. Skirting the table, now set and awaiting lunch for fifteen, I slipped into the warren of tiny bedrooms and skinny, old-fashioned bathrooms that was home to the maids. I liked to sneak back there sometimes, mostly just to scrutinize their lives. The rooms were painfully humble; each had a chair, a small desk, a painted bureau with a mirror on top (now decorated with sentimental cards from relatives back in the Motherland), and a narrow bed made up so skintight you could dribble a rosary across it. On one wall there invariably hung a crucifix bearing an anorexic Jesus, or a picture of the Virgin Mary, looking all forgiving. In Selma's room there were many of both. Taped to her vanity mirror was an ancient, misshapen Pepperidge Farm cookie that Selma swore "on a stack of blue Bibles" was the image of St. Rita, the patroness of all things terrible for females, like tumors and faithless husbands. Selma had shown the face to me, pointing out St. Rita's festering forehead wound, but try as I might I could never see it as anything other than a moldy Milano.

I always felt calmer after breathing in the order of Ann, and Mary, and Grace, and even Selma. After a few deep breaths I reentered the kitchen just as a tray full of sizzling, buttery, sugary palmiers came out of the oven.

I was pretty much over the Ann Rose/Santa debacle by the day of the party. A couple of times I'd even had to work myself up just to give her a show of my lingering indignation. Will and I were dressed up, he in a bow tie and blue blazer, and me in a red velvet number that clashed horribly with my red hair and had a crinoline slip that left scars on my knees. Edward, in Henrietta's arms, was presented in a tiny jacket and a pair of green plaid shorts with suspenders. We were allowed to run free, and did just that, our bloodstreams so charged with Coca-Cola and sugary carbs that flying was a real possibility.

The warm smell of wine mulled with cloves and cinnamon and raisins and almonds was the first thing that hit people when they walked off the elevators and into the long gallery, where a Viennese orchestra played and the Christmas tree rose in a ridiculous blaze of artificial light over the goldfish pond. (Actually, you could smell the wine even before you got to the sixth floor, because the doormen traditionally began drinking the stuff with the first run of guests and didn't stop until the last of them had left, eight hours later.) Waiters swam through the currents of guests, proffering caviar and hors d'oeuvres that resembled shiny mosaic tiles. People lined up at the three bars, where it took a team of men to pour champagne from the fifteen-liter bottle of Moët.

By seven my caffeine quarter had run out. It was exhausting having your cheeks pinched and your hair patted by so many pterodactyls. I was taking a break in my grandparents' bedroom, now the ladies' cloakroom, where, to the horror of the attendant maid, I was flinging myself repeatedly onto the bed piled high with the overflow of minks that couldn't be squeezed onto the teeming coat racks. There must have been fifty of them on the bed alone, in every shade of expensive imaginable. I was interrupted by Mrs. Pell's call of nature.

Pyrma Pell was one of my grandmother's "girlhood friends," and she was a fixture at the annual party. She had been the Pears soap girl back in the seventeenth century, and supposedly a great beauty. She was tiny, with hair like the stuff they put in Easter baskets, and she had a huge face, sort of like Nancy Reagan's. At any rate, there was a lot less of it than she was born with because Mrs. Pell had to have been on her fifth face-lift by the time I started remembering her. She could barely close her eyes. Mrs. Pell had initially gotten my attention because she always wore a Glinda the Good Witch dress to the New Year's party, and this year's outfit didn't disappoint; it was right out of a cotton candy spinner.

Gracing me with a look of intention from the dressing table, Mrs. Pell said, "I understand they're bringing out dinner now." She carefully repowdered her powder-caked nose, and then she rose and came over to where I was stretched out, spread-eagle on the fur bed. "Let's go in together, shall we?" She spoke like she was blowing on a dandelion stem, but I got the point. And I am nothing if not polite under duress, so I struggled to my feet with a dramatic sigh, pulled my party dress into shape, and we went to the dining room together.

When the cocktail drinkers had left, and the party had calmed down, they brought out the real food. Waiters loaded up the marble table in the dining room with hulking crown roasts of beef and the decorated salmon, game pie and terrines of foie gras, wheels of Brie de Meaux, crisp baguettes of bread, golden potato-petaled cakes of Pommes Anna, wild rice, and white asparagus, and haricots verts, and big wooden salad bowls of sherry vinaigrette–dressed mâche. Afterward came Baked Alaska, and Floating Island, and a Bûche de Noël enveloped with spun sugar and meringue mushrooms, and soaked with so much alcohol it was, by my standards, tragically inedible, so I stuck to the petits fours, which I was filling a plate with when my grandfather stood up to make a toast.

After the usual New Year and auld lang syne stuff, he said, "Peggy and I would like to publicly acknowledge a few absolutely marvelous members of our staff that we would be hard-pressed to function without." The chef was trotted out, the butler and his wife, the head waiter who was hired each year for the party, the small, fat, sweaty leader of the Viennese orchestra, my grandfather's two secretaries, Miss Pou and Heidi, and finally George the Nazi. Everyone clapped in drunken acknowledgment, even Ann Rose, who stood in a corner near the swinging door to the pantry, utterly unacknowledged.

After devouring way too many palmiers, iced little cakes, and chocolate truffles, I had to lie down for a while. When I felt better, I didn't want to go back to the party, because everyone was waltzing up a storm and you could get killed just trying to cut your way through them to get a Coke. I decided to go for a restorative snoop in the bathroom that adjoined Ann Rose's office.

It was so cool and peaceful in there, I felt instantly better. The narrow, high-ceilinged room had beautiful prewar fixtures: a wide, curvy pedestal sink, a deep, seven-foot-long tub, and a toilet built for the posteriors of yesteryear. On the far wall there was a mirrored, floor-to-ceiling cupboard with the most comprehensive collection of medical paraphernalia any child with an aberrant sense of curiosity could hope for: enema bags and douching equipment and strange rubber bulbs and bedpans, swabs and forceps and tweezers and *long* needles, and toenail clippers and scissors with peculiar angles to their noses (which I liked to pretend had mistakenly been ordered from a mortuary supply house).

I was standing there, holding one of the ends of a long, thick, pink tube in each hand, wondering what on earth this wonderful thing could be meant for, when I heard the door to the office click open. I stuffed the tube back in a corner of the cupboard and crept to the doorway to see who it was. It was, of course, Ann Rose, and she was pouring something from a tall, clear bottle into a Dixie cup. She saw me too, and on any other day I'm positive her knee-jerk reaction would have been to quickly stash the vodka, or at least pretend it was water, but not that night. She kept on pouring until the cup was full, and then she bent her head and gulped it down. A lesser sleuth would have missed her whisking a scrap of red and green striped paper under the desk with the toe of her shoe as she refilled the cup.

Well it was no real surprise to me. Ann Rose may have vigilantly hidden the traces of her Santa-ing, but I'd seen similar bottles, and then some, tucked behind the douche bags and the Time-Life This Fabulous Century series.

The sorry question I should have asked myself that night in bed, when I was too jacked up on petits fours to sleep, was what did Ann Rose get for all her slavish trouble? For trudging through the slush of holiday-crazed New York to purchase all those trinkets and toys and baubles and gizmos; in short, everything from a Revillon mink to a trick set of squirting nickels? As I'd find out in future years, I'd only witnessed a segment of Ann Rose's annual shopping odyssey. The day before the poodles and I had followed her, she'd also gone to Hammacher Schlemmer, then across town to Zabar's, then down to B. Altman, and over to Macy's, and then through the slush and ice to Verdura, east to the James Robinson Galleries, finishing up in the madness at Bloomingdale's. And who knows where she'd been the day before that.

This is what she got in return: a Christmas bonus and a bottle of Ma Griffe.

And this is what I got for the remainder of Ann Rose's life: a better stocking than Will's—even if he still got bigger presents than me.

Ugly House

A DECADE BEFORE I was born, my grandparents built a house on Mount Desert Island in Maine. They positioned it on the pink granite rocks at the entrance to Northeast Harbor, making it a beacon to anyone who was traveling by in a boat; and in Maine in the summer that means everyone. Even if you looked the other way, you couldn't miss it; the sun bounced off the Belgian hand-rolled picture windows like a paparazzi flash off a Harry Winston sparkler. Natives, tourists, and summer residents gawked as they passed by, and commented freely on the design, the artistic delusion, and the obvious moral depravity of both architect and owner.

When the sea was calm, you could hear the shrewd observations of the lobstermen:

"Jeez, Bert. Thing looks like it got skwashed by a rawk."

"Ayeh."

"Why's your house so weird?" the towheaded heirs and heiresses in my sailing class would ask when we had to tack in front of the house all the magazines had labeled *Trendsetting! Original! The Last Word!* "I don't know," I'd say, waving my hand dismissively like I didn't care, "my GPs are weird."

Summer people on Mount Desert traditionally own "cottages." This is a coy name for the brooding shingled fortresses that populate the island, both the genuine old dinosaurs and the hulking new fabrications that exude the venerable trust fund look parvenus strive for. My grandparents were done with that look; they were hell-bent on the avant-garde. I guess that's one of the only problems with old money—you get bored with it.

Positioned as we were at the mouth of the harbor, and within shouting distance of a picturesque island replete with calendar-worthy lighthouses, tour boats passed by our house all day long. They teemed with sightseers—all cameras and binoculars and lobster T-shirts—who paid to ogle the moneyed piles lining the shore. You could hear the collective intake of breath when they putt-putted round the headland to confront the shock of the new.

"Now this heeah is what we call one of our Down East un-attractions, folks!" the smart-ass tour guide would boom on his PA system. "Had the fella that did the Yoo-nited Nations Building in New Yawk do it for him. Godfrey mighty, if they ain't got his 'n' her privies with a hole in the wall above the soap so's they can talk to each other through the wahl when they're takin' a bath!"

Click, click, click would go all the Polaroids.

"Ayeh—slick as a smelt, this one is. Drives a cah can take you to Ellsworth and back in an hour, and that's the truth."

On cue, my brother Will and I would rush out and wag our butts, dancing around for the tourists like the predictably demented offspring of a wealthy eccentric.

On the morning of the day my grandparents' chef bit me, I hurried down the gravel path from the cottage my brothers and me and our governess, Henrietta, slept in. The sun scattered diamonds across the ocean in a path to the rocky beach that circled our point. I was halfway to the kitchen when—*THWACK!*—a seagull smacked into the colossal living room window. "Number Fourteen," I noted aloud, and ran back outside. By the time the screen door slammed behind me, this one was dead, a tiny smudge on the thick glass and a drifting feather the only signs of recent mortality. I picked the bird up, and it felt as weighty and warm and limp as the newborn baby someone had once mistakenly tried to get me to hold. Breakfast could wait; I hopped off the terrace onto the immaculate lawn that ran between the beach and the west side of the main house, and, skirting the wall but scrupulously avoiding the panoramic windows of my grandparents' bedroom, I ran to the kitchen garden. At the far end I had a little summer project going.

Along with snooping, collecting is another of my genetically coded destinies. My cousin Carter Burden spoke for the entire family when he said, *Collecting is in my blood. It never stops. It just keeps getting more expensive.* My grandparents were into modern art and French wines and first edition novels and Schlumberger jewelry (and sleeping masks and prescribed barbiturates). My mother was into tans acquired in different parts of the world, and anything shaped like a turtle. Uncle Ham–Uncle Ham hoarded Nazi relics. Uncle Ordway had already amassed an exhaustive stockpile of pornographic literature and would go on to curate the authoritative collection of Brooke Shields memorabilia. My initial foray into this family arena had been eraser rubbings. The summer after kindergarten, I went through a case of Eberhard HBs to get about a quart's worth of shredded pink filings. This summer I was concentrating on a dead bird collection. To be specific, I was chronicling (meticulously) mortification of the flesh—specifically, seagull flesh. I had my own little morgue going behind the English cucumbers, which, owing to the latitude of Northeast Harbor, no one had as yet gotten wind of.

Ten minutes later I was in the kitchen (hands washed) sitting on the red Formica counter and banging my sneakers against the white painted cabinets below. Three perfect circles of batter sizzled on the griddle of the massive black range, awaiting consummation by yours truly. A plate stacked high with flat, crispy bacon was keeping warm on the shelf above, and I stole a piece, cramming it into my mouth like a stick of Juicy Fruit.

"You know, I don 'ave all the day to cook for you." Arturo, the new chef, winked as he flipped the pancakes over. We were at the zenith of the houseguest season (plane met at Bar Harbor airport twenty-six times, sheets in the guest cottages changed forty-nine times, signature lobster dinner prepared and served nineteen times). He turned back to his preparations on the work-table: an elaborate picnic lunch he and one of the kitchen girls were in the process of assembling and packing into creaky wicker suitcases. Gloria, a sluggish native with a showcase bosom and bountiful rear, simpered at him. Arturo was the most exotic piece of Mediterranean manhood she had ever seen outside of the Bar Harbor Criterion movie theater. Arturo rewarded her with a grin and a clack of his long white chops, something he was unfortunately prone to doing. A drop of oil slid down the forelock he vainly positioned each morning to escape the hold of his toque.

It had taken a leap of faith for my grandfather to hire a non-Gaul, and it never would have happened but for the publication of Elizabeth David's *Italian Food*. Arturo had exploded onto our domestic scene only a few months earlier, all springing black hair and ion-charged machismo.

"I think they're ready," I announced to him, jumping down from the counter to see what was more important than my blueberry pancakes.

Arturo turned the pancakes onto a warm plate and left me to get the butter and syrup myself.

"I gotta get the peek-neek ready so you must do for youself," he said, pouring a stream of smooth red gazpacho into a steel thermos. He wedged it into one of the baskets, beside a corpulent slice of Brie and a stack of cream-colored Bakelite cups. "'Ay! Not so theeck!" He admonished Gloria, who was slathering sandwich bread with egg salad. Arturo politely moved her aside. He added some chervil and a stick of soft butter to the bowl, and then demonstrated to his devotee how to smooth a thin layer of the mixture onto the pieces of brown and white bread; and how to cut off the crusts just so, and then the square into triangles, so what you were left with was an elegant little sandwich with the caloric testosterone of a Big Mac. "You finish this, then you do the ros bif. And *theen, theen, theen!* Not fat like your kine a san-wich!" Gloria's response was to bat her chalky blue eyelids and squeeze her elbows together so that her breasts struggled to leap out from her pink uniform.

∽

As the summer progressed, the menus my grandfather planned became increasingly elaborate as more and more houseguests arrived on the shuttle from Boston. He began each day by ringing his secretary in New York.

"Miss Pou," he would pronounce into the telephone, lying in his bed with a crackling morning fire, gazing out the window at yachts and sailboats and Boston Whalers coming through the Western Way.

The William A. M. Burden Company was at Rockefeller Center, where the titanic bronze Atlas struggled under planet Earth at the entrance to the building, and upstairs, on the thirty-second floor, Miss Pou struggled under my grandfather. She had been hired during his ambassadorship to Belgium and would remain until his death, which she would fervently wish for throughout the last ten years of his life. The offices took up the whole of the floor and had killer views from every window of the modern, hard-edged space. The carpeting was a shocking yellow, the leather chairs and sofas black, and the built-in desks smooth white Formica. Workers moved discreetly past paintings and sculptures by Léger and Arp and Diebenkorn and Warhol and Brancusi.

There were only two people on my grandfather's payroll to whom my mother was civil, and one of them was his secretary. Miss Pou's first name was Mildred, which cracked Will and me up almost as much as her *pee-you* last, and her daily recommended vitamin C intake came from whiskey sours, which is probably the biggest reason my mother liked her. She was from Shreveport, Louisiana, and had once dated Elvis ("Nothin' but a wet kisser, darlin' "). She changed her hair color once a month, but my favorite thing about her was that she had no belly button because the surgeon had forgotten to put it back after her tummy tuck.

"Miss Pou, the president of M.I.T. is arriving tomorrow at three and I would like to serve grouse for dinner."

"Certainly, sir. Though I believe it may be a bit early—"

"Miss Pou. My food calendar states that mid-August is the season for grouse, so I am certain you'll find a resource."

"Yes, Mr. Burden. I suppose I can call Scotland."

"Marvelous. Bring twelve. Catch the eight-thirty flight. Good-bye."

After dressing for his ten o'clock doubles game at the Harbor Club, my grandfather held a morning consultation with Arturo in the living room, seated beside the floor-to-ceiling window that faced the ocean, in his favorite bright yellow Eero Saarinen chair, a Chesterfield smoldering in the ashtray beside him and a pencil poised above his customary brown spiral notebook. "Arturo," he would begin, adjusting his steel-rimmed glasses and signaling with his long fingers for the chef to take a seat. "This Wednesday I'm hosting a luncheon for some important people from Washington . . ."

My grandfather was a devotee of chaudfroid. This is the culinary technique whereby ordinary foodstuffs such as poultry and fish are transformed into gleaming, elaborately decorated *objets* that seem hardly edible. A lot of white sauce and rubbery aspic is involved, fortified to cementing capability with abundant amounts of gelatin. It stands to reason that chaudfroid has gone the way of pillbox hats and employing leeches to bring down a fever.

Arturo was also excessively fond of chaudfroid. His kitchen could produce a buffet worthy of depiction by Tiepolo. He was Bob Mackie with a stewing hen; tied up and into the pot she went, and out that bird came to be placed on a jittery stage of aspic, enrobed in gelatinous ivory sateen with intricately stenciled truffles and greenery running up and down her showgirl breasts. Arturo knew how to please the ladies. For my grandmother, a Kon-Tiki enthusiast, he fashioned Tahitian cucumber outriggers with little oars carved out of carrots, filling them with composed salads of lobster or crab or tiny diced vegetables, bound with copious amounts of mayonnaise, aka French luncheon glue. These vessels were set to sail on the table between the dishes of glorified poultry, fish, and pastry-wrapped terrines. "Oh, Arturo!" my grandmother would exclaim. "You are so very talented." And she'd hum a snatch of "E Le Ka Lei Lei" as she helped herself to one.

⤲⤳

After I'd polished off my pancakes and a dozen strips of bacon, which my mother would have been horrified to witness (*Jesus, Toots! How fat do you want to be?*), and after I'd checked on my birds, and been forced to bury two of them due to mortification of the flesh so extreme that if left unchecked might lead to olfactory discovery, I returned to the kitchen because I had nothing better to do until we set sail for the picnic later in the morning.

Arturo and his sous-chef were making tortellini. They were shaping and sealing the delicate spinach dough with the economy of assembly line workers. Arturo asked me if I would like to make one, and he showed me how to do it with unexpected patience. I watched as he caught up a spoonful of the filling, a pink and green mixture of raw veal and fresh herbs, and plopped it on the square of dough. He brushed the edges with water; then deftly folded the square diagonally, then into a sort of croissant shape, sealing the tips together with a tender little pinch. He might have been diapering a baby.

After a couple of village idiot efforts, I shaped one perfectly. In recognition of my accomplishment, Arturo clapped his hands, threw me up in the air over his head, and soundly bit me on the ass.

Well, what do you *think* I did?

Wailing like a fire engine, I ran from the kitchen, leaving the bewildered chef standing there with his arms stretched out and a *ma?* on his lips, and ran straight to my grandparents' bedroom. They were getting changed after their morning tennis game and were, as was their habit, walking around in their underwear, oblivious to anyone who entered the room.

"Hello, dearie," said my grandmother. "You're just in time to hook me up, isn't she, girls?" The poodles stared blankly from the nest of expensive French linen they had clawed around themselves at the foot of the bed. I began fumbling with my grandmother's long-line bra/panty/girdle contraption, halting along the way to tuck in the ripples of her soft back.

"Arturo BIT me," I told her, exhibiting the spot on my butt and pointedly wiping tears from my face with the hand that was fastening her up.

"Well, I'm sure he didn't mean it. Brothers can be like that!"

"Arturo. The CHEF," I said.

"Oh, well that's different. Thank you, dearie." She got up with a small *brfftt* and padded back to her dressing room, humming "All Things Bright and Beautiful."

I turned to my grandfather, not my usual ally, but my impatience got the better of me.

My grandfather was a big man. Once slim, he now had a paunch that cantilevered impressively over his British Y-fronts and the long stick legs below. He looked like an Edward Lear drawing of old secretary bird wading around in a marsh. There was a vulnerability to him when he was seminude, making him look almost cozy.

I blubbed my story out to him in a stream of snot and vituperative barbs. He stood in front of me idly scratching his white-haired chest as he listened with a bland expression. Midway, I became distracted by the pointy look of his underpants and the consequent thought of his hoary old penis, which caused me to splutter to an end far less intelligently than I would have liked.

"I feel certain you'll recover," said my grandfather with a bemused smile. "Good chefs are hard to find."

His tone of voice suggested that it would be more likely for the Cold War to end than for him to let a chef go at the height of the season.

All I could think of to say was "ERRRAGHH!" as I ran from the room and headed back to our cabin.

Edward was sitting in the middle of our living room, surrounded by a wall of blocks and basking in his achievement. Henrietta was in the tiny kitchen, out of range, so I knocked the wall over and headed for the telephone next to the stone fireplace. My mother wasn't home so I didn't have to lose face with her too. I slammed out the cabin and headed for the dock.

It was considered déclassé to have a pretentious yacht if you were a summertime Downeaster. Ours was a pumped-up version of a lobster boat. Her name was *Spindrift*, and she was comfortably broad, with an ample rear for entertaining, a large but simple galley, and enough sleeping bunks below to overnight six. Due to my grandfather's love of speed, she had a big BMW engine and could make thirty knots in a following sea.

Captain Closson was the ex-navy man who ran my grandfather's boats in summer. Every day during the summer season, Captain drove over from Southwest Harbor, rowed a dinghy out to where our boat was moored in Northeast Harbor, and brought her over to tie up at our dock and await orders. You could be as sure of finding him down there at nine o'clock, dressed in his khaki uniform, black knit tie, and thick-soled black lace-up shoes, as you could of waking up in the morning.

Captain was a big man with a face the color of the salt pork he liked to use in his chowders. He parted his thinning gray hair with a twenty-nine-cent comb and a handful of Vitalis, and you could see his freckled scalp through the furrows the teeth made. His arms and hands were scarred from bear traps, knives, and fishhooks, and he could catch anything in the sea—cod, bluefish, mackerel, flounder, stripers, haddock, shark, pollack, and even the odd lobster. He had the strength to pull a forty-pound cod up on a deep-sea line with one hand, while holding your feet and dunking your bratty little head in the ocean with the other.

When Captain was in the war, he caught two bullets from the Japs. One went through his throat, which gave him a weird dent there, and the other lodged in his privates, or so it was said. He talked about the war when he took us cruising a couple of times each summer. It would be five or six completely torqued-up kids and him. We'd moor up Somes Sound by Treasure Island, or in Burnt Cove Harbor next to Swan's, and in the morning we'd wake up and there he'd be at the stove in the galley, frying up bacon and sausages, unshaven and groggy from staying up all night telling dirty jokes and ghost stories.

Confidant, prankster, philosopher, Captain was the patriarchal pinch hitter. I'd adored him since before I could speak. When I was at camp earlier in the summer, about an hour away from my grandparents' place, Captain would come visit every couple of weeks. He'd arrive in his station wagon, a seagoing vessel itself, and after a half hour joking and giggling with all the girls in my cabin, he would take me out for lunch at the local Tastee Freez. On the way back he liked to pull to the side of the road to "cuddle." He'd slide me over beside him on the front bench seat and start kissing me on the lips. I'd try to wriggle away with an "Oh my God I'm going to be late," but he'd say, "Let's just sit here a little longer." Then he'd drive me back to camp.

This is how stupid I was: I tried to talk to my mother about it. As for a lot of eight-year-olds, it was excruciatingly awkward for me to discuss anything sexual with an adult, but she really helped me deal with it.

"Honestly, Toots," she laughed, "I don't know why you're having such a cow over it. Let an old man have some fun! Anyway, he got his nuts shot off in the war, so it's not like he can really *do* anything."

I forgave him. Anything to keep the family together.

❧

Forward, in between the bow and the anchor storage, there was a rumble seat cut into the deck of the *Spindrift*, which was where my brother and I sat on the way to the picnic, bumping up and down with the waves, the saline wind whipping through our hair when we popped our heads up to scan the ocean for dolphins. I had given myself a singularly unattractive haircut at camp earlier that summer, the kind of blunt bob that is too short to contain and too long to stay out of your eyes. My hair was lacerating my eyeballs and my head looked like a whipped-up bale of straw, so I huddled back down against the warm red leather seat and curled my bare toes over the lip of the deck.

We began playing the Would You Rather? game. Or rather, Will did. He loved the game, and it was about the only time he broke out of his monosyllabic pattern. I was still seething from the morning's crime, and preoccupied with planning revenge.

"Would you rather sneeze dog shit or vomit rubber cement?" Will asked.

"Neither."

"Okay, would you rather go to the bathroom through your eyeballs or smell stuff with your butt."

"*Quit.* I don't want to play," I told him sharply. I needed to concentrate. I was thinking rat poison in the Wild Turkey bottle. More interesting than the old liquid-nicotine-in-the-aftershave trick, it would provide a cripplingly painful death. Any self-respecting soul sister of Wednesday Addams knew the effects of rat poison on a person. According to the encyclopedia of poisons I'd found on the bomb shelter bookshelf, all it would take was one gram of barium chloride; that was a fatal dose.

But how to do Arturo . . .

"All right, all right," said Will, "would you rather have to listen to Petula Clark sing 'Downtown' all day long for the rest of your life or leave a trail of calamine lotion wherever you go?"

As Captain Closson slowed the boat to pass into the cove of Placentia Island, where we would go ashore for the picnic, snatches of conversation floated forward from the stern.

". . . And if LBJ even *thinks* about backing down from those slit-eyed pinkos—"

". . . Honestly, darling, Paris is overrun with the things!"

"A ha ha ha! You don't mean he sold it at a dollar ten a share, the muddleheaded bastard . . ."

They were the tones of self-confident, self-satisfied, unabashedly tipsy grown-ups. Getting them to shore for a picnic would be tricky.

The first rowboat carried precious cargo: the bar and, even more essential, the shaker of drinks—the butler. Adolphe wore formal attire even when presiding over an al fresco event such as this. Adolphe had never learned to swim. Still, he maintained the dignity of a wrongly sentenced monarch as he suffered himself to be transported, sitting stiffly upright like a pasha in the bow of the dinghy. When Captain plowed its nose into the sand and leapt out, painter in hand, Adolphe scampered with surprising agility ashore and onto higher ground to take up his critical station, shaking up martinis and daiquiris and sours.

Will and I leapt off the boat and swam like maniacs through the icy water to shore. We lingered over the beach, ripe with the pleasant stink of things washed up from the sea, and popped seaweed pustules at each other. As they arrived, the grown-ups made their way to the picnic spot with varying degrees of dexterity. I prayed my grandfather would trip over a granite boulder and break his head open, but he made it okay despite practically needing a walker. By the time everyone gathered, a smoky driftwood fire was ablaze, keeping the mosquitoes at bay, and the picnic hampers had been opened. The party perched on logs and boulders while the help passed out cups of chilled gazpacho and vichyssoise, glasses of cold white Burgundy (as if they needed it), and plates piled with the sandwiches made by the slut and the pedophile that morning. (Which I did not touch.)

I was working my way through each ruffly papered compartment of the assortment box of Pepperidge Farm cookies, envisioning Arturo lashed to one of the buoys out the Western Way (the ones that have dead men clinging to them below the waterline, in various stages of decomposition), when my grandmother came up to me. Her hairnet was escaping off to one side, and her piped wool blazer sported a smear of Brie.

"Here, dearie," she said with alcohol-sweet breath as she pressed a packet of Wash'n Dri on me. "Are you feeling all right? You're unusually quiet today."

My sweet grandmother. She tried so hard to make everything right, even without the tools. She purposefully had no memory of what I'd told her this morning. She was wasted, and it would take Captain and his mate to get her back to the rowboat and then up the ladder onto the *Sprindrift*, where she could hopefully snooze it off in a deck chair all the way home, in time for a nice bath before getting dressed for the cocktail hour at six.

I was the first off the boat when we tied up to our dock, pleading an urgent desire for my own john. In truth I needed to check on Number Twelve, who had that morning begun to exhibit a major larva infestation that needed further documentation.

I ran smack into Arturo. He was bouncing down the back

path from the dock where he often went fishing during his break. His toque was in place, wobbling away on top of his oily head. His sleeves were rolled up over his Popeye forearms, and the double-breasted jacket of his kitchen whites was unbuttoned at the top so that a flap hung down to one side, revealing a lurid hedge of the thick dark hair that undoubtedly covered all unseen parts of his body. A small ray hung on the end of his line; its white belly caught the light as it slowly spun, like a dead man on a rope. I tried to scurry past, but Arturo blocked my path. Clacking like a windup set of dentures, he gestured at me, including me in his merry game. He held out the ray. From his jacket he took a knife and dropped it, blade first, into the ray's pocket of a mouth.

"*Sick*," I said.

I suppose he was trying to get me to laugh, maybe in some sort of completely weird expression of regret for the morning's wrongdoing. When it didn't work, Arturo shrugged his shoulders skyward and trotted off to the kitchen, proudly holding out the grotesque *nature morte* for all to see.

❧

That evening Will and I were allowed to sit with our grandparents and their guests before they had dinner. We drank Coca-Colas with crushed ice that the maids, in their formal black-and-white uniforms, so at odds with the primal rock and sea, offered us from a silver tray. Relaxing a little, I inhaled the scent of ocean and lilies and mold.

The living-dining area was a curved, open-plan space that was divided by a strip of earth planted with baby spruce trees and neon green moss. Normally, Will and I spent the cocktail hour leaping through the trees, from the elevated dining area down to the living room and back up again. When we tired of that, and when our grandparents were focused on Walter Cronkite, we climbed to the top of the bookcases that rose fif-

teen feet above the length of the built-in sofa, and plopped repeatedly down on to the feathered cushions below. But now I
was being momentarily held hostage by a florid man wearing a
yellow ascot with crabs on it. He was interrogating me about the
upcoming fourth-grade syllabus when Obadiah shambled in.
His timing always was impeccable.

Obadiah was the adorable puppy with Dumbo ears that my
mother had snatched out of a pet shop window, only to have him
grow up to be a basset hound. Animal lover though she was,
every chance she got she packed him off with us to visit our
grandparents. He was fat, engulfed in his own saliva, and endearingly bent on parasuicide. *En vacances* in Maine he was fond
of casting himself into the ocean, typically between the boat and
the dock so that he could be crushed between them as he
drowned. You'd think this would be a safe bet; as each wave
passed by, Obadiah would get sucked under and slammed against
the struts of the float and the wooden hull. Slightly less dramatic
were his attempts to run away from home. I'm pretty sure the
idea was to either starve or get run over by at least one automobile along the way. As he set off at a snail's plod, you could almost see the miniature hobo sack swaying on a pole over his
shoulder.

The main reason Obadiah never succeeded in completing his
mission was that he required an audience. He would lumber
down and heave himself off the dock only when there was a
crowd of people to watch. Invariably someone dragged him out
by his collar, usually falling in as well from the sodden effort of
the recovery. Likewise, when Obadiah decamped for parts unknown, he would alert everyone by standing at the top of the
driveway for about an hour, staring at the house for a misty-
eyed final look. Sighing heavily, he would eventually set off.
The way out to the world at large was half a mile long. Whoever
saw him during the two hours it took Obadiah to reach the main
road would alert a rescue squad, who in turn had plenty of time

to repot a dozen begonias, read *The New Yorker* cover to cover, or prepare a Baked Alaska before hopping in the car to go pick him up.

I'm convinced Obadiah was welcomed into my grandparents' house not because they were particularly fond of him but because he looked remarkably chic licking his privates under the Milton Avery landscapes or snoring on his back on the Bertoia furniture. Obadiah was photographed frequently beneath the boomerang-shaped Noguchi dining table, a layered inverted pyramid of honey-colored maple that might have come from a scrapped NASA project. In many of the pictures he is caught gazing balefully into the camera lens with an empty Baccarat goblet next to his elephantine splayed feet. As clumsy as the dog was, he knew how to treat the stemware with respect.

Now Obadiah traveled slowly across the living room to pose beside my grandfather, who was conversing with a deeply tanned West Coast sort who leaned toward him attentively, popping macadamia nuts in his mouth every two seconds from the hors d'oeuvres tray. Obadiah fixed his runny eyes on the trajectory between the man's mouth and the tray. Freed from my cross-examination, I was studying my grandfather as he talked, as he smiled his dry smile and emphasized his points with languid gestures. He recrossed his legs with the help of his hands and, draining his glass, signaled Adolphe for another. Telepathically I signaled to him that he had one last chance to apologize, and to fire Arturo so that we could get on with the rest of the summer. I gave him exactly seven minutes, while I sipped my Coke, pretending to leaf through *Paris Match*. During those seven minutes, my grandfather and Mr. Hollywood covered the topics of post–World War Two Brazilian aeronautics, the disappointing fledgling '63 California vintage, and the shocking trend of Harvard's anticipated diversification, but my grandfather did not apologize.

Adolphe whispered to my grandmother that dinner was

served, and the grown-ups went up the low stairs beside the fir trees to the table. Will and I remained behind, lying across the huge cushions on the sofa, sucking on the sugary crushed ice at the bottom of our Coke glasses, he reading the funnies from the *Ellsworth Times* and I one of the vintage *Vault of Horror* comic books that I kept stashed behind the American Heritage series on the fifth shelf. I watched as the butler pulled out my grandmother's chair for her, and she carefully set her drink down beside a trio of wineglasses before half falling onto the slippery, modern plywood seat. Gathered around the table, the grownups looked like crazed surgeons in a slasher film, their faces flushed above the silly bibs they'd tied around their necks, and sharp instruments for torturing crustaceans lying menacingly alongside their place mats.

An enormous bowl of steamed clams was borne in. Adolphe stood unflinchingly beside my grandmother as she tussled with them, then he continued round the table as if he had the entire summer left to serve just this course. He reappeared to pour Taittinger champagne into the oversized V-shaped Steuben glasses, each so heavy you needed two hands to lift it. A skinned white peach was wedged into the point at each base; as the meal progressed the fruit flavored the champagne and the wine macerated the fruit.

That left Selma with the lobster. She stumbled a little under the weight of the scarlet carapaces, her old-fashioned spectacles opaque from the steam. Anna trailed with a bowl of buttered peas from the garden. Next out the swinging door of the kitchen would come corn on the cob, and then the golden ballooning popovers, and then a refill of champagne. I knew the drill like I knew bedtime followed brushing your teeth, and maggots followed flies on the decomposing body of a seagull.

Obadiah had singled out a woman at the north corner of the table, though she was as yet unaware. At dinner parties, he liked to position himself exactly in the middle of the diners and, from this advantageous position, choose a patsy. Plonking himself down at the victim's feet, under the table, in line with his or her crotch, he would gaze steadfastly up, the deep red pockets of his eyes sparkling with eye goo. If pressed, Obadiah might even moan a little. Should the victim need more encouragement, he'd give his or her ankle a lick. During summer, most of these ankles were tanned and unsheathed, and the startling effect of Obadiah's long, hot, dripping wet tongue usually resulted in something being thrown at him. If it happened to be food, he scarfed it down with the speed of a raptor. Obadiah had flashes of real intelligence.

Back on the sofa, I'd moved on to a moldy issue of *Chamber of Chills*. A grisly pictorial of zombies ransacking a kitchen afforded me a sudden brainstorm.

"Hey, Will," I said to Will, nudging him with the toe of my sneaker.

"Mmm."

"I just got an idea and it's a really good one."

"Uh huh." My dyslexic brother was laboring through *Mandrake the Magician*. I kicked him.

"What!"

"Listen—when everyone's asleep after lunch—"

"Ayeeeee!" cried Obadiah's quarry, upsetting her champagne glass and elbowing her popover to the floor. Obadiah snatched it up and waddled briskly off through the fir trees and out the screen door.

Will and I slunk out the other way; he was, after all, our dog.

A fog had crept in during dinner, rolling silently off the ocean to hang in droplets from the needles of the pine trees and the thorns and blossoms of the wild rosebushes that grew at the top of the seawall. It clung to my hair and stood out in tiny wet granules on the thick wool of my sweater as we walked up the gravel path from the main house to our cottage. Obadiah clambered to the top of the stairs ahead of us. As I let him in, light spilled out onto the red painted steps, and the welcoming bulk of Henrietta spilled out after it. Edward was on her hip, sucking on a block, and he glared at me. I told him I was sorry for wrecking his wall, and he broke into a smile. "Bedtime," said Henrietta, hugging us with one arm, and exhaling the smoke from her Winston over our heads. That suited me fine. I had a night of planning to do.

⤖

The following day we waited until it was the quiet hour when the adults were sleeping off the effects of a morning in the sun and a boozy lunch, and the help watched soap operas behind their bedroom doors or dozed in green wicker rocking chairs on the porch overlooking the vegetable garden.

Will and I started with the walk-in refrigerator. Silently, we picked up a massive blue enamel pot of bouillabaisse, and last night's tin-foiled lobster carcasses, destined for tomorrow's stew. Then we filled a laundry hamper with brown paper bundles of beef tenderloin and stewing chickens, and the waxed packages of smoked salmon and sturgeon from Zabar's in the City. We moved on to netted sacks of grapefruit and oranges, bundles of leeks and carrots, wooden crates of Bibb lettuce and spinach and corn, and newspaper-wrapped cones of arugula, and mâche and frisée picked in the garden that morning. I pricked my fingers grappling with the artichokes, and broke more than a few of the quail eggs when I threw them on top of everything in the hamper. Working as a team, Will and I emptied the room systematically, transporting everything with buckets and a pulley system to where we cached it behind the three massive chimneys on the dead-flat roof.

Nothing was spared. We loaded up packages of bacon, a bunch of bananas, the four mackerel my brother had caught off the dock yesterday, a bundle of Italian parsley, half a crème caramel, and all the stinky cheeses flown in from France. We took the basket of local chanterelle mushrooms, and the bags of mussels, the barnacles on them scratching us through the burlap as we hoisted them to the roof. Up went a white enamel tray of lavender-colored squab (neatly dressed and lined up like the dead of battle), matchstick bundles of haricots verts, wooden pints of raspberries from the garden and *fraises du bois* from the woods, and cartons of tiny blueberries handpicked by my brother and me at ten hard-earned cents an hour. We stacked the remains of our grandfather's black-and-white striped birthday cake (inscribed "TO POP WITH OP") on top of some crates of Coca-Cola and ginger ale, and lugged it all up, only breaking a few of the bottles in the process. We left Arturo's ray.

When we'd cleaned out the walk-in, we emptied the kitchen and pantry refrigerators, taking all the milk and cream, the cottage cheese and ham and mustards and mayonnaise and jams and jellies, and the pitchers of iced Constant Comment tea and the orange juice squeezed that morning, plus about a hundred eggs, and fifteen pounds of Land O'Lakes butter (salted and unsalted), and every kind of Pepperidge Farm bread they made back then (whole wheat, sandwich, very thin, and toasting white), and the twelve packs of Thomas' English muffins that my family went through in a week—with at least ten of the one-pound packets of the (salted) butter.

We took a short breather before clearing out all of the drawers, cupboards, and bins. Flour, sugar, chunks of Belgian baking chocolate, cornstarch, rolled oats, tins of anchovies and StarKist tuna, tomato paste and Campbell's chicken noodle soup, baking soda and candied violets and vinegars and Tabasco, Grape-Nuts and Corn Flakes and Cap'n Crunch. We left nothing—with the exception of my grandmother's essential All-Bran (out of respect). By the time we'd packed the hamper with Triscuits and Finn Crisps and Martinson coffee and Fauchon tea, dried prunes and Fizzies, and boxes and boxes of Pepperidge Farm cookies

(Assorted, Bordeaux, Lido, Milano, Pirouettes, and shortbread), and macadamia nuts (twelve jars) and After Eight dinner mints and Lay's potato chips, which I ate while I worked, we were dead tired. We tossed a couple cans of Alpo and a box of Milk-Bones on top and lugged the final load up to the roof. Back in the kitchen we sat panting on the cool gray linoleum floor, and realized that we'd overlooked the freezer, but it was perilously close to teatime. As a compromise, we wound it up with a roll of duct tape. After a quick check on the progress/decay of Number Four and Number Nine, Will and I hopped on our bikes and rode into town for ice cream.

Seated on the glittery stools at the soda fountain, we giggled a little at each other while we waited for the ice cream to be dipped and then packed into the sugar cones.

"Boy are they ever gonna get a surprise when they go to start making dinner," I said, swinging my legs nervously. It *had* been a bold reprisal. "Maybe Granddaddy'll have a heart attack when he finds out and I won't have to do the rat poison thing."

"Yeah," said Will.

"I hope Arturo has to go back to stupid Italy. Maybe they'll fire Gloria too—wouldn't *that* be great."

"I guess."

Will was looking a little pale—and more than a little uncertain, the pansy.

I said, "You know I was never *really* going to poison Granddaddy." And I wouldn't have. It was just that I like to plot big.

The euphoria of our delinquent deed was beginning to sour. In our unfolding awareness, I found I'd lost my appetite, even for a double-scoop cone of fudge ripple. We were like a couple of terriers that had gutted a herd of goats in a blood orgy and, now that the adrenaline was subsiding, were thinking, Holy shit—why did we do that? Our master is going to *kill* us.

We charged the melting ice cream to our grandparents' account and coasted silently home.

$\mathcal{DC}$

MY MOTHER WAS nothing if not practical. She owed this trait, her saving grace, to her ancestors. The end product of twelve arrogant generations of New Englanders descended from a handful of Plymouth Colony founders, Leslie Hamilton was the only issue of an army colonel and a melancholic ex-spinster whose sole objective in life was to search out, examine, cross-reference, and interpret every branch, twig, leaf, and aphid of her family tree. According to my mother, her mother's premature death was due to hypochondria, but I'm convinced she was a victim of *genealogical nervosa*, a debilitating disease that attacks the brain cells of the afflicted with the speed of a tanker's oil slick. Research has correlated the illness to membership in societies such as the Colonial Dames Society, the Daughters of the American Revolution, and the Mayflower Society. Sadly, there remains no cure, only preventive abstinence.

In a celebratory wrap-up of her first—and final, as she saw it—year of widowhood, my mother relocated us to the arty environs of Georgetown. The house we moved into was a comfortably disheveled federal row house on Reservoir Road. It was painted a peeling biscuit color and was set back from the herringbone-brick sidewalk by a wrought iron fence with the world's clangiest gate. There were three skinny floors, a basement, and a cool finished attic. Naturally, my brother got the attic.

I had the front room on the second floor, and a bunk bed, which I did not ask for. I am not a bunk bed sort of person. Edward had his crib in a cubicle next to mine. My mother's master suite took up the rest of the floor. Henrietta had her smoky domain in the basement, and hanging out with her down there, watching TV, shooting the prepubescent breeze, felt like patronizing a grotto nightclub.

Behind the house, a narrow garden ran twenty feet or so down to a freestanding garage barely large enough for my mother's new Austin Healey Sprite. The garage was accessed by one of the alleys that ran behind the houses of Georgetown like convoluted but biologically necessary plumbing.

Alley life was like ant farm life. The cramped thoroughfares were not only practical, they were highly social. They were where you took a shortcut to the bus stop, or met up with your friends, or roller skated, rode your Stingray, skateboarded, and jumped rope even though there was a continual flow of pedestrian and motor traffic and the pavement was maybe as wide as a 1965 station wagon.

A lot of artists had studios in the old garages and carriage houses, and my mother had hers two alleys over, in a lopsided structure that had once been a car repair shop. Before that, it had purportedly been the shanty of a freed slave, though that was never validated and was probably a stab at historical sensationalism on the part of the Realtor. It was a ramshackle little space made airy by a glass-windowed garage door on one side. When it was warm out, everyone kept their doors up or open, and neighboring artists would trickle by when they grew bored with their own endeavors.

My mother did mostly animal sculptures, stylized turtles and seals and otters and bears that she carved from huge blocks of alabaster and soapstone, or chiseled from stumps of wood the size of small cars. I adored being in her studio. It was at once cozy and macabre, a cross between the school art room and a serial killer's lair. The room smelled of earth and stone and wood, and everything in it was coated with a lovely soft, carcinogenic dust. Torturous tools of the trade—rasps and files and chisels and mallets—lay about on the worktables amid sculptures in various stages of progress. On the rough wood shelving photographic reference books leaned up against boxes of sandpaper, drills and their bits, and buckets permanently lined with a coating of hard white plaster. Next to an old laundry sink was a ten-pound block of modeling clay, swaddled in thick plastic sheeting to keep it malleable. Aprons, welding masks, and safety goggles hung from pegs along a wall. Sacks of plaster of Paris used to make the molds the finished bronzes would be cast from lay in a heap in a corner. When you opened the sacks up, they smelled divine, just like a dank mausoleum.

Normally our mother didn't have the time of day for us, but in her studio she took on her birthday persona. We could run amok in there and she just laughed. We ripped into the clay like mice into a bar of soap, and made action figures (Will—soldiers and guns; me—horses and victims for the guillotine), and dipped our arms and legs in buckets of wet plaster she made up for us so we could pretend we were victims of ghastly car wrecks.

If a homework project called for creativity, and she happened to be in town, our mother became a wildly enthusiastic collaborator. The Nagasaki After the Atom Bomb project she helped me build for Social Studies was not to be believed. I considered it the apogee of my five years of combined elementary school training, and if the terrain displayed over the four-foot length of chicken wire and painted plaster was more doomsday lunar crater than Japanese ground zero, the care that went into depicting human carnage and vegetative devastation was justly rewarded. But I couldn't have scorched the model trees without her knowledge of acetylene torch work.

Gomez and Morticia would have been so proud of my A+.

As it turned out, so was my mother. When I presented her

with my inscribed gold star, she stunned me by putting her arms around me and awkwardly kissing the side of my head. I, in turn, nearly forgot myself and leaned in to receive it—but then I remembered that she had only just arrived from Miami and was leaving for Haiti in the morning, so it wasn't too difficult to remind myself of all the literary mothers she wasn't, which was one of the formulas for hating her that I followed. Blame it on the lower school English Department.

Lamenting the fact that I wasn't an Addams was really only 75 percent of the equation; the rest of the time I longed to be my favorite character from *A Wrinkle in Time*, Meg Murry, if only to have her mother—the gifted, beautiful, wonderfully vague but fiercely doting Mrs. Murry who was always there to support her nearsighted, ugly duckling daughter, someone I resembled not a little. The fact that Meg Murry's father (also achingly brilliant) had vanished, and was subsequently found to be not dead but merely on another planet in a glass tube, the prisoner of a giant brain named IT, would have no bearing on my obsession with this book.

Matters ran smoothly at home when our mother was out of town, thanks to the domestic superintendancy of Cassie Diggins and Henrietta. When she was home, everything went out of whack. Like I couldn't go to the bathroom. Which is why I remember November 22, 1963, the day that President Kennedy was shot, as the day of the Kennedy Poo, because my mother had left for Mexico that morning.

Other than that, things were okay. Meaning, I was mostly having a decent childhood, other than the glaring hole of deprivation caused by my not having a pony. Since my father hadn't had much of an impact on my life when he was alive, I can't say I missed him. It's hard to miss someone you didn't know in the first place. To save my brother from the dishonor of having to repeat fifth grade and be in the same class as me, Will was sent off to boarding school. But we were already beginning to part ways gender-wise, so I didn't really miss him either.

The most cherished thing in my possession then was an autographed copy of Charles Addams's book *Nightcrawlers*. I had purloined it from my grandparents' library in the city, along with *Homebodies*, *Drawn and Quartered*, and *Dear Dead Days*. I deserved them more than my grandparents. Besides, they were friends with the Maker himself, referring to him as "Charlie" even, so they could get more copies anytime they wanted. I'd met Him once, when He was over for lunch in the country. I'd been suitably starstruck, and uncharacteristically polite, but He hadn't found me amusing enough for conversation. The whole thing was reminiscent of my meeting with Walt Disney, when, during our visit to California, my brother and I had knocked on the back door of his Beverly Hills house. Old Walt had actually answered the door himself. I don't remember what my expectations were at the time. I was five, so undoubtedly they were vast, but they probably weren't that Mr. Disney, creator of *Cinderella* and *Bambi*, would glare at us and snap, "Scram!" before slamming the door in our faces.

Oh, happy mournful day! On September 18, 1965, the Addams Family came to television. Even though I much preferred her two dimensional persona, I stepped up my slavish emulation of Wednesday Addams. I even built a replica of her guillotine. This was a crude but fully functional piece of engineering that I constructed with pieces of wood from my FAO Schwarz riding stable after watching the episode where Wednesday chops off the head of her Marie Antoinette doll. The blade was problematic, since Cassie Diggins would have missed even a piece of Saran Wrap from the kitchen, so I had to make do using a pocket mirror and pair of industrial-sized scissors that I snapped at the exact moment the mirror fell, which was sort of cheating but ultimately had the desired effect.

I quickly ran out of things to decapitate. Will wasn't around much, and I was too attached to my hamster. I considered martyring the baby, but Edward was too enthusiastic to be a worthy victim. He would have gladly laid his gurgly little melon on my guillotine, but he didn't deserve the honor. And Mary Falusi, the old lady who sometimes filled in for Henrietta, would die of heartbreak. She loved my little brother like he was the young John the Baptist. (Mary Falusi was very religious.)

The last time I'd behaved magnanimously toward Edward was on the night he was born. This event had long been anticipated, mostly with intense skepticism, and had finally occurred when my mother hit the eight-month gestational mark and began running up and down all four flights of stairs. Thirty-six hours later her water broke, three weeks shy of her due date (though she'd later say she'd been aiming for four). She lined the seat of her Willys jeep with a towel, put the top down, and drove herself to the hospital to have the baby on her own goddamn schedule, thank you.

A witness was dispatched from Burdenland to see what color the baby was. Despite all in-house predictions, the squalling pupa in the hospital basinet was the spitting image of his rightful father, grandfather, great-grandfather, and so on. He might as well have had a tattoo of the family crest on his right butt cheek. The signature pink hair and humongous Burden testicles were enough validity, and the baby was hailed as a prince—a boy!—and proclaimed second in line to the throne. The night we heard the news, Will and I had danced arm in arm, celebrating our new sibling. We hadn't much noticed him since.

❧

The only suitor to have appeared since our father had accomplished the opposite was Charles Thomas, a darkly handsome foreign attaché whom I liked to imagine my mother had fallen hopelessly in love with. For a long time I retained a single, far more saturated memory of him than any of my own father—

that of Charles swinging me in his arms in the kitchen while I laughed my brains out. It was my only clear vignette from the weeks after the funeral, other than Henrietta accidentally pouring a baby bottle of boiling water on my hand and me watching in silent awe as the skin peeled back on either side like the biblical parting of an ocean.

Down in the grotto nightclub, watching television on Henrietta's bed with Obadiah and Piddle, our corpulent dachshund, I'd sometimes ask her what had happened to Charles, but she never wanted talk about him.

Nor did Cassie. "Don't you go asking about that man" was all she would say, and point to the pancake turner if I ragged on about it further.

Enter Mr. Love.

Mr. Love's attentions started up shortly after we moved to Georgetown. In the beginning, he seemed nice enough, but then so do most people who arrive bearing gifts, even if they're as lame as saltwater taffy. When she was in town, Mr. Love took my mother out to Trader Vic's, and Harvey's for oysters, and Georgetown nightclubs and discotheques, which he nerdily referred to as the "heppest new thing." As far as I could tell, my mother didn't like dancing. She certainly had no rhythm, and from watching *Shindig* I knew that that was what discotheques were all about, so it worried me that she might like Mr. Love for something deeper than what I imagined people did on a date. Even worse, she seemed to be sticking around town just to date him, and it was wreaking havoc with my bowels.

Mr. Love was so anxious to get at my mother that he always arrived early. It fell on me to entertain him while she did her getting ready thing upstairs. He would mosey on in and make himself a cocktail in the kitchen, like he lived there or something, and then he'd go plop himself down on the living room sofa and read the paper.

For the first few dates I tried to soften him up for her, like I was sent in to warm up the audience before the main act came on. My routine went something like this:

"Hey, Mr. Love, you wanna see me do the Bongo Board? I can do it for an hour straight."

"Uh, that's nice, hon," Mr. Love would reply. "Maybe another time."

"How 'bout I show you the bullwhip? I can crack it five times in a row. Sometimes I can even break a glass with it."

"You know, I think I'll just sit here *quietly* and read the paper."

"Wanna see my hamster? Or my guillotine? How about the two of them together? I bet you didn't know we have a dog that's trained to kill people."

This was partially true. My mother had gotten Greta, a German shepherd attack dog, about a week after we'd moved into the new house. She seemed to think being a widow with young children called for accessories like the switchblade she packed in her Gucci handbag, or the bullwhip she kept under the seat of her car. Maybe it was because we were geographically on the wrong side of Georgetown's tracks. Maybe she thought my grandparents had taken a contract out on her. Sadly, she never divulged to us what the command for Greta to attack was. And Greta wouldn't do it unless you uttered the one word that she knew meant go ahead and disembowel the indicated target.

Shortly after Greta had arrived, Obadiah developed a full-blown case of Munchausen syndrome, and started eating his own ears when any attention was paid to the new dog. Piddle dealt with the change in hierarchy by sinking her teeth into all visitors under the age of twelve.

They needn't have bothered. The words *German* and *shepherd* said it all. Greta was remarkable in that she had no personality, except when she was ordered to kill. Then she was a one-dog blitzkrieg.

Mr. Love's fatal mistake was in allowing me to overhear him

(and with such a vested interest, who wouldn't spy?) tell my mother that she should sell her car and he would sell his car, and then they could buy a new one together. Which almost made me laugh because the guy had nine, count them, *nine* children and my idea of a new car was more in the line of an Aston, not an airport van.

From then on, it was no holds barred.

The first plan I came up with involved Greta. The idea was to accidentally get her to kill, or at least maim, Mr. Love. So when he arrived for his date, forty-five minutes early as usual, I was crouched with the dog behind the curtains in the living room, whispering every conceivable word of combat I could think of. I even tried saying them in a German accent, but nothing triggered her Teutonic killer reaction. The humorless beast just sat there, calmly panting. With twenty minutes to go, I figured I'd have more success using an accomplice with an established canine compulsive disorder, so I traded Greta for Obadiah. I seated the two of us next to Mr. Love on the sofa and fed Obadiah three plastic cars. Obadiah loved to eat toys. He was never happier than when munching on a cowboy or an Indian or a farm animal. (Trolls made him gag because of the hair.) In lieu of digesting, he either barfed them up later or had his stomach pumped by the vet.

Mr. Love was unfazed. Evidently he was not an animal lover.

With only five minutes left, I made a last-ditch effort and tried to annoy him to death by singing all five verses of "The Worms Crawl In." By the last one, I was shouting because he hadn't once looked up from the paper.

Mr. Love raised his eyes from the Real Estate section. "Why do you persist in persecuting me?"

"It's nothing personal, Mr. Love. I just don't want you to marry my mother."

"Who said anything about getting married?" he said.

I told him how I'd overheard his icky line about buying a car together. "And if you think I'm okay with having nine new brothers and sisters, you're nuts."

Mr. Love started laughing, and continued until he had practically cackled his Brylcreemed head off his shoulders, and I was in tears. I spun around, heading for the stairs, and ran smack into my mother.

"Hey!" she said, but I streaked past her and up to the second floor.

And when she came into my bedroom later that night, and put her hand on my head in the dark, I kept my breathing in a regular, careful simulation of sleep. *Traitor.*

By date number five, however, I pulled out all the stops. I answered Mr. Love's ring at the door in Wednesday's black cardigan and braids.

"Why hello, Mr. Traveling Salesman," I said.

Mr. Love gave me an exasperated look and brushed past me into the house. I pretended to be perplexed by his odd behavior, but was all milk and naïve kindness as we Addamses always are when dealing with outsiders, however bizarrely they act. He fetched his drink and went to his spot on the sofa, snapping open the paper after giving me another suspicious look. I glided about the room, pretending to eat bugs off the windowsills. Then I got a vase and arranged some dead flower stalks and sticks from the garden, murmuring, "The thorns are *so* lovely this year," à la Morticia. Mr. Love spiked his hairy eyebrows at me, but continued reading. So I went and got Hammy Hamster from my room, got a pan from the kitchen, put him in it, then carried the pan around the living room, chattering about what spices I was going to fry my hamster up with. Mr. Love, widower and father of nine children, wasn't going for it.

So I marched into the kitchen, slammed the pan down on the stove, grabbed the matches, and twirled the dial so the gas went *hissssss.*

The living room was over and down a little set of stairs, and you could just see the stove if you were sitting on the sofa. When Mr. Love heard Hammy scrabbling around in the pan, cutting the Teflon to shreds with his desperate toenails, he merely rustled the paper. But when he saw me expertly strike that Ohio Blue Tip on the side of the box and hold it to the gas, which ignited into a bonfire the witches of *Macbeth* would have been proud of, he leapt to his feet, yelling, "Leslie! Leslie, your crazy fuckin' kid is cooking the hamster! She's setting the house on fire and *she's cooking the fuckin' hamster!*"

Oh my God, it was *great*.

Henrietta stuck her head out from behind the basement door, took one look, and retreated. Luckily, Cassie Diggins had gone home for the day, or her entire *batterie de cuisine* would have been taken to my backside. My mother stormed into the kitchen, furiously tucking her orange Pucci blouse into her skintight black Capri pants.

"That's it, THAT IS IT!" she bellowed. She scooped up Hammy and gently placed him in a Tupperware container, crooning, "There now, there now, you're fine." Then she let me have it with a slap across the head.

"Why do you have to be so goddamn macabre all the time? Like the sun is never out?" she growled, shaking me, though not as hard as she wanted to because she was angry with herself for whacking me in front of her date. "You apologize to Mr. Love this instant."

I looked at my feet and muttered that I was sorry, though all three of us knew I wasn't in the slightest. After all that wildly imaginative insubordination, my punishment was mundanely formulaic—I was sent to bed without supper.

I sat in the corner of my bedroom and ate all the Reese's peanut butter cups I had saved from my Halloween candy. Then I reattached the heads of my Barbies with Scotch tape, and reguillotined them. It thoroughly irked my mother, this morbid little world of mine. In fact, it was like it scared her. She must have thought it was congenital. Maybe it was, but at the time I was only whistling past the graveyard.

Turns out I should have cremated Hammy when I had the chance and saved him from a gruesome death. Will, in retaliation for my telling Henrietta that he let me touch his scrotum in the bathroom, let Hammy out of his cage, whereupon Hammy made a beeline for the cellar and gorged himself on the rat poison. When Hammy showed up a few days later he was fat and satiated, but his skin was turning inside out. Ordinarily I would have found this textbook example of rodenticide anticoagulence scientifically fascinating, but it was Hammy—so I went berserk, and my mother, who was home, but packing for the Bahamas, had to take the poor thing out in the garden and bash him over the head with a shovel. To her credit, she killed him with one good swing.

As for Mr. Love, it took voodoo to get him to cave. Among the artifacts and souvenirs brought back from exotic places by my mother and her forebears was a family of stuffed dolls with crudely stitched faces and yarn hair. They resided among the magic stones, Eskimo carved animals, antediluvian ornaments, dinosaur turd fossils, and scraps of ancestral Pilgrim wedding dresses in an old Chinese chest we called the "Beast House." My favorite thing in there was a long necklace of beads made from human skulls. My mother claimed that each of the beads was from a different skull. The beads all looked the same to me, but I pored over that thing like a nun over a rosary, trying to tell them apart.

The spirit of Mr. Love was transferred to the male doll with an appropriate incantation and a sprinkling of scotch from his bottle in the kitchen. Then I savagely stuck about two hundred pins in him. Mr. Love didn't die, but he stopped coming round.

❧

It was the kind of sultry Washington, DC, evening when the sky is orange and the humid air is so dense the lightning bugs have to swim through it. I was out in the backyard, rearranging the pebbles over Hammy. I tended his tiny grave like it was my husband's. A thunderstorm was brewing, and Henrietta was trying to get me to come inside.

"I'll no' be telling you again—now get in before you're struck by lightning!"

"What?" I pretended I couldn't hear, as a DC-10 screamed overhead on final approach into National Airport.

"I said, get in here now!"

"What for?"

"So you live to be ten. You heard me."

"But Cassie said I could stay out till bedtime."

"Rubbish."

"Okay, well Mommy said I could."

"Oh, did she, now, lassie. Well I'll just go and confirm that—"

"Oh, okay!" I finally shouted, and stomped up the back steps just as sixteen-ounce raindrops began to fall.

The new guy was coming to take my mother to dinner. His name was Pete, and I had yet to meet him. Not that I wanted to. I was still smarting from Mr. Love, and had decided to relight the torch for Charles, the foreign attaché. To avoid the new guy's entrance, I went off to scuba dive in the bathtub.

Pete had gotten my mother seriously into scuba diving, probably because it involved a bathing suit. She in turn was trying to get me interested in it, probably because it involved getting a tan and exercise, which usually leads to a loss of weight. She'd enrolled us both in the diver's certificate course at the YMCA. Will escaped by being away at school, but if two-year-old Edward had been able to swim, she would have enrolled him as well. Breathing underwater was the easy part. Learning decompression charts in order to avoid getting the bends was proving more difficult. Hey, I was lucky to maintain a D+ in math. However, it delighted my mother to see me making an effort to do something that might alter my body shape, so she got me a small scuba tank and a regulator, and I practiced at home in the bathtub.

I was pretending I was on a deep-water dive in the Indian Ocean, looking for great whites, sea snakes, box jellyfish, and anything else listed in the course manual as hazardous to divers, when the flipper of a leatherback sea turtle poked me. It was my mother, in a bright pink linen skirt and fitted jacket, looking like a scoop of tutti-frutti sherbet. I sucked in my stomach (always my knee-jerk reaction), and then surfaced, even though I knew I would die getting the bends from coming up so fast.

"Listen, Diver Dan, it's going to thunder and you can't stay in the tub during an electrical storm because it's very dangerous, so you need to get out, okay?"

My mother's concern surprised me, so I said okay, but as soon as I saw she was leaving, I slunk back down in the ocean. Only now I was Honey West, on a dangerous aquatic assignment in the Bahamas. Bruce, my pet ocelot, was swimming beside me in a specially constructed wet suit, and we were going after suspects in a hidden treasure heist. Suddenly, a shadow loomed from above. But instead of it being the hull of the getaway yacht, there was my mother again. Even from fifty feet below, I could see she was tapping her foot. I was alarmed enough to surface.

"Believe it or not, this is for your own safety, Toots. *Out*."

I tried to mumble, through the thick black rubber in my mouth, that it wasn't even thundering.

She squatted down beside the tub so her face was closer to mine. She smelled deliciously grown-up, like hairspray and perfume and alcohol. I went so far as to take the regulator out of my mouth so I could breathe her in, and I waited for an argument strong enough to convince me to do as she said.

"Pete says he had a friend who was electrocuted while swimming in the Amazon."

"Wow!" That sounded terribly exciting to me.

"Pete says that if lightning were to strike the house, you could be killed. Water conducts electricity—you know that."

"I don't see any lightning," I remarked, getting fidgety.

"Well, Pete says—"

"Pete says, Pete says!" I snapped. "*Charles* would've let me stay in the bath!" I couldn't believe I said that, but now I was on a roll. "And why doesn't Charles visit anymore?" I continued, fanning the flames. "*Charles's* who I want you to like."

"Enough!" She snatched a towel from the rack and stood up. "Charles isn't coming back, okay? Now, get out."

"But . . ."

"That's *enough!*" she shouted. "Charles is not coming back. Period. End of story."

She was as angry as I'd ever seen her. Well, two could play this game. I popped the regulator in my mouth and slid back down under the water. Even a monkey could have lip-read the ensuing barrage of "brat," "bitch," and "allowance," but the steady whoosh of my pressurized breathing had a tranquilizing effect. Hell may have been breaking loose above, but all was amniotic peace in my little world below.

Stark raving livid, but not inclined to ruin her outfit hauling a child with scuba gear out of a bathtub, my mother threw the towel at me and stormed out of the bathroom.

I pretended I was on the deepest of deep-water dives, and the fish around me all had lanterns on their heads and huge sets of pointy teeth, while my mother was yelling at me to get out. I was down *Guinness Book of World Records*–deep—like five thousand feet—but she was really *really* mad, so I had to do what she said without stopping to decompress, and all the nitrogen in my bloodstream was boiling up in my body and clogging my arteries, and I was becoming paralyzed and was without a doubt, according to the manual, going to die.

I sat up and took off my mask, and oh God, there was Cassie Diggins, her dark face about an inch from mine, her pancake turner cocked and ready to strike. She gave the surface of the water a tsunami slap, and my ocean reverie dissolved into the murk of tepid soapy water. I scrambled from the tub, scuba tank clanking, just as a colossal clap of thunder rolled heavily over the roof of our house.

Why They Invented Florida

EVERYBODY HAS TO pay the piper sometime. My mother paid up during spring vacations, when our grandparents went to Paris, Henrietta went home to Scotland, Cassie Diggins remembered she had a husband, Edward went to stay with old Mary Falusi, and camp didn't start for another two months.

For me, getting there was more the point of the vacation than the destination: the fabulously pink Roney Plaza Hotel, on South Beach, in Miami. At Union Station we boarded a Deco streamliner train called the *Silver Meteor*. It left at seven in the evening, and by the time we pulled into Miami the following afternoon, just when some of us were dying for our mai tais at the hotel bar, Will and I would have forensically covered every inch of the diners, sleepers, coaches, tavern, and the round-ended observation car at the end of the train, where the caboose should have been.

Leaving freezing cold Washington in a cloud of steam, just like in the movies, the *Silver Meteor* would slowly gather speed and settle into an initial rhythm. I always looked out the window for the first ten minutes to make sure we really were on our way, and watched as the dark rail yards, and the cluttered backyards of the poor, and then the factories on the outskirts of the city, generalized into a blur of dull Northeast Corridor landscape.

After my mother had freshened her makeup, and made sure

her children were presentable—shirttails and stomachs tucked in ("Remember, you are a reflection of me")—we'd head off to the smoky tavern car in the back, finding our sea legs and swaying exaggeratedly like we were drunks. While she had her cocktail(s), we ate dry roasted peanuts and drank Shirley Temples with a dozen extra cherries in them, which is why Will and I will eventually succumb to cancer of the Maraschino, if melanoma doesn't get us first.

When our mother was "relaxed" and Will and I were thoroughly cranked up on sugar, we'd have to run to make it to the second seating in the dining car. The cover of the menu invariably featured a travel agency illustration of a tanned, carefree Barbie and Ken sitting under a palm tree on the beach. It also invariably featured Oysters Rockefeller, pan-fried trout, Steak Diane, and prime rib so enormous it hung off the plate. The waiters were seasoned, old black men with big pink hands and kind faces, graceful in their starched white jackets. They waited on you like they had all the time in the world, carrying the thick china and heavy hotel silver in layers up their arms as if they weighed no more than leaves.

After dinner we'd go back to the tavern car and play bingo for tubes of Sea & Ski suntan cream. I would have preferred cash, or a Zenith color TV, but when in Rome and all that. Sometimes they showed movies, but watching them in a swaying train with a full stomach made you want to throw up.

Our mother's plan was to get us all in bed by Petersburg, North Carolina (10:05 P.M.). Barring that, by Raleigh (12:20 A.M.). Then she gave up and locked her door, having rung for the porter to come to Will's and my room. When he showed up, all smiles and aren't-you-up-late jokes, he opened up the beds with a special key, and down they plopped, fully made up and good to go. Even though I avoided mine at home, the top bunk in a first-class sleeper was a veritable delight of Let's Play Tree House, or even Mortuary. It was engineered in such a way that you could spend hours up there with nothing but a few toys and the three toggle switches: one for the white reading light, one for the blue night-light, and one for the porter—although you got sent to my mother's Hell if you messed with that one. There were built-in places in which to store your comics, flubber, Silly Putty, and trolls; and pockets to stash contraband like Cheez Doodles or exploding caps. Even if you were a grown-up, you got to be netted in by a web of canvas so you didn't tumble out if the engineer had to slam on the brakes in the middle of the night for broken-down cars, or dumbstruck cows, or blondes strapped to the tracks by Snidely Whiplash. (The latter of which would be the case on a night train we once took from Chicago when, somewhere between Syracuse and Utica, we plowed into a woman who had lashed her own self to the tracks, for obvious reasons.) Best of all, when you went to sleep, the beautiful blue light stayed on like a guardian angel, so you never felt scared, even if you woke up discombobulated in the middle of the night and wondered what planet you were on.

At the crack of dawn Will and I would pop up like prairie dogs and look out the window to find ourselves in the midst of boundless orange groves. This view always struck me as exotic and as foreign as if I'd woken up in Egypt and we were speeding through a landscape of pyramids.

Riding between the cars was obligatory on the way to breakfast. They left the windows on the platform open, and you could feel the speed of the train on your face as you leaned through the curves, and the slam of displaced air when a train passed from the opposite direction. When our cheeks were numb we'd go stand between the cars, one foot on each wildly sawing edge like we were straddling a couple of wild animals. Gulping in the diesel-laden air, we'd claim we smelled the ocean even if it was still a hundred miles away. Then we'd stick our heads back out the window and pop blood vessels screaming as loud and as long as we could.

Our mother was always in a spectacularly good mood when she was southward bound. As soon as the train crossed the Florida state line, it was like she *really* forgot she had children. And until we crossed back over it on our return, she pretty much ignored us.

Being left to your own devices in a five-star hotel is still my idea of a really good time. Will and I had the keys to our room. If we were hungry, we could charge any meals we wanted. If we wanted to swim, there were lifeguards at both of the pools and on the private beach. And if we really needed her—"but it had better be for a damn good reason"—we knew exactly where to find our mother: from nine to five, she was either in her favorite deck chair, or at the bar. After the sun's rays were too oblique to tan, she had a bath and a clothing change in her room, and if she didn't have a date, we all ate out somewhere. But she almost always did, so usually Will and I ordered room service and watched TV all night. When we were younger, our mother would conscientiously hire a sitter, and then we would watch TV all night with the sitter.

Mornings after a date, my mother would lie wasted in her deck chair and, if prodded, would recount her evening to me. The mid-sixties was the height of the discotheque craze, and all the big Miami hotels had them. Go-go dancers were a phenomenon I found repellently fascinating.

"So which one did you go to?" I'd begin the inquiry.

"Oh God, let's see. Well, we started at the Eden Roc—"

"That's where they have the girls in the cages, right?"

"Yup. In Harry's Bar." (Yawn.)

"And what were they wearing? What were their boots like?" I was really into the outfits.

"They had on gold lamé short ones," my mother answered wearily, taking a long suck on her Bloody Mary. "And white fishnets, and gold hip-hugger skirts so short you could see their asses."

"Neat-ohhhh . . ."

"Then we went on to the Shelbourne, where they go-go on top of the tables, and one of the dancers had her wig fall off. I'm afraid she was not a blonde, after all."

"Whoa . . ." Wardrobe malfunction of such mythic proportion was beyond my juvenile imagination.

"Quite." She stirred the ice cubes at the bottom of her empty glass with a stalk of celery and took a bite off the end. "Hey, rub some of that oil on my back, would you?"

My mother's rotisserie timetable was very specific. First, she would lie on her back with her legs spread eight inches apart at the calves, her ankles turned out, and her arms by her sides, but not touching lest it occlude the path of the almighty UVs. Then it was a half hour with the knees slightly raised, the feet now flat and pointed a little in, and the arms above the head to permit exposure of the pits. Then it was onto her side, with a half hour on each one, her legs held in a scissor position. (Tanned inside knees are the mark of a master.) After a dip in the pool to cool off, she flipped onto her stomach, and followed the same routine, first with her head turned left, arms up, and then with her head twisted the other way, with arms down so her elbows could get their share. Then it was time to scoot all the way forward. With her arms hung over the top edge of the chair and her feet splayed, she looked like a cutout person that had fallen straight over. This was the position in which my mother devoured her bodice rippers.

You'd never have guessed this woman could read Greek and Latin. Or that she had a degree in anthropology from Radcliffe, and would go on to earn a doctorate in philosophy from Oxford. The only thing you'd catch my mother reading, other than a textbook, was something from the drugstore rack with a cover depicting a woman standing in front of a brooding English castle. My guess is these romances diverted her from the mess that was her real-life love life.

I always figured my mother would die of skin cancer. (She wouldn't.) Certainly her obsession with being tanned was of the age, but she went beyond the trend by insisting we be tanned too. She considered a good burn as meritorious as a battle scar, and until we were a color somewhere between magenta and carmine, and our shoulders were sloughing off in sheets, she wasn't satisfied.

"You look like you've been growing under a pot. Now get out and enjoy the sunshine!" (Get out and get some second-degree burns!)

Red-haired, blue-eyed children of near-Lapland ancestry have been known to blister under fluorescents. Basal and squamous carcinoma cells were choosing teams on my epidermis even as I rubbed the oil on my mother's leathery shoulders by the banks of the Roney's Roman Pools of Salt Water.

In reciprocity my mother would indulge me by taking me on her back and swim-walking around in the shallow end. Her skin was always hot from the sun, and slippery from the tanning oil. It smelled of her own bittersweet perfume: coconut, perspiration, Diorissimo, Prell shampoo, citrus, and booze. I would close my eyes and rest my cheek on the warmth of her shoulder, and pretend she was the momma koala bear and I was her baby.

If it rained, the three of us drove to Monkey Jungle, where our mother got all misty-eyed over her old pet spider monkey, a horrible creature no one missed but her. (Like the alligators, and the various snapping turtles that outgrew the bathtub, the monkey had been anonymously donated to the Washington Zoo when we'd moved to the house in Georgetown.) We always visited the Seaquarium, where glided, and skulked, all manner of gloriously toxic marine life. At the entrance there were vending machines that would make a blue plastic dolphin while you watched, then spit it out at the bottom, all warm and sweaty like it had just been born. We watched them milk the cobras at the Miami Serpentarium, or we went to the Flipper School and

swam with the dolphins—a supposed "treat" I found disconcerting, since they've been known to mate with humans. The
last thing I wanted was to be deflowered by a dolphin.

But it hardly ever rains in Miami. And there wasn't a whole lot
to do at the Roney except swim, and get into trouble. Will spent
most of his time hanging around the games room, trying to get
a bulls-eye on the darts board. I spent mine doing field experi-
ments on toxic invertebrates, namely Portuguese men-of-war.

Like Camp Tan, Camp Man-O'-War also kept to a strict
schedule.

9 A.M.: Canvas beach in search of subjects. N.B. Handling
poisonous *physalia* is not for the faint-hearted. I used a net
I had found by the pool and a tennis racket someone had
left by their cabana. Even dead, those men-of-war could
reach out from the grave, launch their neurotoxic poison
into your bloodstream, and, in a matter of minutes, pull
you in. I wanted my research efforts to land me with the
Nobel Prize for science, not in an iron lung.

10–11: Assemble and record subjects according to size and
color of air sac, length of tentacles, and state of life or
decay. Assemble tools to test them with.

11–12: Testing of subjects' toxicity with various apparatuses:
twigs, tennis racket handle, pencils, carrot sticks or
chicken thighbone from lunch buffet, etc.

12–1: Lunch. If time, consultation with hotel encyclopedia.

1–3: Dissection. Experimentation with independent variables
and control medications: rum, toothpaste, Psssssst, orange juice shot through a water pistol, Off!, Coca-Cola,
etc. Record results in logbook.

3–4: Bury dead subjects that are starting to smell.

Will doubted my theory that a dismembered tentacle could
be harmful.

"So you're saying that even if those jellyfish've been dead for weeks, you can die if they touch you," he said.

"The nematocysts can still discharge their toxins—sorry, *poison*," I answered condescendingly.

"Yeah, right," said Will, and he proceeded to systematically pop the bubblegum pink and blue bladders I had placed in careful rows in the sand.

Before he could destroy my camp, our mother arrived for a viewing. She stood there for a while, hands on her hips, surveying the lineup of jellied cadavers.

"Fascinating," she deadpanned.

"Actually, it is," I protested, and pulled out my logbook to show her. "See, that one there, for example—his name is Hydro—well, his tentacles started going crazy when I sprayed some Off! on them, but they didn't when I sprayed deodorant."

"Ducky," she said, crouching down to get a better look. "I think it hurts them when you do that, poor things. Hey, move over a little, you're standing in my sun. I mean, how would you like it if I sprayed you with insect repellent and poked you in the stomach with a stick?" She pushed her fingers into both Will and me and we giggled. Then she started in tickling us, something I feared more than her anger, because she tickled too hard and too long, and I always ended up gasping and purple and sobbing for her to stop.

One (obviously) boring afternoon, I was in the games room with Will. He was demonstrating his newfound skills at the dartboard. The darts back then looked like hypodermic needles from a James Bond movie interrogation scene, and they assumed the weight of a hand grenade when wielded by the uninitiated. Will threw a few, and missed. He threw a few more, and managed to hit the black outside circle. It might have been the most boring five minutes of my life. I told him I was going to the beach, and headed for the door.

"Waitwaitwait!" cried Will. "One more. I'll get it this time, I swear."

He took careful aim, did a few back-and-forth motions with his shooting arm, and then let her fly—just as a man wearing nothing but muscles and a Speedo walked in the room. While the victim writhed in astonished agony, his eyes fortuitously clamped shut, Will and I escaped.

We hightailed it down to the pool, to where we knew we'd find our mother. But all we found was her empty deck chair, a towel, a can of Tab, a pair of "boy watcher" sunglasses, several plastic bottles of tanning oil, and a copy of *The Carpetbaggers*. I started thumbing through the thick paperback, looking for the bedroom scenes.

The cute lifeguard saw my brother scanning the horizon as if he was the mother, and she was the lost child. Like a big zoo cat he oozed down from his white throne and made his gorgeous way over.

"Hey kids," he said in a *Beach Blanket Bingo* way. "You, like, lookin' for your mom?"

"Yeah," we said, blinking at him with stars in our eyes.

Was it mere coincidence *The Carpetbaggers* lay open to page 459?

> She came down into his arms, her mouth tasting of ocean salt. His hand found her breast inside her bathing suit. He felt a shiver run through her as the nipple grew into his palm, then her fingers were on his thigh, capturing his manhood.

I think not.

I was seized with an epiphanic understanding of all that was catastrophically wrong with my body, from my white eyelashes, to my concave chest, to my Wise potato chip middle straining against the gingham of my one-piece bathing suit, to my moon-colored thighs and their faint blue road map of Scotland, my unbecoming heritage.

"Wull, your mom's like over in the Tiki bar, on a long-distance phone call to Chile," said the lifeguard.

Will and I looked at each other. We knew Haiti, we knew Acapulco, and Nassau, and San Diego, but Chile?

"Okay," we said in unison, and tried to look like everything was hunky-dory. After giving us a friendly, if quizzical assessment, the lifeguard went back to his station, and I started planning how best to hit puberty. Either that or kill myself.

I began walking toward the ocean, conscious for the first time in my life of my thighs rubbing together.

"Hey, wait up!" Will pulled alongside of me. Yanking off his T-shirt, he said, "You wanna go swimming?"

"Uh-uh," I said disdainfully, "I've got work to do."

"You do not. Sticking things in jellyfish is not work."

I reluctantly agreed to go swimming. I loathe swimming in the ocean. It takes the poison of a black widow spider a full hour to take effect, that of a Gila monster fifty minutes, a rattlesnake fifteen, a cobra five. But run into a stingray, a Portuguese man-of-war, a scorpion fish, a blue-ringed octopus, or a box jellyfish (something you can't even *see* whooshing your way), and you start to croak immediately. And if the flora and fauna don't kill you, the undertow will.

I followed my brother down the beach to where the lethal briny lapped.

"Race you!" Will yelled, galloping into the waves.

I surged through the water ahead of my brother. He passed me and, well, you know the routine. Except suddenly he wasn't in front of me, he was knee-high in the water behind me, triumphantly calling, "Fake out!" from the shallows, and I was so far out that the water was immeasurably deep, and calm, and yet when I tried to paddle back in, the sea refused to let me.

What a day. First the unquiet stirrings of puberty, and now

the premature onset of death. I'll spare you the details, but picture trying to swim against a herculean current, and getting the reverse of nowhere, and almost pooping in your one-piece because, having seen a photo of a drowned person in *Look* magazine, you knew yours was going to be a grisly crossing of the bar.

When I was quite far out, and had actually kind of given up and was halfheartedly treading water, the current lessened and I found I could swim sideways a little. I eventually managed to make my spluttering, panic-stricken way to a line of partially submerged pilings that must have been put there by Ponce de León, judging from the buildup of barnacles encrusted over them.

There I clung, caterwauling for my mother, dammit, barfing up seawater, and praying for rescue—just not by the cute lifeguard, because that would be a fate worse than drowning.

But there he strode, and there he swam, a merman with look-at-me, gliding strokes, and a flutter kick that didn't disturb the water. He arrived by my side in no time, underscoring my humiliating proximity to shore, and gave a head toss that flipped the hair out of his eyes in a perfect arc. He unhooked me from the piling one limb at a time, as though I were a starfish sucking on to it with all one million of my tube feet.

Oh, the extreme mortification. To be carried through the water draped like a heroine over his arms, and to be a nine-year-old without even the buds of breasts to press against his godlike chassis. For miles he carried me, past gawking families on the hotel beach, past the cabanas where the bronzed men and women nodded and whispered sympathetically, past the pools where the round-eyed teenaged girls sighed and shook their heads in envy, and finally to my mother's deck chair, where she stood, hands on her hips, waiting.

"This had damn well be worth getting me off the phone for," my mother said.

"Will m-made me swim out th-there," I sniveled, as the cute lifeguard deposited me on the deck chair. I was scraped all over by the barnacles, and my bathing suit had little rips on the butt and on the frills above the leg openings.

"Jesus H. Christ, *now* what have you done?" My mother's face was flushed, and she had that look she wore when something bad or scary or emotional was happening, but no way was she going to give in and publicly admit it. Instead, she regarded me with the disapproval she reserved for Obadiah when he gunned the house with diarrhea.

"Omigod . . . this kid is *yours*?" The lifeguard looked at the two of us with idiotlike perplexity.

My mother acknowledged her ugly spawn with a Pepsodent smile and a hand on the lifeguard's golden forearm.

"Thank you so much," she purred. "I'm sure a rescue at sea wasn't necessary. My daughter tends to overdramatize."

"Hey, like no problem, miss," the lifeguard said, smiling back and holding her gaze. The perfect white stripe of zinc oxide on his nose had not been the least bit smudged by our encounter.

Mr. Innocence suddenly appeared, like nothing was wrong. Like he hadn't basically held my head underwater and tried to shove me into Davy Jones's locker.

"Gee whiz! What happened?" my brother said.

"Nothing," said my mother, pushing her boy watchers on top of her head like a hair band. "Birdbrain here did something stupid."

The lifeguard suddenly remembered his duties. "Maybe we should check the kid out. She got pretty banged up hangin' on to that piece a wood out there." He took hold of my ankle and lifted it up, revealing a cross-hatching of bloody scrapes and cuts all along the inside of my legs. As he replaced it, I watched the soft flesh of my upper thigh wobble. Then the lifeguard unfolded my arms, and after he inspected them, he returned them to where they'd been, clamped around my shivering torso. My mother didn't interfere, but stood close by, watching, chewing on her thumb. I thought she was looking for flaws. I couldn't stop thinking of *Glamour* magazine's Dos and Don'ts pages. I distinctly saw myself with the black bar across my face ("That hair! That one-piece! No grooming at all!") and my mother, opposite, on the Dos page in a flattering enlargement.

My cuts were all stinging like crazy from the drying salt, and I was trying not to cry. I struggled to channel my heroine, even though I knew Wednesday was not fond of seaside activities. Certainly she would have been stoic, and delighted by any injuries brought on by a near snuffing.

"Shheesh. You're really bleeding," my brother said.

"Hey, little dude, don't cry," urged the cute lifeguard. He was proving much better at this than my mother.

"Oh, she's fine, aren't you, Toots? They're only superficial cuts. I'll get some Bactine and we'll fix you up." My mother patted me awkwardly on the rump. "Will, go fetch her a Tab, would you?"

Turning back to the lifeguard, she said, "Listen, I wish there was some way I could thank you properly." She reached into her bag by the chair for her Fabergé lipstick and started piling it on.

Gross, I thought. I knew the signs. I stood up, wrapped a towel around myself, and demanded the room key. I could look after my own first aid.

She figured out a way to thank the cute lifeguard all right, starting with the mai tai she bought him at the Tiki bar when he went off duty. As for the person on the other end of the interrupted long-distance call, turns out he only wanted to know her ring size.

A Dose of Religion

THERE MUST BE a trillion ways to deliver bad news by letter.

I'm sorry to be the one to tell you . . .

By the time you read this . . .

Someday this will all seem like a horrible dream . . .

My mother dispensed with the usual epistolary protocol. On a postcard from Cozumel she wrote:

Guess what! Pete and I were married last week! The dogs are fine, and we've moved to Virginia! You're going to love your new school! It's co-ed! Love, M.

P.S. Henrietta got a new job.

Like she could fool me with exclamation marks. What she was really saying was:

Listen up, Toots, your life is about to get ugly. I've gone and married that sleazy Austrian gunrunner, Peter Beer. You know, the guy that was your father's best friend? Yeah, him. The one with the accent and the ugly pointy nose. The guy that

sweats a lot and doesn't use deodorant. So you've only met him
a couple of times, big deal. You'll get to know him soon enough.
And you'll get to hear us doing it all night long and on Saturday
and Sunday mornings because your bedroom is right over
ours, and the house is one of those new ranch types they built in
under a minute. Whoops! Forgot to tell you we moved to the
middle of nowhere. You're going to hate your new school.

P.S. Pete thought Henrietta was fat and lazy so he
canned her. Guess it's just me from now on! There's a
chore list already up by the back door and you're down
for about sixty hours a week.

Too bad camp can't last forever, M.

Since my mother was conceived, born, and raised without a
sense of humor, I couldn't regard her bulletin as anything other
than the stone cold truth. The few times I'd met Herr Peter
Christian Beer were enough to convince me that my new stepfather and Hitler had been littermates. I already knew I hated everything about him. Like the way he answered the telephone
with a razor-sharp "Beer here!" Or how when he patted the
dogs, he did it so hard they fell over. It would have been more
humane if a soldier in uniform had shown up at the door of my
cabin with a folded flag.

Summer camp had been sort of a bust that year anyway. I
couldn't figure out who I was supposed to be, nor could I find a
niche among the jacks-playing, skinny-legged, madras-wearing
Brookes and Whitneys. It was hard to be ghoulish in a cabin by
a lake under sun-filtered pines, with campfires, and s'mores, and
"Kumbaya" ringing in your ears. After a couple of fruitless
weeks combing the Maine woods for hemlock (not that I knew
what it looked like) and recording the effects of formaldehyde
on bats snared by the camp nurse, I gave in and learned to play

jacks (horribly), swam and canoed, and played Capture the Flag.

Next to Breck shampoo, the hottest seller at the Camp Four Winds supply store was stationery. The amount of summertime mail that went in and out of the Sargentville, Maine, post office was of North Pole magnitude. Following lunch there was a mandatory rest period during which letters were furiously penned by the homesick inmates. The rusty springs of ancient bunk beds squeaked with the force of all those Bics, and tears were staunched by autographed stuffed animals and Lilly Pulitzer sheet ensembles. Even I had gone so far as to miss my mother. Whether this was a genuine sentiment, or one born of peer pressure, it didn't last longer than the time it takes to skim a postcard.

Home was suddenly a low-ceilinged, split-level ranch made entirely of brick—both real and faux, but mostly faux. The floors were brick, the walls were brick, the shelving and the alcoves, the stairs and the basement, they were all brick. There was a brick patio off a living room that had a brick fireplace, and the brick kitchen had plastic brick counters and brick-colored Kenmore appliances and a linoleum brick floor. Even the cupboards had brick-patterned contact paper. It was like living in a kiln that had been air-dropped onto the middle of an eight-acre field. Over the summer, my mother and her new husband, whom she addressed as "my Lord and Master," had put up ten linear miles of raw wood fencing and erected a barn, into which they had moved four horses: hers, a big gray named Puck; his, a palomino killer named Mighty Mo; Will's once coveted but now bratty and loathsome pony; and an obese bovine piebald named Beethoven. It was like the Instant Grow version of *Green Acres*, minus the pigs.

My stepfather was an arms dealer. He and my mother had not been brought together by serendipity alone; he had been my father's closest friend, their initial bond having been an obsession with all *objets de guerre*. As manager of an American organization called Interarms, he bought and sold surplus weaponry to governments and civilians all over the world. The founder of Interarms wasn't picky about who was pushing the shopping cart—Castro, Batista, or Nixon—because he claimed neutrality, and thus was able to equip home guards, national reserves, civil wars, revolutions, defense wars, and insurgencies alike. My stepfather was paid very well, and then some, for his hazardous line of work, and he put the money into his stable of cars, as well as the vault full of gold bricks that he kept in Zurich.

Applying the managerial skills of his business to the home front, the Lord and Master's first official act had indeed been the brutal firing of my beloved Dewar's-slugging, Winston-puffing Henrietta, whom he detested. (In a double whammy, Cassie Diggins felt compelled to quit in protest.) My mother had been aghast, but her new husband had bullied her into going it alone. I was bereft. I'd been looking forward to taking care of Henrietta in her demented years, after she had hand-reared my own children. That's what Scottish nannies were supposed to do—stay on till death. The other side of my family, the happy, well-adjusted Uncle Shirley side I dreamed of belonging to, had one. Her name was Magoo (or something like that), and she was about a hundred and fifty. Her adoptive family had built her a little apartment in their gargantuan house in New Canaan, Connecticut, a place I would have given my heart and lungs to have lived in. Magoo toddled down for meals and babbled in atmospheric Scottish gibberish in her designated corner throughout. Since three, I'd been planning to build Henrietta a wing on my English country estate, complete with her own tap-room and cigarette and candy vending machines.

On the hot September day we arrived at the new house, Will and I stood in the kitchen and gaped at the chores chart the Lord and Master had bolted to the wall. We had never been assigned chores before.

"I changed my mind," I said, turning to my mother in total neurogenic shock. "I do want to go to boarding school. I do. In fact, I *insist*."

"Too late," my mother said, swinging six-packs of Tab onto the pantry shelves. She was organizing her supplies, something she did on a weekly basis. My mother stocked up like the Russians were scheduled to drop the Big One at 0800. There was a spare for the spare for the spare that was the spare for the item in use, be it salt or Bacardi or Comet. Her personal staples, Lipton Iced Tea Mix, strawberry Carnation Instant Breakfast, Metracal shakes and cookies, Sweet'N Low, and Tab, she bought by the case. There was a measurable blast of carcinogens whenever you opened the cabinet doors.

My mother stood back to admire her work. She frowned, and then switched the five jars of Bac-Os with the five boxes of Rice-A-Roni. Still not satisfied, she transferred the Rice-A-Roni to the shelf above, and put the seven bottles of Good Seasons Lo Calorie dressing in their place. Obadiah was rooting for crumbs beneath her, and she kept tripping over him and sliding on his slobber as she struggled to place the Rice-A-Roni far enough back to accommodate six tins of roast beef hash and five of deviled ham on the front of the shelf.

"There!" she said, emerging from the tiny pantry, which was really a cupboard stashed under the back (brick) stairs. "Anyway, Toots, school starts in a week, and you'll make lots of new friends, just like you always do. Some of them might even be boys." She wiggled her eyebrows suggestively as she unscrewed a jar of powdered iced tea. I caught a whiff of the nuclear fallout from ten feet away. She spooned some into a glass, added water from the tap, and pulled a tray of ice cubes out of the freezer. Slamming it on the counter, she gave the frosty handle a yank, which sent most of the cubes thumping across the counter and onto the floor. Obadiah dove after them in a commendable burst of energy. My mother wiped her hands on her bikini bottoms.

"So you might consider laying off the potato chips for a while." Inspired, she wrote out *DIET!!* on a piece of paper and Scotch taped it to the fridge, where a dozen similar notes were already displayed. She claimed these motivational reminders were for herself, but she made a point of being reminded by them whenever I was around.

Will leaned against the screened back door, smirking. He left for school in a couple of days.

"Shut up, jerk," I hissed, turning on him. "I wouldn't want to go to your *re*-tard school anyway!"

"Ah, ah, ah!" cautioned my mother. "Now, that's a little unfair. Glayden is for kids with dyslexia too." She smiled at Will as she sipped from her glass. If this affirmation of my brother's school really being for retards insulted him, he didn't show it.

"At least I don't have to live here and shovel shit and wax cars," he said snidely, and slammed out the door into the stifling humidity.

I went back to staring at the Lord and Master's work detail. Jeez. The guy had no clue how to go about doing this. He had never been married before, plus he was old. Like forty-something. There wasn't enough time in the day for all the tasks I was supposed to perform. Spoiled? You bet I was. But this was hardly a case of not wanting to take out the garbage or feed the dogs. This was about mucking out the horses in the dark before school, whitewashing all that fencing in the middle of a heat wave, picking up every Monday after school the shit three dogs had broadcast over eight acres, and waxing one of my stepfather's stupid sports cars every other Wednesday.

That afternoon found my brother and me doing time with buckets and brushes, working on our own little chain gang. As soon as you applied the paint, the thirsty wood instantly slurped it up like a sponge. After a couple of hours, we felt like we were getting nowhere.

Our mother came out with some Kool-Aid, and her two tortoises, Mr. Turt and Miss Tort. Obadiah greeted her by rolling onto his back and flapping his dinner-plate paws. Will and I collapsed beside him in the long buggy grass and feigned heatstroke.

"Honestly, you two," she said, setting the tortoises down gently in the deep jungle, whereupon they instantly slammed all four doors shut. "You'd think you were being worked like darkies down on the old plantation." With her face turned to the sun, she managed to locate and remove a tick the size of a baseball from Obadiah's neck. She flicked it into the grass, sparing its evil little life so it could live to suck the blood of basset hounds again.

I glowered at her from under my paint-streaked bangs.

⨞

For the first time since bearing them, our mother actually had to take care of her children. Will was mostly away, either at school or camp, or at our grandparents', but Edward made up for Will's absence by being an omnipresent toddler. Without Cassie Diggins we were suddenly, horribly, at the mercy of our mother's cooking: Early New England Regional Cuisine as Interpreted by an Alcoholic with an Eating Disorder.

Everything went into the Teflon frying pan: Spam, hot dogs, "grilled" Velveeta cheese sandwiches, steak, spaghetti, hearts of palm, fish sticks, and any and all leftovers, which, with an addition of onion, were then relabeled "hash." Meanwhile, my mother rarely deviated from her own regime of cottage cheese, diet soda, Ayds candies, and raw hamburger meat dipped in Lipton onion soup mix—except when she was loaded. Then she sucked up drippings from the roast or frying pan with a straw.

The cook soon became *fed up to here* with cooking. In the nick of time someone invented Shake 'N Bake, Birds Eye boil-in-the-bag frozen vegetables, and a coffee cake mix in a plastic bag that you added an egg to before squirting it out into its own little baking pan. Those technological advances, along with Chun King sukiyaki in a box, helped my mother evolve.

The Lord and Master left for work at dawn, so it was relatively peaceful in the mornings. Edward would watch cartoons in the living room, while I'd sit at the kitchen counter before school and watch my mother fry eggs in bacon grease. On certain Fridays, I went to visit my grandparents for the weekend. I hated flying, especially alone. I was torn between my fear and wanting a breather from my stepfather's autocratic domain, not to mention babysitting my little brother, a drudgery that was hardly worth its twenty-five-cents-an-hour compensation.

"I hate flying more than *anything*," I grumbled, and refolded my paper napkin so the corners were more perfectly aligned.

"Poppycock," said my mother, sliding a couple of eggs that looked like brown lace onto my plate. The toaster popped, and she scraped the tiniest amount of margarine imaginable over an English muffin before handing it to me. I glared at her. She herself was so terrified of flying someone had to crowbar her out of the airport bar in order to get her on the plane.

"And just think," she added, "you get to be waited on hand and foot by those Irish biddies *and* pork up on butter, and drink Coke until your teeth rot." She had a knack for making the things you looked forward to sound terrible.

"Yeah, well at least I'll be away from Adolf," I said through a mouthful of toast. My mother whipped around from the sink, a bottle of dish soap in one hand, a sponge in the other. She narrowed her eyes at me, like smoke was heading her way. Whether my sobriquet for him insulted her, or whether it hurt her feelings, I couldn't tell, but clearly she was pissed. Not that I cared. Now that we were at last spending quality time together—something I couldn't believe I used to wish for—my mother was becoming less of an enigma and more of a liability. The bottle of Dawn slipped from her grasp, beaning the new dog, Dropout, on his massive head. Blue soap leached out like gore as we stared at each other. The arty metal cutouts of turtles and otters and porcupines on the kitchen walls looked down accusingly at me until I lowered my eyes, and my mother bent to clean up the soapy mess, apologizing profusely to Dropout, who squirmed and thrashed his tail like a delighted sea serpent.

(Greta, to no one's regret but my mother's, was history. Upon her arrival in rural Virginia, she had adopted the mind-set of a homicidal psychotic. One minute she would be all heroic and Rin Tin Tin–like, posing with her keen eye upon the horizon, looking out for the 101st Cavalry, and the next she'd be enacting the canine version of *The Texas Chain Saw Massacre*. After she'd redecorated the neighbor's henhouse with the blood of its residents, my mother was forced to ship Greta to the nearest active war zone. On her way home from the cargo terminal of National Airport she picked up a replacement. Dropout, as the name suggested, had failed attack school. He was the world's largest German shepherd. He was entirely black, sweetly complacent, and lazy—and would eventually get mistaken for a bear and shot to death—an event from which my mother would never fully recover.)

"Yes, yes, yes!" she now said to the behemoth creature. He clicked around her with joy, crashing into Obadiah, who fell over, and Piddle, who snapped at him before retreating under my stool. I gave Piddle my bacon and then put my plate on the floor for Obadiah, who was forbidden to have fried eggs because he liked to drag his ears through them, and then all over the house.

Lightbulb: "Why can't I just stay with Gaga and Granddaddy, and go to school in New York?"

My mother took a swallow of her morning Tab and sighed, considering this wonderful possibility. "Fine by me," she said, "but your grandfather would never go for it."

"Why not?"

"Because you ain't a boy, Toots, that's why." She scooped a

handful of butterscotch Ayds from an economy-sized box and put them in a Baggie. "Better pack these," she said, handing them to me. "I don't want to have to go buying you new clothes before spring. Speaking of which, you better hurry up and get dressed for school, and pack your suitcase too. We still have the horses to do before the bus comes."

Weather took all the fun out of owning animals. It was barely December, but there was already a foot of snow on the ground.

"The neighbors all have farmhands. Why can't we hire someone to do all this stuff?" I asked my mother. I was cracking the ice out of the buckets in the barn so the horses could drink, while she threw extra flakes of hay into their stalls.

"Oh, stop your grumbling," she said, though not without sympathy. "You know how Pete is. He thinks we should be the lords of our own fiefdom, but he doesn't want to pay for the serfs."

"Yeah," I laughed, and went to help her buckle extra blankets onto the horses, their warm breath rising in grass-scented steam all around us.

I had to feel for my mother; I was old enough now. Still, I would look at her sometimes and wonder what on earth she saw in her odious husband. I sensed she had little control over her domestic situation, even though she had put herself—and, more importantly, *me*—into it. It had to have been like toxic shock, her being thrown into all those different layers of servitude. Out in the sticks, Trader Vic's and Dead Zombies a thing of the past, her studio gone and her artistic life confined to a room in the basement, her children requiring meals at least two times a day, her husband requiring sex the same amount (not to mention slavish devotion in between); when Pete was history, my mother would confess she'd married him because he was the most exciting man she'd ever met.

My stepfather would have been delighted to have me permanently packed off to live in Burdenland. There was no love lost between us. I continued to hate him for any number of reasons, not the least of which was because he seriously sweated. No one in my family sweated like that. They maybe turned pink after a couple of sets of tennis, but never did quarts of perspiration drip from their noses or course in rivers from their pits. The Lord and Master claimed sweating was healthy. He eschewed the use of deodorant and antiperspirants, saying that to block it was unnatural.

"Why do you drink so much if your just gonna sweat it all out?" I had asked him one broiling hot Indian summer Sunday before the weather had turned. My mother had been trying to kill two birds: getting me tanned, while encouraging a little family time. The Lord and Master was intermittently sunning his armpits, elbows raised to the sky, and slurping grape soda from a work crew–sized thermos that rattled with ice cubes every time he hoisted it up. I was working on a five-thousand-piece jigsaw puzzle of migrating Assateague ponies, that I had carried out on a card table. (Nothing leveled me better than a few hours spent on a good jigsaw puzzle—other than a stack of *CREEPY* comics and a big bag of Lay's.)

"I am like an Olympian, cooling the surface of my skins!" he proclaimed, turning himself slowly, like a vertical rotisserie, beside my mother's deck chair on the patio. His thick Austrian accent only underscored his operatic delivery of anything— from the time of day, to a lecture on the proper way to simonize a Berlinetta Boxer.

Olympian, my ass. He was a sweaty, disgusting satyr. He might not have had the pointy ears, but he sure as hell had the horns. And I knew from Greek mythology that satyrs went hand in hand with drunken, lewd behavior. They were always fornicating with nymphs, and goats, and little boys.

I repeated my question about his excessive consumption of liquids.

"Because it is excellent for one's body to sweat!" he sang in reply, mopping his face with a towel. "This is merely thermo-regulation! Men who are working, athletes who are running, they produce a gallon of sweat an hour!" His left eye, a wanderer, rolled around in a sickening manner.

"Yuck," I said.

"And you will see, you will begin to have this sweat yourself, when you will have breasts!"

"Eeuw."

"Yes, this is true. With this puberty will come these hormones, and these will produce the sweat glands from under your arms, and in your groin, and from your nipples!"

"*Gross me out.*"

The Lord and Master winked at me, and smacked my mother on the butt. "Women, they love sweat from a man. This is how we communicate our sex drive!"

I stomped off inside, just in time so they couldn't see the waterworks. Honestly, how could my mother be with such a complete perv?

I may have been an idiot savant in terms of mortuary science, but I still had clichéd ideas of love and sex, Harold Robbins excerpts notwithstanding. Up until my mother's unfortunate union I'd been able to pretty much ignore her proclivities. Now I felt like I'd been thrown into the carnal sea, not only on the home front, where the newlyweds kept to a regimen of hyperactive coitus in the master bedroom below mine, but at my new school as well.

The Flint Hill Preparatory School had an erudite name, but venerable the place was not. My sixth-grade class was a mixed bag of future hucksters, sluts, and farmhands, albeit in regimental blue uniforms. On the playground with my classmates at recess, I'd watch as the ten-year-old boys stuck their hands in the panties of the obliging ten-year-old girls, withdrawing their fingers for all to smell.

Will had it just as bad. Burgundy Farms Country Day was an

"alternative school." Before he'd gotten permanently assigned to boarding school, I'd gone there with him for fifth grade. Unmitigated disaster. All I got out of it was a phobia for sandals and a talent for eating mud. Fourth grade had been at the National Cathedral School for girls, praise the Lord. Now I was enduring everyone else's puberty at Flint Hill.

All of which contributed to my becoming a drug addict by ten.

~∞~

It began innocently enough—but then that's what they all say. In New York for the weekend, I'd been stricken with nausea during a routine perusal of Ann Rose's office. For the record, I have a world-class vomit phobia. I'd rather overdose on rhubarb leaves and bleed from my eyeballs than throw up. After the initial wave, I crawled to the towering cabinet of pharmaceuticals in Ann Rose's bathroom. Next to the Pepto and the milk of magnesia was a giant-sized bottle of BiSoDol antacid tablets. Panting, I unscrewed the cap and sniffed—*mint*. My mouth was filling with that nasty gush of saliva you get right before you're about to blow, so I ate a couple of the thick white tablets. Then I prayed to God not to throw up and guess what—it worked!

You bet I brought the miracle drug home with me. I hid it in the headboard shelf of my bed, behind a propped-up copy of *Happiness Is a Warm Puppy*. It freaked me out that I became conscious of the BiSoDol's presence at all times. In the beginning I'd just take the bottle out, open it up, and smell it. Then I started shaking a few tablets out into my hand and looking at them. One thing led to another, and before I knew it, I was taking one every night before I went to bed. Shortly afterward, I found religion.

It could have just been a chemical reaction from the sodium bicarbonate, but within seconds of ingesting my nightly wafer, an inexplicable urge to worship came over me. The chalky mint would spread over my tongue like a shroud, staunching the flow of saliva, and assuring me that no matter what I had eaten—a whole box of Cap'n Crunch, mud, or an entire jar of Jif—God, and BiSoDol, would keep me from throwing up. Accordingly, I gave thanks, and lots of it. This was a peace I'd never known. My mother would have died if she'd seen me on my knees on my floral Dacron bedspread, swaying like a fly rod and praising Jesus and the Lord Almighty in a whisper.

I'd tinkered with religion briefly as a six-year-old, when, in a desire for what I mistakenly considered to be textbook normalcy, I'd marched over to the local Catholic church and signed myself up for Sunday school. They didn't seem to care that I was unaccompanied, nor did they inquire if I was a Catholic. In the true spirit of Christianity, they welcomed me with open arms.

Sunday school was a huge disappointment. It was all about coloring pictures of Noah's Ark or Jesus in the Temple with an incomplete set of Crayola crayons. We sat at a long, oilcloth-covered table, and, after a couple of graham crackers and Dixie cups of lukewarm grape juice, the teacher handed out pages torn from religious coloring books for us to work on. The other children filled in the robes of Mary's dress with whatever colors were at hand—orange yellow, or silver, or salmon—carelessly running amok outside the lines. They scribbled the lilies with pine green and mulberry, but then they all fought for the flesh crayon, even when I showed them you could color skin the same with a very light shading of melon.

The teacher, a kind enough spinster in an ankle-length prairie dress, walked around peering at our efforts. When she stopped at my shoulder, I covered my drawing with my hands. I saw it as vastly imperfect. The teacher asked to have a look, and I shrugged and told her I would have given Jesus rosy cheeks if there'd been any carnation pink.

"I'm done with this one," I said. "Do you have any others, like of the dead guy coming out of his grave?"

"You mean Lazarus?" the teacher said with skepticism.

"Sure. Anyone'll do. Or I could work on a puzzle if you have one. But it has to be over a thousand pieces."

"First let's see how you've done with Jesus walking on the water, shall we?"

I leaned back and uncovered my picture. The teacher looked down at it and put a hand to her throat.

"Oh my God," she whispered hoarsely.

Ask any control freak and they'll tell you how brilliant they were at coloring. When everyone's picture was pinned up on the bulletin board at the end of the class, I already knew I wouldn't be back the following week. How could I, in good faith, create masterpieces while surrounded by aesthetic imbeciles? The teacher begged me to stay, but I'd lost interest. Besides, I was an imposter—I was Episcopalian.

❧

In the future, I'd be able to resolve all kinds of things by invoking the proverbial "suffering is redemptive" theory. Like if my mother hadn't married that dictatorial sphincter, I wouldn't have acquired a sense of self so early in life. Or learned to drive a stick at twelve. And if my father hadn't killed himself, I wouldn't have inherited a few million at twenty-one. But that philosophy wasn't working for me then, and I was as tortured as St. Augustine. I was serving God, but God had yet to reward me by smiting my stepfather. Therefore, He too was torturing me. And I was no Job. Switching gears, I decided to miss my father. It was the first time I'd given serious thought to him since his death four years earlier. A shrink might have told me I was embarking on a deferred period of mourning. I can tell you I was perihormonal, hooked on antacids, and living under the same roof as the Antichrist.

But wait a minute . . . if God could stop me from vomiting, maybe he could bring back my father. It seemed like a parallel miracle to me. It was a long shot, but I worked it anyway. Every night when I took my BiSoDol, instead of praying for God to kill my stepfather, I prayed like a fundamentalist for God to produce my father. Initially I referred to him as Daddy, but it sounded really weird to me. I was obliged to ask my mother (when she was toasted—I wasn't stupid) what Will and I had called him, but she was flippant and said things like "Well *I* don't know, for Christ sake, what do all kids call their damn fathers?" When Will and I were together one weekend in New York, I asked him, and he responded by punching me in the stomach.

I didn't feel the least bit guilty that I hadn't missed my father before drugs had reintroduced us. It was as if he'd never been there in the first place. I had maybe two memories of him, and both of them were at night. The first was of my father going after a giant bee in my room, which turned out to be a half-dead bluebottle. The second was of being in his arms on the Snow White ride in Disneyland, when the wicked witch held out the apple to our little cart as it swung past on its tracks. I was scared out of my mind, and he protected me.

I remembered protecting him. Whenever it rained during the night, I would sit outside my parents' bedroom door and monitor the puddles on the street and the sidewalk. I dreaded rain. I was convinced it would never stop, and that the world would flood, worse even than when Noah was around. I'd sit all night outside that door, ready to warn my parents when the water rose and began to tug at the tender walls of our house.

In an attempt to discover any traces of my father, I combed our sterile house, but all I could find was an old check register containing his carefully recorded expenditures, like a check to Best & Co. for thirty dollars and fifty-eight cents (*clothes for Willy and Wendy*), or one to Johnson's Garden, fifteen dollars even. I spent hours analyzing my father's handwriting for clues, trying to identify my DNA in the dot of his *i* or the curve of his *c*. I hated having only half of myself accounted for.

That was about all I had to go on in the memory department, so I settled for missing the *idea* of him.

One is either born with the capacity to believe in God, or not. Apparently, I was not. About the same time I ran out of BiSoDol, I came to the conclusion that whereas God had neither resurrected my father nor drowned my stepfather in the boiling sea of shit and piss and vomit he deserved, He, She, or It clearly did not exist. This led to a disturbing chain of thoughts that culminated in the epiphany that everyone and everything was going to die. More importantly, *I* was going to die, and there was going to be nothing after that. As in forever and ever and ever. This got me screaming into my pillow, and making lists, and imagining ordered rows of shoes, or trolls, or jellyfish on the tide line of a beach. If you were born just to die, and then be dead for infinity, you might as well have never existed, so what was the point of anything? No wonder my father had killed himself.

My mother, on the other hand, believed in lots of gods. She exhibited the primitivism of early man, and made few distinctions between animals and humanity. She was surrounded by her daemons and totems, and she glorified the animal spirit deities by treating her pets—her dogs and horses and chinchillas and tortoises and prairie dogs and coatimundi and old spider monkey—as equals, even though the latter would spray a fountain of go-away urine on anyone who walked in the door, and then bite them for good measure.

It should come as no surprise that after my brother's evil pony bucked me off in the field, and I staggered to the kitchen door, my arm like a twisted car wreck, the radius sticking out at a forty-five-degree angle, my mother took one look and said, "Jesus fucking Christ! Is the horse okay?" Luckily, shock had already set in. As red-faced as an India rubber ball, my mother called an ambulance, taped my former arm to a two-by-four, and then walked me back across the field to catch the pony.

Hoisting me into the saddle, she grimly reasoned, "Listen, Toots, if you don't get straight back on, you'll be scared to do it again."

She had dealt with my compound fracture in the same pragmatic way she'd administered to Piddle when her throat had been ripped out by a neighbor's werewolf. Upon discovering the three-quarters-dead dachshund in the garage, my mother had calmly fetched a bottle of rubbing alcohol and a needle and thread. While I held the dog, trying to ignore the gushing blood and exposed windpipe, my mother stitched her throat closed. The vet said he'd never seen such practicality. My mother told him she worshiped the damn dog, so she did what she had to.

A few days after I came home from the hospital, the doctor made a house call. My mother was on her way into town to meet the Lord and Master for dinner, and she fussed about my room in an attempt to hurry the doctor. She was wearing her new Yves Saint Laurent "Mondrian" shift and her favorite black Roger Vivier patent leather shoes with the Myles Standish buckles on them. It may have been late winter, but her legs were bare, and of that peculiar pumpkin color only QT can deliver.

Examining me, the doctor remarked on the size of my stomach.

My mother came to stand by the side of the bed and tapped her foot. "I *told* her to lay off the Fritos," she said, shaking her head. "But honestly, Doctor, what can I do?"

"I'd say this is more than just a case of snack food," said the doctor, palpating my distended, rock-hard abdomen. "Your daughter looks like she's in her second trimester."

"*What!*" my mother shrieked. She sank backwards into a beanbag chair, her pocketbook spewing lipstick, change, keys, and switchblade across the carpet. "Are you telling me—I mean, there's no *way* she could possibly be—"

"Yes," said the doctor, sternly. "I'm afraid this poor child is *severely* constipated."

My mother made a sound like gas escaping a balloon.

The doctor regarded his Timex, and snapped his black bag shut. "Do you know how to administer an enema, Mrs. Beer?" he said, giving her a dubious look over his glasses.

Mother and daughter looked at each other in profound horror. Shit. If only I'd read the label on the bottle of BiSoDol. *Not for children under 12. Adverse side effects include constipation.*

Never has a procedure been invented that so tests the mettle of the participants. My mother and I hadn't been that intimate since I'd come through the birth canal.

❦

Spring arrived, my arm healed, Piddle was taken off the respirator, and the snowshoes were put away for the year. While the Lord and Master and his bride went scuba diving in the Bahamas, Will and Edward and I went to visit our grandparents in Hobe Sound, Florida.

The Jupiter Island Club was once the most stultifyingly WASP enclave that closed society had ever produced. The town of Hobe Sound itself was nothing, a hole-in-the-wall with a Winn-Dixie and a Bible college. The club was on the adjacent barrier island, in between two game preserves. To be a part of it, you had to own a house on the grounds, but to own a house on the grounds you had to be a member. The Atlantic sparkled along a white beach on one side, and the Indian River, swarming with fat, amiable manatees, separated the island from the mainland on the other. Sun-kissed, fair-haired men, women, and children tooled along on bikes and in golf carts, and behind the Bakelite steering wheels of old Mercedes-Benzs. They went back and forth from the courts or the fairway, to the beach club or the snack bar or the clubhouse, to one another's houses for cocktail parties. My mother only dreamed of such a Nirvana—sun, the beach, hot and cold running servants, flora and fauna, and an open bar at all hours.

My grandparents honestly tried to make things fun for Will and me, but it was their idea of fun, not ours. Edward was happy to sit all day long in a sandbox with a pail and a shovel and a starfish mold and several doting caretakers, but for us they scheduled tennis lessons and swimming lessons and golf lessons and deep-sea fishing excursions, and even signed us up for tea dances. They rented us ugly bikes and brought Captain Closson down from Maine to drive us around—to no avail. Hobe Sound was my idea of Hell. I hated tennis, I hated golf, I hated swimming lessons, I hated lying in the sun—and I had no friends because I was inept at doing all those things. Lollygagging about the house with the grown-ups was supremely boring, but I endured it because I was too embarrassed to be out with Will, riding around on crappy rental bikes.

Suffering, in addition to being redemptive, can sometimes be portentous. On a day that would herald the close of the Addams era, I was introduced to two wondrous things: Gothic literature and the obituary page.

One of my father's brothers, Uncle Bob, was staying with us in Hobe Sound. We had all just returned from the beach club snack bar, where the four of us had lunched respectively on stone crab and noon balloons (the club's signature rum punch with an added floater of 150-proof Myers's); salad and a glass of milk with two raw eggs in it; and bacon cheeseburgers with fries, multiple Cokes, and a couple of brownies. My grandparents had teetered off to their beds for the usual post-lunch sleep-off. Edward was being forced to do the same, and was wailing his head off in a far corner of the house. Will had (unbelievably) found a friend to hang out with and was gone. It was too hot to do anything other than drape oneself across a Bruno Mathsson chaise and get lost in the newest issue of *CREEPY*.

Uncle Bob was reading *Scientific American*. He was blinking heavily behind his thick horn-rims, and making his trademark groany-grunty sound—something he did so habitually that we referred to him as Uncle *urr-hhhhh-uuuuhhh* Bob. I could see why he'd never been married. With his blue chin and gross hairy back, Uncle Bob often reminded me of Fred Flintstone.

Finishing his article, he came over to see what I was up to. Over my shoulder he studied the black-and-white drawings of a body-snatching that was taking place in a dark, rainy cemetery. Rotting flesh and bone-bared limbs were sticking out of coffins and body bags, and worms were playing pinochle on decomposing snouts everywhere. The omnipresent narrator, Uncle Creepy, leered and cackled his trademark *heh, heh, heh* all over the pages.

Uncle Bob straightened up and grunted. He asked me if I'd read the short story by Robert Louis Stevenson. I shot him a look that said, *Are you nuts?* Like I would read school stuff on my own? But then he told me the name of the story was "The Body Snatchers."

"Really," I said.

Was it a red-letter day or what. That very morning I'd been in my grandparents' bedroom, rearranging my grandmother's jewelry and makeup on the dressing table while she had her breakfast in bed with the octogenarian poodles and Edward lay ripping up Babar books by her side.

My grandfather was in the bathroom with *The New York Times*, doing big business with the door open, as usual. We heard the toilet flush and he shuffled back into the bedroom, the ties on his Savile Row pj's undone, the bottoms half off and trailing over his long pale feet.

"I say, Peggy, look at this." My grandfather rustled the paper in the direction of his wife and cleared his throat to read.

"Babar!" shrieked Edward, and stuffed a page in his mouth.

"What is it, Popsie?" my grandmother said, her eyes locked onto the *Today* show.

"In the obituaries there's a woman who's died. Some Bolshevik. Name seems familiar."

"Mmmm hmmmm," my grandmother replied, sucking on the pit of a prune, eyes riveted to Barbara Walters.

"See here, Peggy." He squinted at the paper with his glasses down his nose. "This 'aide of Lenin,' they call her. Well wasn't she that female your mother used to have those nonsense séances with?"

Brfffffttttt. "I'm sorry, darling?" My grandmother was following the directions the guest chef was giving with small movements of her cereal spoon, building the Pineapple Surprise right along with him.

"What's an obituary?" I interrupted.

"Ca-ca! Doggie ca-ca!" laughed Edward, lunging for a poodle turd on the floor.

"Yes, I'm certain that was the woman. A hawkish type. Dour. No wonder," my grandfather said, padding around with one hand scratching his stomach. His pajama bottoms suddenly dropped to the floor and he stepped out of them.

"What's an obituary, Granddaddy?" I asked louder.

"What?" He looked at me, surprised as usual by my existence, and said, "Look here, that's an obituary." He handed me the paper, pointing to a few columns with a fuzzy photo of a woman. Then he wandered off to the closet to get dressed for his tennis game. A commercial had come on, so my grandmother offered an explanation.

"An obituary is a story they write in the newspapers where they tell about a famous person when they've passed away." She reached for her lipstick on the bedside table and began to haphazardly apply it.

"Gaga! Gaga, ca-ca!" said Edward, holding the turd out to her.

"Do they talk about how the person died?" I asked, suddenly remembering that early sighting of my father's.

"Thank you, dearie," she said to Edward. "Sometimes they do, but only if it's because they were killed in an avalanche or sank with the *Titanic*, like that poor Astor cousin. You are too young to remember. Think of it as a sort of book report on a distinguished person's life."

"Huh," I said, scanning the rest of the page, but there were no interesting details. Then I had a completely brilliant thought.

"Gaga, do all papers have them?"

"Right-o, dearie," my grandmother mumbled through tissue, blotting her lips. The poodles exchanged positions, and *The Today Show* returned from station identification.

"Right-o, Gaga," I said, and trotted off to the kitchen to see if there was anything more explicit in the *Palm Beach Post*. There wasn't, but in due time I would discover British journalism.

The next day, Uncle Bob returned from town with a couple of books, both of collected short stories. The first was by Edgar Allan Poe and the second by Stevenson. By lunchtime I had read "The Body Snatchers," and by dinner "The Raven," with Uncle Bob's help in translating that bugaboo "Night's Plutonian Shore." By bedtime I had penned my first obit—a heartfelt, if sophomoric, send-off for the Lord and Master:

> *Peter Christian Beer, an international arms dealer, died yesterday of horribly severe and unnatural causes. He was around 50 . . .*

I could have built a substantial career on the thousands that were to follow.

When I returned to school after spring break, I decided to reinvent myself. Throughout the fall and winter terms I'd put in my usual time in the principal's office for misdemeanors ranging from Extremely Poor Attitude to coauthorship of a slam book, which is basically a compendium of the filthiest words in the English language.

Now I resolved to become a good student, starting with my

English class. I remember exactly what I was wearing when I finally got an A for something other than an art project. It was free dress day and I was proudly dressed in geometrically patterned go-go boots, beige windowpane tights, a faux leopard hip-hugger miniskirt with a white plastic belt, and a black skinny-knit poor boy sweater. *God*, I was cool.

"My, my," said the teacher as she handed out graded papers to the class. "Somebody had a wake-up call this vacation. Either that, or some very much needed tutoring."

I accepted mine from her and checked out the big beautiful A. "I've been reading," I said.

The bell rang and students started leaping out of their chairs. Miss Gleason rapped her desk with a ruler for attention. "Quiet down! Now listen, it will be your own choice for next week's book report, so I will expect creativity. And remember, comics and record liner notes do *not* count."

I smiled and patted my book bag. I was halfway through "The Monkey's Paw." Future book reports would practically write themselves.

Oi, Yank!

IN 1967 THE Monkees sold more records than the Beatles and the Rolling Stones combined, which was about the only thing that kept an American like me from being stoned to death in England.

Call me unpatriotic, but if you'd been trailed home from school every day by a pack of mercenaries in blazers and kilts who, because of some genetic xenophobia, felt the need to verbally disembowel you (*Get lost, you bleedin' Yank! Go back to the colonies! Yeah—fuck off an' bloody stay there!*), you'd have cut up your American passport with pinking shears too.

The annual exploding postcard arrived during the last week of camp, informing me that we were emigrating because of the Lord and Master's promotion. The house had already been sold, and the dogs and horses given away. The life of the chosen one, Will, remained unaffected, meaning he got to stay in a stateside boarding school and spend his vacations in Burdenland, while my younger brother and I were measured for English school uniforms. Had Edward been older, no doubt my grandparents would have claimed him as their legal property as well. I was temporarily placated by a Vidal Sassoon wedge haircut before we sailed from New York to Southampton aboard the SS *France*, but I shouldn't have been; it was hideous.

England did not turn out to be a Yardley Slicker commercial

after all. I emerged from the train at Waterloo station expecting to see the youthquake in full action: birds in oversized caps and textured stockings running in and out of red telephone booths; blokes with striped bell-bottoms and Edwardian jackets lounging on Jaguars; and benevolent bobbies everywhere. The magazines I'd consumed on the passage over had alerted me to possible sightings at any given place or time of the Beatles or Herman's Hermits or, at the very least, Lulu.

In reality, suburban London in the late 1960s was a dreary postwar scenario with rag-and-bone horse-drawn carts, blocks of dismal council flats, and a core population of spinsters and widows all vying for the parish vicar's favor like they were trapped in a Barbara Pym novel. There was nothing fab about the place at all. The authorities had been forced to come up with commercially crazy places like Carnaby Street just to keep people from eating their young out of depression.

Home sweet home was initially a small leaky house on a street named Strawberry Vale, in a town called Twickenham, in a suburb on the southwest side of London. The narrow garden behind gave on to the Thames River with a slippery cement quay that was perfect for accidental drownings. The interior of the house was furnished like a bordello: the squashy sofas and armchairs were upholstered in molting red velvet; the lamp shades were fringed; and all of the oddly sized mattresses had been stuffed during the Middle Ages with coarse black horsehair. Heating anything—air, water, or food—necessitated shoveling coal into the furnace, a quaint task whose novelty wore off within a day.

We all pined for something—my mother, for Miami and iceberg lettuce and Tab; me, for Cheetos and American bacon. The Antichrist wished that his wife's children would disappear. Only my little brother had what he wanted: unlimited Matchbox cars and his mother, whom he continued to adore unconditionally.

Despite a yearlong crash course in Virginia, domestication

continued to prove difficult for the lady of the house. "God-damn it!" my mother would erupt with when the fat popped at her from the (non-Teflon) frying pan in the cold gray dawn. Somewhere she had read that English schoolchildren began their English school days with a stomach full of eggs and bangers, those pink phalluslike sausages the Brits love. She really was trying.

"SHIT!" she would expostulate twenty times or so during the drive to school, first down our busy road and then into the traffic flowing into Twickenham, then past the Odeon and onto the congested high street that ran parallel to my school.

"Jesus H. Christ! That goddamned mini almost hit me! Oh God, if only I had a *tan* I could handle this. Look at me! I'm the color of that shiny gray toilet paper the Limeys use!"

You don't know the meaning of fear until you've driven with a hungover, sunlight-deprived woman who is grappling with a stick shift on the wrong side of the road, and whose head is swiveling every two seconds because she is searching for a shop that just might, by some miracle, sell Shake 'N Bake or QT. In less time than it takes to say "public transportation," I was commuting to school on my own.

Twickenham County Preparatory School for Girls was another school with a fancy name. However, this one was your basic state-subsidized institution: an assemblage of scarred desks, leaky fountain pens, and chalk dust in an archaic Edwardian setting that was permeated throughout with the odor of boiled cabbage and governed by teachers who enjoyed a good caning the way the landed gentry enjoyed blood sports.

My school uniform was an all-inclusive one: itchy wool underpants, kneesocks, dorky sandals, drip-dry ecru polyester shirt, pleated kilt, V-neck sweater, necktie, crested blazer, wool overcoat, and felt boater. Listed by the outfitters as "Nigger Brown," everything was the color of cheap chocolate cake.

The academic curriculum for Year One included fourteen

subjects and an overview of every competitive game played on British soil since the time of Cromwell. "God Save the Queen" was respectfully sung every morning at chapel. Refusal to participate on the grounds of unconstitutionality was not recognized as exercising one's inalienable rights. It wasn't long before I was on speaking terms with the top brass.

"Don't you guys know about the separation of church and state?"

"The only separation you need to know about, Miss Burden, is your desk from the other students. You will sit in the corner until you are repentant and ready to honor the monarch."

The headmistress and I often met for these cozy chats in her office.

"And I see, Miss Burden, that once again you have been using *ink* in your rough book. In our rough books, we use pen-sill and *only* pen-sill. Furthermore, Master Grimshaw informs me that you recently submitted an assignment—in your *neat* book—in ballpoint ink! Really! Let me remind you that here, unlike in the colonies, we use prrrroper ink and prrrroper fountain pens, and we practice the discipline for a *rrrreason*."

Sitting in what I would come to think of as my own, very straight-backed chair, I faced the headmistress and her suspiciously tidy desk. "I don't see why I can't use a Bic (wear earrings, sit out cricket, boycott lunch)."

"If you persist in demoralizing this institution with your slovenly ways then we shall have trouble, my girl, that we shall." She stood up and reached for the Magistrate, a splintery yardstick that had produced more than its share of martyrs.

"George the First should have never allowed tea into the colonies. Hands out, please," and she drew back for a mighty lash.

They say the English are an accommodating breed; after all, they've been invaded and infiltrated for thousands of years, inviting everyone to stay, or at least not asking them to leave. They didn't seem to feel that way about me, though. Being considered a foreigner had never occurred to me, what with the *Mayflower* and all that. So what if I spoke differently; on paper, wasn't it all the same playing field? Explaining this fact, or my documented chromosomal connection to Charles II, had little effect on the enemy, and I found myself routinely pinned against the WC wall with a razor blade by large girls with lavender thighs who didn't like the way I said "hi."

Eventually I picked up a few friends, losers who found an American curiously compelling (as in something offensive that you can't keep away from); wets with names like Roxanna and Felicity. But the friendships came to a grinding halt when they tried linking arms with me and I'd squeal, "Hey! You a lezzie or what?" What is it with English girls always touching one another and falling in love with horses and getting crushes on their female gym teachers?

My mother was quick to point out my unpopularity. "When I was your age I was making out in the cemetery every weekend. What in blazes are you doing home on a Saturday night?"

My mother liked to tell the story of how she and her classmates would down a couple of aspirins with a Coke (back then it still had traces of cocaine in it) and then go neck in the local graveyard. Since I knew my parents were dating in high school, I liked to imagine the two of them, young and in love and making out all over the headstones.

We were sitting at the dining room table. I was doing homework—with fourteen subjects it was pretty much a constant activity—and eating a slab of heavily buttered bread the size of my state-owned chemistry textbook. My mother was cataloging a set of medieval floor tiles she'd recently swiped from the ambulatory of Salisbury Cathedral during a smoke-screen stampede of Taiwanese tourists. Her can of Diet 7UP was close at hand. It wasn't really Diet 7UP, it was 90 percent Bacardi, but everyone went along with it in the interest of harmony. The only problem was that it was impossible to count the number of drinks she had consumed, so I had to rely on the expression on her face and the tone and delivery of her observations.

I told her I was home because I didn't have any friends.

"And why don't you have any friends?"

"Because everyone hates me," I explained. I burrowed my nose more deeply into the effect of temperature on equilibrium.

"Poppycock," she said, pulling lustily on her straw, "you just need to put on a skirt. But with black tights—they're slimming, you know."

We both glanced down to where I was straddling the chair. My high-waisted corduroy pants were so tight they were practically cutting off my heartbeat. It wasn't as if I was legally fat, or had ever even been fat. The issue was that I wasn't thin.

My mother was thin. And beautiful. I would have given my ovaries to look like her. She arranged the brown and yellow tiles into a pattern. "You know," she said, looking down at her work, "someone remarked the other day that if you painted those lower lashes under your eyes and lost ten or twenty pounds, you'd look just like Twiggy."

"Hmmm. I'll bet that someone was you," I said.

"And so what if it was?" she retorted. This was not a new approach, my mother's attempt to get me to look like Twiggy—or rather to try to get me to starve myself to look like Twiggy. She regrouped. "I'll bet you haven't tried marching yourself right up to people and being friendly. Ask them what they're up to on weekends. If they know any boys! You're old enough to be dating regularly."

"Oh, come on. I'm a twelve-year-old kid in school. I'm getting judged every minute of the day by someone. By my teachers. By other students. By boys I pass in the street. By you and Adolf—"

"Don't call him Adolf!"

"School's bad enough. The last thing I need is to be condemned for being a Yank at the movies or a dance or, or playing spin the bottle!" With that, I packed up my neat books and rough books and textbooks and fountain pens and blotting paper and ink bottle and ink eradicator and stormed off to my room. It's a waste of time trying to have a conversation with anyone in a see-through crochet dress, let alone your own mother.

Anyway, it's not like I had time for a social calendar. That first year, my weekends were spent hanging around gloomy churches and Celtic burial sites while my mother pursued her fascination with antediluvian British history, and trying to steal it. Like a good American tourist, she had discovered brass rubbing, the art of transferring onto paper the funereal engravings of medieval knights and their kin. Our hallways flapped with their morose, wraithlike effigies, clad as they were in chain-mail hoods and armor and the pointiest metal booties imaginable. I had to brush past their papery guard on my travels to and from the bedroom, bath, or kitchen. I may have been into the dead, but my mother was into the deader.

My childish interests hadn't been for naught. Tucked away in those Cimmerian churches, burrowed in the vestries and sacrarium, I managed to find something to amuse me: relics. Most churches possessed one—the arm of St. Philip, the eyelid of St. Euphemia, a splinter of the True Cross. This martyred cadaver jerky was cached in everything from jeweled crystal boxes to clumsy wire cages, and you didn't even have to go to the crypt to see it, which was a travesty in my opinion. Some churches had gift shops where you could buy postcards of their relics, the image rendered deliciously putrid by substandard photography and cheap printing. In an obscure Norman church in Gloucestershire I even found a relic for sale. It was the (purported) big toenail of a local virgin and charlady, Mildred of Chipping

Whopping, who had been martyred at the hands of her sexually deviant master.

The woman who ran the gift shop had my number. "Lovely, innit?" she simpered, hovering beside me as I gazed longingly at the scat-like thing. "I'll just wrap it up for you then, shall I, luv?"

Now really, what did I want with someone else's toenail when I still had my own collection from three summers ago? I was hemming and hawing, trying for once to be economical, when I spied out of my little eye my mother preparing to burgle. She had entered the church in her yellow tartan reversible cape (now you see me on the yellow side, now you don't on the black) and when last seen, like two minutes ago, had still looked like a school bus in a cave full of bats. Now she was a bat. I'd seen her do a double take at the ornamental stonework by the baptismal font. If I was going for the toenail, I'd better hurry.

"I'll take it!" I called to the shopkeeper, a little urgently. She bustled on over.

"You'll get plenty of use out of this, you will," she said. "Why, I've a bit of her ear meself, and when me and my Stan have a row I go straight to where I keep it in a tin, and I ask her for help, I does. American, are you?" I swallowed hard as I held out the ten-bob note I'd been planning to spend on a couple of Mars bars and some salt-and-vinegar crisps.

"Ta, ducks." She handed me my relic in a small brown envelope. "Care for some snaps of her torture chamber to go with it? Only half a crown . . ."

I apprehended my mother just as she was preparing to chisel a pint-sized gargoyle from its perch of several centuries. She hissed at me as I shoved her off her mark, using my little brother, her accomplice, as a sort of bludgeoning tool. I had to repeat this several times until she eventually scuttled out the door of the church, damning me to hell in front of God's House. Her unappreciative behavior led me to consider slipping the toenail into her Diet 7UP can. I considered it all the way home, and then, to prove I hadn't lost my Wednesday touch, I did it.

By the following winter my mother and brother and I had been to just about every stone circle, henge, barrow, ring, and hill-fort, every ruined Norman wall, turret, keep, abbey, and urinal, every Celtic cross, Iron Age fortification, medieval castle, Roman site, Neolithic flint mine, Saxon church, and Gothic cathedral within a ten-hour drive—including the Cheddar and Wookey Hole cave dwellings, Grimes Graves, Long Meg and Her Daughters, Ackling Dyke, Bevis's Thumb, and the incomparable Pike o' Stickle (Britain's biggest source of stone axes *and* the alleged home of the saintly nipple hair of the Martyr Thomas Plumtree).

My mother's favorite was Stonehenge, as would be evidenced by our Christmas cards over the next several years.

"Here, kids, back up against that trilithon and let me take the picture. Jesus, Wendy, wipe those crumbs off your face. And don't you have any lipstick? What are you now, thirteen? Oh, use mine. Now, where is your brother? Edward! What do you mean you don't like frosted pink? Just use it. EDWARD! Jesus H. Christ, I turn my back for one goddamn minute—"

Edward was at the developmental stage where boys like to urinate on weird things. He was partial to one of the Station Stones outside the circle.

My mother considered Stonehenge to be her personal archeological site. She had a chip off every stone except for three, and she would have gotten those had they not erected a fence to keep enthusiasts like her out. She was also extremely fond of the Uffington White Horse Hill Cut. In the garage there was a gallon bucket filled with chalk that she'd filched over a number of visits to the site. Once, when I'd allowed our new dog to poop in the vicinity of the horse's head, my mother had become apoplectic. I'd carefully apologized, the way one does to a psychopath, but she'd reiterated that it had been a bratty thing to do and Jesus H.

Christ why couldn't I show some respect for a prehistoric figure dating back to 2000 B.C.? Sparks had flown.

"Oh yeah? Well stealing the chalk the Celts made the thing with, and then carting it home in a Baggie sounds *real* respectful," I'd come back with.

Scooping the stuff as fast as she could, my mother had matter-of-factly pointed out that no one loved animals more than her, especially horses. She was right, of course; and when the sexton would lower her into the hallowed Puritan dirt of her former playground, the Milton Cemetery, the only thing my brothers and I would throw on top of her coffin would be a tattered photograph of Puck, her favorite hunter.

❧

Into our second year, and our third rental, I remained pretty much friendless. Among other things, my accent had refused to adapt, unlike that of my little brother, who within minutes of arrival, had taken on the piping tones of Little Lord Fauntleroy. Even my mother had developed an accent, albeit an ultra-embarrassing, inaccurately feigned Oxbridge one. On a good day I could barely pass for Canadian.

For my birthday that year, a sympathetic and well-paid "babysitter" took me to see *Hair*, the "American tribal love-rock musical," in which a guy gets drafted and a bunch of hippies on acid screw their brains out while they rant about the Establishment. Then the guy goes to Vietnam and dies. I don't remember much else—except all the words to all the songs because I bought the LP as we were leaving the theater and I played it from the second I got home until the needle wore straight through to the other side.

People left the theater saying things like, *Wow, that really blew my mind*, and *Yes, peace* will *guide the planets and love* will *rule the stars*. All I knew was that I had heard more dirty words in an hour and a half than I had in a lifetime, and that fourteen men and women had taken off all their clothes and demanded that I stare at them. Heretofore life had been pretty much about horses, trying to reach the end of puberty, keeping up with modern mortuary science, and steering clear of my mother's relationship with the Antichrist. *Hair* was a hormonal wake-up call.

I had also walked out feeling tight with Uncle Sam again. This was *Hair*—the *American* tribal love-rock musical. Not the British one. And the Brits were spending pounds to see it. I was so proud, I let my accent rain down on everyone in section CC, and then out onto the streets of the West End and into a steamy little café we stopped in to warm ourselves before heading home on the tube. That was a mistake, because the frazzled tea lady behind the counter had not had the pleasure of seeing the show.

People were pressing in on one another, yelling for service and trying to stay clear of the harried waitresses. When my babysitter at last got the ear of the tea lady, she had to shout out our request over the din of crockery and laughter and short-order jabberwocky.

"Whot? You want two cups of tea and a whot?" the tea lady yelled back at us as she simultaneously ladled soup into a take-away container and rang up a bill for a pedophile who kept elbowing me in my future bosom.

"Yes, please," my babysitter screamed back politely, "that's two cups of tea and some buttered toast, please."

"Some *whot*?"

"Er, toast, if you please. Any sort will do. And some butter on it would be lovely, thank you ever so much."

"*Oats?*" she shouted back, her hand to her flabby ear. Good God, the English. This was no time for gentility; I was starving. Emboldened by my patriotic musical experience, I put my face into the tea lady's bestial one and hollered, "*Tea and hot buttered toast, please!*"

Maybe I only imagined that the room went morgue-quiet,

and that everyone heard the tea lady repeat what I said with the most torturous mimicry imaginable. In my head the ruddy English faces moved in with the menace of a lynch mob. The tea lady stuck her dishpan hands on her walrus hips and, wagging her head with each nasal syllable, said, "Sam hat badderrrrd towwwst? Is that what you bleedin' want, now is it? HAT BADDERRRRRRRRD TOWWWSSST?"

I shrank away from the counter in the most intense self-loathing and mortification of my short, miserable life.

On the tube ride home I came to the conclusion that the only way out of this misery was to change my nationality. And what better way to begin than by desecrating my passport, thereby getting rid of the evidence. Following this liberating act of treason, I felt better—until I got in serious trouble, not only with my mother (*Jesus H. Christ, Birdbrain! You think that's going to solve your problems? Contact lenses and mascara are what you need!*) but more enduringly with my grandfather.

En route to Paris, my grandparents had stopped in London for a night. Edward had ratted on me during a lull in the feeding of the sea lions at the London Zoo, where my grandmother had insisted we go following lunch at the Connaught. My grandfather was speechless with rage; so speechless that I thought I'd escaped relatively unscathed—until the quiet dark of the Nocturnal Mammal House unlocked his tongue. We were standing in front of the slow loris exhibit when he let me have it. "That's an act as blasphemous as burning the flag!" my grandfather thundered. The lorises watched, unperturbed, and continued to munch (very slowly) on grasshoppers behind the glass.

In a swell of bravery I lashed back. "I don't see what's so great about being American!"

"I suppose you prefer the dismal mediocrity of socialism to democracy?"

I had no idea what he was talking about, and I said so.

"You truly are the most ignorant girl—have you not heard of

freedom? Or private enterprise? I'll tell you what's so great about your country—"

"Bill!" my grandmother interjected, laying her gloved hand on his rigid arm. "*Please*. The animals are *feeding*. Can't we chat about this over tea and scones back at the hotel?"

"You have no idea what it's like to be an American here. Everybody hates me. The kids in my school, the greengrocer, the bus conductors, they all hate Americans. HATE them. The only time anyone's been nice to me at school was when we watched the landing on the moon, and that only lasted until they turned off the TV in the auditorium. When I won the academic prize at the year-end awards, they practically stoned me. You want me to be patriotic and *die*?"

"Of course not, dearie, we just don't want you to forget who you are," said my grandmother.

"Are you kidding? I won't survive another week here if I don't."

"What utter rot!" blustered my grandfather.

In the near total darkness, his was a disembodied voice, with correspondingly little effect on me. Burdenland might have been in a different galaxy for all it mattered. I had more in common with the dentally challenged, loudly dressed, and hushed-with-wonder family next to us than with my own blood, my grandfather in his pinstripes and homburg, my grandmother in a Givenchy dress patterned with exploding roosters, clutching her poodle-portaled pocketbook. A Bentley waited by the zoo entrance to whisk us all back to the world's most expensive hotel.

"Bloody hell!" piped Edward, nose to the glass. "The little bugger's eatin' 'is mate!"

"That's it," said my grandfather, pounding the floor with his tightly rolled umbrella. "It's boarding school for both of you!"

The populist family shot us a collective look of horror and scooted over to the ring-tailed lemurs.

"Oh yeah?" I hissed at him. "Well you'll have to drag me there!" I turned back to the lorises, who appeared to be watching our domestic exchange with deep interest.

"'Allo, cuntface!" Edward chirped to the small creature staring back at him.

❧

It probably should have bothered me that my older brother and I were like strangers now, but it didn't. Will remained my grandparents' favorite, and I wanted nothing to do with him. Our relationship had quickly unraveled after his departure for boarding school, and now there wasn't even the common ground of Burdenland. For the first three years we were in England, I didn't go back to the States, and Will had come to visit just once. The only thing I can recall of that awkward Christmas break was that my brother capsized his kayak into the winter-cold Thames, and my mother "had to" dive in to "save" him. Like he hadn't spent about ten summers learning to swim at camp. She fake-rescued him while he was hanging on to the overturned kayak maybe two feet away from the quay at the bottom of our garden. Then she hustled him inside and got him undressed and into a hot bath like he was a baby instead of a fifteen-year-old. I was beside myself with jealousy.

Worst of all, she then had to tell me afterward how pleasantly surprised she was by the size of his penis.

Like a lizard dropping its tail to avoid capture, I stopped speaking. I walked the three miles to school rather than have to communicate with the bus conductor. Outside of the house, I transmitted through the written word, telepathy, or kinesics, which meant I did a lot of wild shrugging and facial gesticulation. When displeased, I pretended to vomit; when happy—well, I never was. My teachers were hardly sympathetic, and it wasn't long before my hands looked like I'd been knitting with barbed wire.

At home I practiced in front of the bathroom mirror:

Privacy—pri(not prie)-va-see
Schedule—shed-dule
Sexual—sex-yoo-all
Vitamin—vit(not vite)-a-min
Zebra—zeb-rah

I made a decision to radically alter my wardrobe and began to clothe myself in what I imagined to be the expression of a sexual free spirit with countercultural values. I wore lace-up Greco-Roman sandals, fruit-colored snakeskin waistcoats, long hippie skirts I sewed myself, and Spanish shawls with trailing fringe. I frizzed my hair out and carried hobo handbags that also trailed fringe. I went fringe crazy: I had fringed jackets and fringed Indian boots and fringed leather skirts and wristbands with clacking, beaded fringe. You could hear me before you saw me.

In order to be an insouciant free spirit, I knew I'd have to understand the vocabulary of one. Unfortunately *sodomy* was not in the school dictionary. Fortunately, my mother supplied me with the definition one evening without my even having to ask.

"D'you know what shodomy is?" she said, plonking herself down across from me at the kitchen table where I was doing my geometry homework. The thunk of her soda can echoed in the hard-edged room. We had just moved (for the fifth time) into a house that appeared to be for keeps. It was a small, newly constructed, two-storied brick box attached to a very large six-car garage. My mother had outfitted the rooms with cheap Danish furniture. She'd hung her beloved knights up on the walls, but even they looked uncomfortable. Reimagining herself as the kooky artist, she'd painted the kitchen a migraine orange, and furnished it with a picnic table varnished to a blinding gloss.

"I shaid, do you know what shodomy is!" she repeated, after a deep suck on the can.

"As a matter of fact—"

"I'll tell you what it is. Is fucking illegal, thas what it is."

"Shodomy is illegal? But—"

"Not SHODomy, *shodomy!*"

"Right. Shodomy. S-H-O-D-O-M-Y."

She flapped her hand and leaned over to snatch my fountain pen. She wrote out *s-o-d-o-m-y* on the cover of my rough book—the precious, state-provided, teacher-monitored notebook that only *pen-sill* was permitted in.

"There." She sat back and took another hit. "Shodomy ish fucking in the ASH." She pounded with the soda can for emphasis. Great. Now there were rum stains to enhance the inked profanity.

"Well," I replied, affecting nonchalance, "isn't that what poofters do?"

She drew her head in like a tortoise.

"Poof-ter! *Poof*-ter? What kine of a word ish that? Shodomy ish what your shtepfather doesh to ME." She sat there, fiddling with her straw. I sat there, twirling my compass. I was not entirely sure what I was supposed to do with this information.

"An I don't *like* it," she added, after a long pause during which I considered my options. If nothing else, it was one word down in the song (plus the title) from *Hair*, with only thirteen more to go.

"An I'm wan a divorsh," she said, tossing the straw over her shoulder and tilting her head back to gulp her drink. Gone was the red face of stoicism; she was teary. I elected to act indifferent. I just wanted to get back to trying to figure out the Pythagorean theorem

I don't want to know this, I thought.

"It hurts," she whimpered, wiping her nose with the sleeve of her robe.

She brought this on herself. My father's passport picture flickered in my head. (Oddly, it was the only picture I had of him.)

I stood up and went around the table to fetch her a paper towel. I waited while she blew her nose on it, and then I threw it in the garbage. I massaged her rigid shoulders until she stopped crying. I took a sponge from the sink and cleaned the table where some of the rum had spilled, though I knew I didn't have to. My mother would be wiping the kitchen down late into the night, drinking and wiping, forestalling bedtime with the mechanical and comforting motions of housekeeping.

As I was about to retreat to my bedroom, I had a thought.

"You wouldn't happen to know what *pederasty* means, would you?"

❧

The key to becoming part of a coed peer group is a willingness to exchange saliva. Once I understood this, my social education began to progress in a relatively normal way—if you can call dating a guy with a harelip normal. Melvin Moss was the richest boy I knew. Which wasn't saying much, given where I went to school and the select coterie I hung with. Rich, in my new life, did not mean four houses and a staff of twenty. Rich meant your family owned two cars. It was almost as if Burdenland and the immoderation of my grandparents' life had never been a part of mine.

Melvin was not exactly a hot ticket. You could tell that he was the kind of guy who would eventually require an instructional flowchart to participate in real foreplay, but for my needs he was fine. All I required was a snogging partner in order to gain access to weekend parties. I'm not sure Melvin knew I was American; it's not like I ever said anything more to him than "No—the bra stays on." Melvin, who pronounced his own name *Mayo-vin Mosh*, had been patched up at some point, as evidenced by a seam on his upper lip where the hair of his "mustache" parted. Still, speech did not exactly flow out of him. So what; he wore skin-tight, long sleeved T-shirts and cool bell-bottoms, and he had a snaky little body like Mick Jagger's. More importantly, his parents had a color TV.

Everything was going according to plan until I tried to give Melvin a hickey. We were at his house one Sunday afternoon in the humid company of four other writhing couples, in the den with the curtains drawn. Cream's *Disraeli Gears* was on the turntable, and the parents were at the pub. I had no idea how to give a hickey, or a *love bite*, as the Brits call them, but that didn't stop me from trying. Trouble often evolves from confusing semantics, as illustrated by Melvin's reaction when I bit him. I really was being penetratingly sexy, so I was baffled when he leapt up and shrieked, "Hit! Wash-oo oo at or!" The party came to a grinding halt as everyone popped up his or her head. With both hands clamped to his neck, Melvin sprinted for the bathroom and slammed the door. What a baby. There was hardly any blood.

I picked up my fringed shoulder bag with all the colonial dignity I could muster, and left the house via the back door. Tidying myself as best I could in the garden, I considered my options. The Thames lay in front of me, and I thought about jumping in and floating downstream to my house, because that would have been the easiest way of getting home without having to talk to someone. Judging from the progress of a drifting branch, however, I'd be able to vote before I pulled up to my own backyard. I started walking to the nearest bus stop.

I was waiting for the number thirty-three when a beat-up red Austin pulled alongside the curb. I recognized the dark-haired girl in the passenger seat as Josephine Doran, a typically aloof classmate in my form at school. (So *she* had been half of the pretzel in the armchair.) The driver, clearly her brother, leaned across and said, "Oi, Yank—want a lift then, do you?" Three gangly boys shoved over for me in the backseat, and I burned out my quadriceps trying to put as little of my weight on them as possible.

"You all right back there?" the driver called above the volume of the tape deck. He introduced himself as Chris. "Crikey, Melvin didn't half look bloody daft for carrying on like that!" He laughed a smoker's hack, and I blushed as unbecomingly as a mandrill.

"Don't be silly," said Josephine, thinking my lack of reply came from a puritanical sense of outrage. "Melvin's so sexually frustrated he often needs a proper set-down to keep him in his place. I shouldn't worry if I were you." She flipped her long, curly hair over her shoulder and turned around to read my reaction. She resembled her brother in that both had pasty, troubled skin, small dark eyes, and mouths that were wide and thin-lipped. Her upper teeth had curious tiny ridges along the edges. Josephine was the better looking of the two, simply by nature of her sex and her palpable self-confidence.

The boy named Nigel, upon whose boney thighs I was pretending to lie like a feather, began to mimic Melvin's snuffled inflection. Soon they all were punching one another in the arms and calling one another *fuckin' git* and *cuntface*, which is a charming colloquialism English lads like to address one another with.

Chris shouted above the fray, "Where d'you live, then?"

I mumbled my address in as Canadian a tone as I could muster. Nigel repeated it in a yee-haw twang.

"Don't mind him," Chris said, "he's fuckin' mental. Broom Water Road—that's not far from our house, innit?" I nodded. I had no idea.

The car swerved as Chris extricated a pack of squashed cigarettes from the rear pocket of his Levi's. These were passed around to salutes—*Fuck! Gauloise!* and *Bloody brilliant!*—and lit from a plug in the scratched metal dash. The car rapidly filled with acrid French smoke. Josephine cranked down her window with a look of sovereign disgust and said, "You can leave me off at home first, please, or I shall asphyxiate." Unlike Chris, who employed more glottal stops than someone actually missing a glottis, Josephine spoke a beautifully precise Oxford English.

"I need the fuckin' loo," called out Nigel, to the relief of the others who were desperately holding in an afternoon's worth of lager. We stopped shortly thereafter at the Dorans' narrow row house on the Stanley Road.

I waited self-consciously on the upstairs landing as, one after another, the lads emptied their bladders. My foot was finally on the threshold, so to speak, when a humpbacked old woman came out of nowhere and nipped in front of me, slamming the door in my face. I waited, legs crossed, my teeth sunk into my lower lip. I leaned my forehead against the paper-thin wall and held my hand against the swelling tide below. I pressed my ear to the door and heard only the sound of pages being turned.

Just as I reached the point of no return, Mrs. Doran came up the staircase. She was a comfortably untidy, German-born woman with a far more questionable take on the King's English than mine, particularly as it was punctuated every other second or so by a considerable facial twitch. To me, that spelled kindred spirit.

"Would it be okay if I used a different bathroom?" I stammered sotto voce.

"A different bawsroom? Sorry, love (twitch, twitch), we've only the one. Takin' her time, is she?" She banged on the door. "Here, Granny! Put that bloody book down and get a move on—there's a queue." To me she added, "The silly cow gets stuck in the middle of a Louis L'Amour and you can't get her out till she's finished."

From the living room downstairs Mr. Doran called out, "Tell the Yank if she wants another bog she can use the garden. We won't look."

The furious unrolling of toilet paper could now be heard from within. This was followed by a series of grumblings and grunts and sighs, and the elastic snappings of supportive garments. Suddenly, Granny burst out with the energy of a water buffalo, leaving the flimsy door banging in her wake, and a brown-colored odor suspended like woodsmoke. I slipped in and locked the door.

Plastered to the bottom of the bowl was a chocolate swirl of dung. With averted eyes, I carefully lined the seat with toilet paper and sat down. The residual warmth from Granny's old arse radiated disturbingly into mine, but the release of Niagara was so blissful, I got over it. With curiosity, I looked about the bathroom that serviced an entire family of six. A sarcophagean tub took up most of the space. The paraphernalia of personal hygiene was everywhere: loofahs, acne medicine, Tampax, shampoo bottles, toothbrushes, aspirin, tweezers, eyelash curlers, bottles of nail varnish, shaving cream, eye cream, and thirteen different cakes of soap. Drying panty hose and bras hung from towel racks, and hooks, and the window knobs.

If the room hadn't been so smelly, thanks to Granny's mighty turd, it would have been downright cozy. It was warm, and, like a good English bathroom, it had thick wall-to-wall carpeting. Waist-high stacks of paperback books encircled the toilet and lined the walls. With the exception of a pile of mysteries, they were all American westerns. I selected the well-thumbed *More Brains Than Bullets* and began reading.

A thump on the door brought me up sharply.

"Oi! Yank! D'you fall in, then?" called Chris. I hurriedly wiped up and dashed out. He grinned at me but then reeled back dramatically and clutched his nose.

"It wasn't me!" I squeaked.

"Right," he laughed, and continued to hold his nose as he entered.

I wilted down the stairs. As I entered the living room, Mrs. Doran pressed a large mug of milky coffee into my hands. I looked at it with trepidation, not knowing then that it would be the first of ten thousand four hundred and fifty something cups of instant Nescafé that I would consume under that roof. I was offered a cigarette, which I declined, and then a seat, and then a biscuit. For a good hour I sat on a sprung couch amid a pile of old papers and *Radio Times* magazines and quietly took the place in. The boys from the back of the car had invited themselves for supper and were now going judgmentally through a shelf of LPs under the windows. The working-class, beer-bellied man of the house sat next to the television, smoking and flipping through the evening papers, his eyes up and down on everybody in the room, doling acerbic one-liners out sparingly and to great effect. A dog that looked like a stegosaurus lay with its armored head on the master's feet.

Trying to absorb the dialogue gave me vertigo.

". . . If Manchester don' bloody win next week . . ."

"Shut up, you lot! I can't hear the bleedin' news!"

". . . And the stupid git carried on about the Magna Carter until break . . ."

"Is everyone rich in America, then?"

"Bloody hell . . . Granny's back up in the loo again . . ."

"Ma, Jo stole my nail varnish. Ma . . ."

". . . Oh, don't get your bloody knickers in a twist, Jane . . ."

"D'you know the Monkees, then?"

". . . and that fuckin' Wilson, you wait till the next election . . ."

"Does everyone talk like you in America, then?"

"Oh, leave the girl alone! It's not your fault you speak funny, is it, ducks?"

"No, it is NOT my turn to do the washing up, cuntface."

"Dad, Granny's screamin' bloody murder . . ."

"But why can't I leave school at fifteen? It's no bloody use to me . . ."

". . . with his willie stuck in the effing milk bottle . . ."

"No, YOU deal with her—she's not my bloody mum—"

". . . he got it at the beach fight in Brighton over the weekend . . ."

This is bloody brilliant, I said to myself, trying on Josephine's favorite expression. If I'd wanted to remain silent, it would have been a snap; you had to fight to get a word in edgeways with this lot. But unaccustomed levels of caffeine opened the linguistic floodgates, and I began to rattle on about the number of radio stations on US airwaves, and frozen food aisles in supermarkets the size of rugby fields, and the proliferation of McDonald's and Hot Shoppes and Burger Kings and Roy Rogers and Howard Johnsons and White Castles and Kentucky Fried Chickens, and how many Ferraris my dreadful stepfather had and how it did less than nothing to make him appealing.

"We'll take you in as a lodger in exchange for one of those cars then, right?" joked Mr. Doran carelessly. I prayed he didn't catch the sudden welling of my eyes. If only. I was happy for the first time in eons, happy and stupidly full of hope. And then I remembered that I had my own puny family and they had no idea where I was.

"I think I better use a phone," I said to Mrs. Doran. She told me theirs (their *single* theirs) was in the kitchen. I thought about how my grandparents had his 'n' her four-line telephones on each side of their beds, and next to the toilets in their bathrooms, and how there were two on either side of the sofas in each of the living rooms of their four houses. I thought about how many bathrooms there were in each of those houses, and felt ashamed. In the New York apartment alone there were fourteen.

The phone was answered on the first ring: "Beer here."

"Oh—uh, hi," I said. "I'm, um, just calling to let you, um, know that I'm okay and, um, I'll be home soon, after I have supper which, um, the Dorans have, um, in-invited me to, um, stay for."

There was a silence, and then my stepfather responded, "Do you have any idea how many *ums* you have just said?"

I was pretty well used to this, he having been married to my mother for four years now, so I told him I had no idea, and that I would be taking the bus home.

"No," he said, with the kind of heaviness the air has when thunderheads are getting ready to crash about. "One of us will collect you."

I gave him the Dorans' address, hung up, and began to fret over which was going to be more embarrassing—being picked up by Hitler, or by Barbarella.

The latter, as it turned out.

Josephine and I were taking a magazine sex quiz when the doorbell rang. Jane, the youngest, scrambled to pull open the front door. There stood *ma mère*, resplendent in a white leather miniskirt and matching vest, and thigh-high wet-look vinyl boots that revealed a good four inches of her bare orange thigh. A silver Dino Ferrari was inefficiently parked with one wheel on the curb behind her. Jane gaped. Everyone in the living room rushed to see the apparition, and I felt my lunch percolate near the region of my colon. Lowering her oversized sunglasses, my mother said, "May I come in?" That was my cue to stream up the stairs to the fortunately empty bathroom.

When I came back down ten minutes later, my mother had not disappeared, but was sitting in Mr. Doran's armchair with a glass of water and a napkin folded on her naked knee. Everyone was sitting up straight, minding their Ps and Qs and trying not to stare. My mother was chattering away about her upcoming trip to the Canary Islands, and how these fabulous new bikinis were designed to let sun in so that you could get an allover tan without being nude, and how she had just been accepted to Christ College at Oxford University. With her phony accent, she sounded like Churchill doing a drag act.

"Oxford. How luffly," said Mrs. Doran with a tremendous tick of her nose and upper lip.

"Yeah. But if you don't mind me askin', what on earth for?" said Mr. Doran. He wore a bemused expression, like someone half-tolerating the parlor tricks of a pomeranian.

"Hell no, I don't mind! I'm getting my doctorate in numismatics," my mother explained with a toss of her hair. Her roots were showing and I couldn't wait to tell her.

"What the fuck is that?" asked Chris politely. His pinky crooked out daintily from a coffee mug that depicted Sneezy and Bashful in an act of homosexual congress.

"It's the study of coins. In my case, ancient Greek coins. I'll be doing my dissertation on a particular hoard from the island of Aegina. It's absolutely fascinating because some of the coins have tortoises with three marks on their backs and some of them have four, though they are of the same denomination, which has led experts to conjecture—"

"Time to go," I yipped, snatching up my things and heading for the door.

"I thought you were going to stay for supper," Josephine said. "We can give you a lift home, can't we, Dad?"

"Well, I am a bit hungry," my mother began. I pushed her rudely out the door and down the uneven sidewalk and wrestled the driver's side door of the Ferrari open with so much force it nearly came off its shiny little Italian hinges. I practically threw her in. A small crowd had grouped themselves around the car, but they took off when they saw the lightning bolts shooting out of my eyes.

After a couple of failed attempts, my mother got the engine going and we moved off.

"Let's get one thing straight," I said. "Those are MY friends and you are NOT welcome there."

"Oh, poppycock," my mother retorted, missing the gate on the gearbox for third and grinding the lever back into first. The engine nearly leapt out of its compartment in anguish.

"I'm serious," I said. "You leave them alone. If you don't, I'll dump out every bottle of Bacardi I find from now until I leave home for college."

We had stopped at a zebra crossing to let a group of ladies in blue raincoats and orthopedic sandals cross. My mother had her hands on the steering wheel in a death grip. In a quiet voice she said, "But I'm lonely too."

Poof! I made the sudden (unwelcome) sensation of compassion disappear. "Get your own friends," I said coldly, and turned my face to the window to hide my shame. The car bucked into first and stalled, and we sat there.

Christ. I finally get a life, and I can't shake her. "I'm sorry," I said. I wasn't really, but honestly, it didn't cost me much.

"Yeah, well I'm sorry too." After that, neither of us said anything, we just stared at the black leather dash and the swoop of sparkly platinum metal beyond it, until finally she restarted the engine and turned the car around, bumping up over the center island and scraping the low front of the undercarriage with a sickeningly expensive sound, and drove me back to the house on Stanley Road. I told her I'd be home by ten and climbed out.

The Dorans were having a meal my mother would have appreciated, if not partaken of: fried eggs, fried streaky bacon, fried sausages, fried bread, fried tomatoes, deep-fried chips, and tinned beans. We ate on our laps in the living room with the telly on and the wireless squawking in the kitchen. Mr. Doran and Chris and his friends chain-smoked while they ate. Jane had a crying fit because she felt ignored. She would remedy that situation in the not so distant future by giving birth to her first child at fifteen.

Mr. Doran ran me home in his battered Rover. He dropped me at the end of my street as I requested, too embarrassed for him to see the house I lived in. It was modest by American standards, but a mansion compared to the street of dismal houses and tiny littered yards where I'd just been.

"Night, then, Yank," he called from the rolled down window. His long gray face, his eyes narrowed from the smoke of a No. 6 permanently hooked in his mouth, would become unimaginably dear to me. But I had only an incandescent inkling of that as I hurried down the dark street to my mother's house.

George

THIRTEEN WAS *HUGE* for me. I finally got to see a grown man naked, and I fell in love—although not with the same person. The naked man was my stepfather, and seeing his fruit bowl only increased my aversion to him.

It was late at night and I'd been up reading *Forever Amber.* Ravenous from all that wanton behavior, I decided to make some toast and slather it with butter, Restoration London style. My room was adjacent to the kitchen, which was extremely convenient for nocturnal refreshment, and at night the kitchen became an integral part of my bedroom suite. So you can imagine my irritation when I opened up the door to see my stepfather bare-assed in front of the refrigerator.

I had to stuff my hand in my mouth to keep from screaming. Apart from my two brothers, the *David* was the only male anatomy I was familiar with, and his was the aesthetic penis of high art—a tidy marble package crowned with a pyramid of tastefully coiled tendrils. On backlit view in front of the Tupperware and cottage cheese and orange juice was a limp sea cucumber, one of those nasty, squirting, shell-less things that untalented fisherpersons like myself are forever pulling out of the ocean in a clump of dark, stringy kelp. No wonder my mother hit the Bacardi.

My stepfather was busy chugging a bottle of milk so I knew

he hadn't seen me, even though his wandering left eye seemed to stare out from beneath the Adolfian thatch of hair. I watched until he drank to the end of the bottle. He replaced the foil top, leaving an inch of spittle-laced backwash for someone's cereal in the morning (my brother's, because I wouldn't tell him), farted robustly, and exited the kitchen. I closed my bedroom door on feathered hinges, leapt into bed, and yanked the covers up over my head. My appetite had vanished, probably for life.

One week, sixteen hours, and twenty minutes after my conception of idealized manhood was shattered (teenaged diaries are all about detail), I sat at the kitchen table slogging through a government-issued copy of *The Merchant of Venice*—in German, which made it even more gripping, if possible. My mother leaned against the sink in the late afternoon sunlight, reverentially bathing a head of jet-lagged iceberg lettuce like it was the Christ child. Her recent discovery of the Food Halls at Harrods—and, consequently, other long lost friends from departed shores: Tab, Rice-A-Roni, Chef Boyardee, Chun King, and Carnation Instant Breakfast—had so appeased her, she'd cut back on her dosage of Miltown by 200mgs.

A mound of raw chopped beef lay on a piece of butcher paper beside the sink. From time to time my mother would pinch off some of the meat and dunk it into what looked like floor sweepings.

"How the bejesus have I survived for two years without Lipton onion soup mix? And *dreamy* iceberg," she said, smiling beatifically down at the puny lettuce on the drain board. Slicing a minuscule wedge, she spooned some gelatinous dressing over it and, shuddering with pleasure, took a bite. I flinched from habit as her teeth rang annoyingly on the tines of the fork.

My mother always changed for dinner before her husband came home from work. Tonight she was wearing one of their all-time favorites, the crocheted brown micromini dress. As usual, she skipped the underwear. The dress must have been made with the largest hook on the market, because there were more spaces than yarn, and my mother's nipples poked through them like pencil erasers.

On cue, the rumble of a 3.0-liter V-12 engine could be heard turning onto our street. It revved to a wail as it streaked past the four Victorian row houses before our hideous detached modern brick. The Ferrari 250 GT spun through the gate and squealed to a halt in front of the only noncommercial six-car garage within forty miles. Out sprang Herr Peter Beer, as immaculately groomed as when he had left the house ten hours earlier. His gray flannels were still sharply creased, his shirt tautly tucked in, his custom John Lobb side-buckled shoes as glossy as when they'd come out of the box, and the black Hermès briefcase he gripped had barely sustained a scratch in ten years of service. The Ferrari gleamed as well, but he had me to thank for that: punishment in our house was dispensed in the form of a tin of simonize wax and an afternoon of flunky labor.

It was lucky I still didn't have much of a social life. Given my propensity for screwing up, waxing my stepfather's sports cars took up a fair amount of my time. There were six of them: a Porsche, three Ferraris, a Mercedes-Benz Gullwing, and its 300 SL roadster counterpart. Each perfectly maintained specimen was painted with about a million coats of silver lacquer that my stepfather insisted be buffed, burnished, stroked, and rubbed in a particularly exhaustive (and punitive) fashion.

My mother waved to her husband out the kitchen window, then returned to the stove to dump a cylinder of frozen orange juice over the pale carcass of a duck. She shoved the pan into the oven, licked her hair into place, and took a suck from her 7UP can that could have drained a wading pool.

"*To—ré—a—dor, en gar—dé! To—ré—a—dor!*" the Antichrist belted as he fussed about the Ferrari, flicking the road dust off with a feather duster, unrolling the fabric car cover, and enfolding his baby in it for the evening. He fancied himself a misunderstood tenor and sang opera far more than was necessary. He sang it all with theatrical gusto, in the seven languages he was fluent in.

The garage door ground shut. Smooth leather heels sounded on the front path. And then, *"WAA HOO!"* hailed the Tenor. The front door sprang open with a rush of 4711 cologne.

"HOO WAA!" returned my mother, whipping off her apron. "Where are you, little one?"

"Coming, my Lord and Master!"

That was always my cue to exit stage right so I wouldn't have to watch him suck out her tonsils and make bread out of her butt.

Beneath the stairs in the core of our house was a triad of tiny gun rooms. These were referred to as the outer, the middle, and the (high-caliber) inner sanctums. Within were samples of what was represented in the tens of thousands at my stepfather's arms factory: Soviet AK-47s and Dragunovs, Israeli submachine Uzis, German Walther PPK pistols, Belgian Brownings, Italian Berettas, French Chatelleraults, Chinese and Dutch hand grenades, American M-79 grenade launchers; you get the picture.

My stepfather was all for sharing his enthusiasm for the weapons industry.

"Look at this beauty," he said one evening after dinner, placing a rifle in my seven-year-old brother's lap. Edward sat on the floor, still in his gray flannel uniform shorts, his shirt untucked and spotted with spaghetti sauce, his tie askew. He'd been playing with his Matchbox cars and was justifiably uneasy at having been singled out for enlightenment. My mother glanced over from where she was slunk in a black butterfly chair (in a leather mini and fishnets) working on her thesis. She was in her second year of graduate school at Oxford.

"Some jokers think this is an AK-47," said my stepfather. "Ha! It is not!"

Edward stared dolefully at the weapon. Inspired, the Lord

and Master leapt up and exited the living room to return a moment later with another hulking assault rifle.

"*This* is an AK-47." He leveled the gun and peered with his non-roving eye down the sight at Inky, our recently acquired pound dog, who exhibited her hallmark stupidity by yawning back at him.

Taking up the original rifle from my brother, he stroked it lovingly from its slotted forearm to its cutout skeleton stock. "And *this*," he crooned, "*this* is an SVD: a Snayperskaya Vintovka Dragunova—the first rifle specifically designed for sniping!"

"Blimey," said Edward, dutifully, and looked toward his mother. But she had given up trying to shield him from these stepfather-stepson moments. Her hands tightened on her notebook, but she said nothing.

"That old Dragunov, now he knew how to design a rifle! The magazine alone took eleven months and twenty-three days to design!" My stepfather said this in an awestruck, Russian-accented whisper, as if he could hardly fathom such a feat of creation.

"They may look the same, but the likeness is strictly cosmetic." He was trying to transfer some of his zeal to this pathetic child. "The critical difference is the *gas* system. The Dragunov has a short-stroke gas piston, do you understand?" Edward's lip trembled and a tear rolled down his cheek. He knew he was failing in the role of stepson, but he was powerless to act any differently. Like all of us, he was terrified of the man.

"Ach!" said the Lord and Master, sitting back on his heels in disgust. "Leslie, your son is a coward."

"Waaahhh!" cried Edward.

My mother remained in her chair, conjugating Greek verbs, and sucking hard on her 7UP can. She'd make up for Edward later, in bed.

❧

Puberty had not been going too well for me.

After school one day my mother had marched me into the underwear department of the local Marks & Spencer.

"Listen," I'd hissed to her as, one after another, she snapped through the racks of gargantuan brassieres, "I don't even want a bra! Everyone at school will laugh at me—even *more* than they do already."

"Oh, poppycock." She had signaled to the saleslady, a steel-haired matron with a proud, two-acre chest, as I slumped in my mortification.

"I can't believe you don't carry a 32AA." I clutched the glass counter at my mother's pronunciation of "can't" as *cawn't*. Her fake accent was a constant source of public humiliation.

"I am most dreadfully sorry, madam," the woman clipped back, her metal spectacles disdainfully down her nose, her hands in prayer over her *balcon*.

"Just what do you expect girls this age to do?"

"Why, we expect them to grow, madam. I shouldn't worry, time will take care of her." She turned with dismissal to the next customer, a spotty girl with double Ds who stood arm in arm with her quadruple-E mum.

My suddenly American mother had grabbed the saleslady's pink arm. "Well we don't *have* time. My daughter needs some boobs *now*." With her free hand she continued to rifle through the bras. "Just find me four of the smallest goddamn bras you've got, already."

In the end, her Yankee ingenuity overpowered my modesty. In front of *The Avengers* that evening, my mother stitched me a set of breasts. She cut the padded cup of a generic brassiere along the seam, brought the bottom half up over the top, and sewed it back into place.

"The sooner we get you into one of these, the better," my mother had said through the pins in her mouth.

The result was a spongy but credible B-cup bustline.

I wore my new chest out shopping the following weekend, and imagined the admiration of every boy along the high street. I came home and actually hugged my mother. This was a mistake—it convinced her she was making headway.

On the morning of my fourteenth birthday, while I was inhaling a celebratory stack of toast drenched in butter, my mother presented me with a small, carefully wrapped present. Wiping my hands on my school uniform, I took it from her.

She beamed. "Go on, open it up."

I did, and sat frowning at a round plastic container. "What is it?"

"It's the Pill, nitwit. Do you love it?"

"The Pill? I don't need birth control."

"Bullshit," she laughed, unwrapping the cellophane from her own breakfast, a caramel-flavored Ayds candy, and popping it in her mouth. "Maybe you don't now, but you will soon. Trust me."

"Did you send Will a six-pack of rubbers when *he* turned fourteen?"

"Are you kidding? He's just like his father. He's so sexless he wouldn't know what to do with 'em."

I stashed the thing in my bathroom with all the unopened boxes of Tampax she continued to buy me every month.

∝⧉

Within hours of becoming friends with Josephine Doran, I had adopted her family. All that was lacking was the paperwork. In their compassion, the Dorans allowed me to live at their house pretty much full-time without actually residing there, which greatly improved my view of humanity. It amused me no end to think of my grandparents coming to visit me there, my grandfather having to use the Doran household bathroom, or my grandmother being offered Nescafé in the mug with the fornicating dwarves as she perched on the edge of the sprung mohair sofa in a pink shantung Mainbocher with Dino the stegosaurus salivating freely against her side.

Despite her imperfect features and pockmarked skin, Josephine was pure jailbait. There was something minxish about the way she hiked her pleated brown kilt high up on her thighs and slunk her kneesocks down around her ankles before trotting past boys, men, and grandfathers even.

In her wake I began to make progress. After I left the house on school mornings, I would emulate the master by stuffing my brown felt boater in my book bag and rolling my kilt up at the waist so that the hem barely reached the bottom of my regulation brown wool knickers. We timed it so that Josephine and I caught the same bus to school. I'd get on five stops earlier and wait for her in the front seat at the top of the double-decker bus. When we reached our stop near school, we'd flounce down the twisty stairs and hop off in front of the butcher shop. With our noses in the air, we'd traipse past the lab-coated apprentices as they staggered from truck to shop under enormous, stiff carcasses. Swiveling around to gawk, they'd bang into one another like stooges, tripping over the sides of beef and mutton hind ends. It was a revelation that all I had to do for attention was wear falsies and show my underpants.

Naturally my mother endorsed this new trend.

"Hey, Toots," she said to me one afternoon. "I passed you on the high street today when you and that Doran girl were walking to school. I like the new look. You know, the skirt-up-to-your-ass look. Just don't let your teachers catch you."

I folded my arms and sunk my chin into my fiber-assisted chest, and stared mutinously at the floor.

"But you know," she went on, "your legs would look a lot better if you'd lay off dairy products for a while."

"But do YOU know," I spat, "if you were normal, you'd be mad—like Josephine's mother would be, if *she* caught *her*."

My mother whirled around from the stove.

"Maybe you'd prefer I was one of those sagging old bats that hang around the house, porking out on the stuff they cook for their fat families." She shook a wooden spoon at me, making her huge Diver Dan self-winding Rolex go *whirrrrrrr.*

Sulkily, I shook my head.

Emma Peel (M-an-A-p-PEAL) was the fashion icon my mother lionized. Accordingly, today she was all in black in an *Avengers*-style stretchy faux leather catsuit and stack-heeled patent leather knee-high boots. She had on her favorite lipstick, Fabergé Nude Pink, which made her look like she'd been eating pink marshmallows. My mother probably had a couple more good years to carry on this Bond girl stuff, but she was thirty-nine and looked like a J-O-K-E in my opinion. I, on the other hand, was ever so slightly pudgy, and wore glasses, and was understandably resentful as hell. When not in my shit brown school uniform, I tended to cover my body up in floor-length hippie skirts or patch-adorned, bell-bottomed jeans; when my mother wasn't Mrs. Peel, or the Girl from U.N.C.L.E., she was the Girl from Chelsea in Mary Quant shiny plastic raincoats with upturned collars, and wet-look microminis, and skinny-rib sweaters. I tramped around in Roman-style lace-up-to-the-knee leather sandals, or short, fringed suede booties; my mother was into thigh-high white patent leather boots. My drawers were stuffed with shapeless, long-sleeved T-shirts. She had a closet full of YSL see-through blouses.

Poor thing, she must have really thought I'd had a break-through when she spotted me on the high street.

What she should have appreciated even more was that summer's Herculean efforts to make peace with the Lord and Master. Naturally, there was a motive: I needed the surveillance equipment from the middle sanctum to track the movements of the deity whose family had just moved in across the canal from us. His name was George, and I was throbbingly in love with him. He was the quintessence of summer, androgynous youth, and exquisite pathos. He was tall, nicotine-stained, and consumptively slender, and had straight, straw blond hair to his shoulders. His beautiful open face was sunburned, and his wide-spaced eyes were the color of his faded Levi's. A study through a pair of German Zeiss military eight-by-sixty binoculars revealed fingernails bitten to the quick, a gold St. Christopher medal, and an appendicitis scar I wanted to lick.

Most evenings, when it began to get dark, George would wander down to the canal, untie the blue dinghy that lay moored there, and set himself adrift. The canal was maybe thirty feet wide, running the length of the two streets whose houses backed up on it, and it flowed westward into the Thames. George never followed it though; he just allowed the dinghy to swing gently about in serpentine patterns, as if it were stuck on a Disneyland ride, unable to stray from an underwater track.

An elderly beagle always accompanied him, and the two sat in silence, the dog's nose stretched toward the twilight scents, George chain-smoking. I'd watch him until the night grew solid and the boat fused with the dark water, and the only discernible details became the glow of George's cigarette and the woofling nostrils of the beagle opening and closing.

You're wondering how on earth I could see those nostrils in the pitch dark. That's where a night vision device—an NVD—comes in mighty handy. My stepfather kept one in the middle sanctum, and, once I'd sighted George, I began to barter Ferrari waxing time against the use of it.

The first time I used the night vision goggles to spy on George I just about threw up—not from guilt, but from motion sickness. I hadn't read the label on the inside of the head strap that said, "Proper Scanning Critical to NVG Operations." Looking through the goggles was sort of like looking down a tunnel to a green television screen. There was no peripheral vision, so you had to swing your head from side to side, which, if you're bumbling about in a dark place with a weird thing strapped over your eyes, can make you feel pretty ill. I couldn't see much farther than four hundred feet, but that was far enough. George looked heavenly in pistachio green.

He didn't seem to mind it when I got the nerve to insinuate myself into his conspicuously ample downtime. I began to sit with him in his dinghy in the evenings, and on Sunday afternoons he'd allow me to accompany him to the pub down the street, the beagle in perpetual tow. We'd sit out back in the grassy garden that fronted on the slow-moving Thames of summer, a couple in my mind. George would order room-temperature bitter, which he drank silently, in deep drafts, while I had to settle for shandy, a lager-and-lemonade mixture invented to placate the meek and underage. We'd share a Ploughman's Lunch— two slabs of bread with a hunk of dry, aromatic cheddar cheese in between. "Share" isn't the right word really. George would have one bite and chain-smoke while I nervously demolished the sandwich, wallowing in the hazy nimbus of his sweet pollution. On the rare occasions he spoke, I'd give him the consideration of an oracle, gazing at him with more reverence and veneration than any god has ever been afforded. As he stared out at the river, or at a cloud, or at the beagle, I'd venture shamelessly lovestruck glances. When I'd look at his mouth, an unfamiliar worm would flip around in my future uterus, and when the golden hairs of his forearm accidentally brushed against mine, I'd envision our dogs mating.

When George finally invited me *chez lui* for dinner, it wasn't the formal, hand-delivered note and forest of roses that I'd fantasized about, but rather a casual offering from his embankment as I drifted downstream in a kayak.

"It won't be much," he said, studying the path of a bumblebee on the gunwale of his dinghy. "My parents are out."

How terribly disappointing.

I would have long since petitioned George to come over to my house, but for the obvious deterrent: my mother. I knew from experience that she would attire herself in one of her favorite slutfits—like the chrome yellow leather micromini and matching zip-up vest (no shirt, no bra)—and would ambush George as he made his way up from the water. Or, as she had done on my only two previous dates, she might appear in her après-dinner togs, a filmy leopard print negligee left open to reveal a crotch-length, see-through baby-doll. There was always a reason to bend over, to offer some beer, which she kept conveniently on the bottom shelf of the refrigerator even though no one in our house drank the stuff, or to myopically check the dog's water bowl. Whoops! Why, she forgot to put on any panties! (Again!)

The problem with my mother was her looks were peaking— big-time. Her beauty was the kind that is not only strictly physical, but of an era. Once she took her glasses off, she'd looked great in the fifties, and fantastic in the sixties. Now it was the early seventies and she was still hot, but definitely on the downside. To get a sense of the evolution of my mother's looks think Brigitte Bardot then (minus the boobs) and Brigitte Bardot now (minus the hairpieces).

In preparation for the big night I bathed slowly, with extreme care. "This is the last time I'll lie in this bath as a virgin," I said aloud. "This is the last time I'll shampoo my hair as a virgin. This is the last time I'll pluck the hairs out of my mole as a virgin . . . step into these underpants as a virgin . . . brush my virgin hair with the hairbrush belonging to a virgin." I had high expectations for the evening.

At the appointed hour I traipsed beguilingly down to the water's edge in a tail-dragging multicolored paisley skirt, a gauzy Mexican embroidered blouse, and cork-soled platform sandals. My hair was nearly waist-length, and I wore it loose in cool-hippie style with two little braids at the sides. I concealed my glasses in a fringed shoulder bag, along with a hairbrush, three pots of No. 19 lip gloss, and a tube of spermicidal jelly I was forced to shoplift from Boots the Chemist because I was too embarrassed to buy it.

George appeared thirty minutes later and punted languidly across to my side. The beagle grudgingly moved over, and I settled my voluminous ensemble, posing and composing myself for the ninety-second passage to the other side.

From my side of the canal it had been difficult to observe much of George's house through its protective screen of shrubbery and vines, but now I saw that it was disappointingly middle-class, and thoroughly devoid of all previously imagined topiary, turrets, and cupolas. We entered through graceless French doors that led to a back hallway papered in an enthusiastic, if faded, chintz. A gray-haired wedge-shaped woman wearing an apron emblazoned with a psychedelic map of the London underground transportation system came forward to greet us. She turned out not to be the serving maid or tenured housekeeper but George's mother. I suppressed a cry of dismay. What the hell was she doing here?

Cooking dinner, it turned out.

"You two go on up to Georgie's room," she said, waving her hand toward the rear of the house. And I thought my household was loose. I followed George up the narrow staircase to the third floor, the beagle struggling behind. At last, I was able to look out instead of in through the large garden-facing windows of George's bedroom, and I did so with smug ownership. The room might have belonged to a six-year-old; there were no posters on the walls like in other boys' rooms that I'd seen, and the shelves held only juvenile literature—picture books, Enid Blyton stories, and the graphic tales of Tintin. The only concession to the maturity of the occupant was the double bed and a pair of enormous sneakers in the corner.

In his own domain George became uncharacteristically chatty. He walked about, showing me his things like a kid with a new friend over; memorabilia like a Jerusalem hotel ashtray;

his original front teeth, which had been knocked clear out of his head when he'd slammed his Triumph motorbike into a wall; and his collection of hash pipes, which I obligingly gawked at. (He does *drugs*. How cool.)

"And this is the pistol I had to carry when I worked on a kibbutz in Israel." He indicated something that looked like a prop and laughed a bit sheepishly. "I'm afraid I kept it."

I was thinking, You call that a gun? Come over to my house and *I'll* show you a gun. Still, I followed him around, hyperventilating in what I hoped was an adorable fashion, trying to tell him through an admittedly beginner level of body language that it was quite okay for him to ravish me whenever he felt like it.

There was a tap at the door. "Hullo!" called the motherservant as she staggered in under the weight of an enormous dinner tray. I pushed the sudden image of Selma, my grandparents' octogenarian maid, out of my head. George rushed forward and took the tray from his mother, setting it down on the bed. On it were two plates heaped with roast chicken and potatoes, a bowl of salad, a lemon tart, and a straw covered bottle of Chianti. I half expected George's mother to wink as she backed out the door. George inserted a Ravi Shankar cassette into the tape deck, then uncorked the Chianti and poured some into a pair of heavy pewter goblets. "Cheers," he said, raising his wine and lighting a fresh cigarette from the butt of his old one.

We ate, the beagle between us on the bed, periodically rolling his tongue out for the master to place bits of food on. The newly loquacious George yakked on about the last three years he'd spent on the kibbutz, and I lay back on one elbow, trying to look like a sexpot while I frantically channeled Julie Christie and Marianne Faithfull.

When the meal was finished, meaning I had stuffed myself and George had rolled and smoked at least five cigarettes, he yawned and gave a long, slow stretch that was mind-blowing. I actually left my body as I imagined George taking me roughly into his arms to ply me with his manhood. But instead of ripping off my clothes, he picked up the dinner tray and headed for the kitchen. The beagle fired a salvo of farts and flopped over on its side, whereupon it fell instantly asleep and began to snore. I got up and checked my teeth in the mirror above George's bureau. I ran my fingers through my hair and under my mascara-smudged eyes and then returned to the bed, where I shoved the beagle to the floor and arranged myself in what I hoped was an irresistibly salacious pose.

George was taking his sweet time. Was he doing the dishes? Was his mother giving him advice? I checked my teeth again, then re-coiled myself on the pillows, hiking my skirt casually up one thigh. Had he run out for condoms? Was he washing himself? That would be good; I could deal with a clean unknown better than a smelly one. I was worried about my lack of experience. Really, when faced with the business end of a penis, how could a first-timer possibly know what to do? The wine had made me sleepy, and I closed my eyes (for the last time as a virgin) and drifted.

George plopped suddenly down beside me. I caught my breath. This was it. I slid my eyes toward his with what I hoped was an encouraging gaze. George smiled down at me—and then he reached under the bed and pulled out a colossal textbook. He opened it up across his lap. I sat up to examine the title: *Skin Diseases of Sub-Equatorial Peoples.*

"One of my father's medical books," George said, giving me a conspiratorial grin.

With a yellow fingertip he directed my attention to a close-up of some poor native's skinny foot, and its huge, ulcerated wound filled to the bubbling brim with a zillion wriggling maggots. I fished my very unsexy glasses out of my bag. It looked like raw hamburger left in the garbage for a month.

"Poor sod," said George, shaking his head. "Severe myiasis."

"What?"

"Myiasis—the invasion of tissue by dipterous larvae. Flies. Disgusting, really." He skimmed to another page. Slavic children wearing diapery undergarments lay in cots. Crusted, cracking lesions covered their sunken little stomachs, their hands and feet encased in scar-tissue mittens and gigantic blister bubbles.

"Recessive dystrophice epidermolysis bullosa," George said, pointing at a whimpering toddler holding out stumpy arms with paper basketballs for hands. "Kid's a goner."

My stomach put dinner on *blend*.

George tapped his cigarette on the face of a dark-haired woman who would have been beautiful if her left eyeball and nose hadn't been rotting away. "Funny that the principle chronic infections—you know, tuberculosis, syphilis, leprosy, and leishmaniasis—all have rather a fondness for the nose." Flipping to DNA mutations, he said, "Check it out," indicating a picture of an infant's head. It looked like a Mayan frog. "Anencephaly. Absence of the cranial vault."

"Anencephaly?" I looked fearfully at the blob.

"No brain." He turned the page, humming along with the sitar on the tape deck. God, I loved him for that. We were talking about a baby with NO TOP TO ITS SKULL and he was like, ho hum.

He stopped at a picture of a little blond girl with a charming Dutch girl hairdo, and eyes that were fried eggs running off on either side of her face.

"Treacher Collins syndrome," stated George. "Bloody sad, really."

We were straying way too far from the task at hand. "You know," I interjected, as George turned to a page of African men with elephantiasis, one proudly displaying his scrotum in a wheelbarrow, "I used to want to be a mortician."

"Did you now," said George politely.

"Yeah," I said, warming to the task of impressing him. "I

wanted to concentrate on preparing the bodies of children." I was completely bullshitting, of course. What idiot would want to embalm kids?

"Did you think that would be easier?"

"No. I just wanted to make them beautiful, preserve them really well, so that the grieving parents could sort of, you know, keep them around?"

George finally put the book aside. Gathering his papers and his bag of tobacco, he began to roll the next ten cigarettes he would smoke in nearly as many minutes. I felt my face and neck flush with embarrassment. I knew he knew I was lying.

But he was a gentleman. "For one thing," he said, running the tip of his tongue along the gummed edge of a rolling paper, making my armpits gush in the sweat of desire, "that would only prolong the grief. For another, it would be highly unsanitary."

"What do you mean?" I was appalled he thought I'd do a bad job on the embalming.

George struck a match against the zipper of his jeans and put it to his cigarette. He sucked on the burning taper, squinting his eyes against the little cinders that flew up as the tobacco caught. Inhaling deeply, he turned back to me and said, "With a dead body there's no immune system functioning to keep all the disease organisms in check. Microorganisms, bacteria and germs, all kinds of shit proliferate after the death of the host. Within twenty-four hours autolysis has gone mad—"

"Autolysis?" I squeaked.

"Yeah. When we shove off, the enzymes produced by the cells in our bodies break down the very cells that make them. Although embalming reduces the bacterium in a corpse by ninety-nine percent, rotting is unavoidable. Embalming is basically just for the funeral, so everyone can have a look-see."

"I knew that."

"Course you *could* use a greater concentration of formaldehyde in your solution when you embalm the kiddiewinks."

George looked out the window and smoked contemplatively, as if picturing pickled dead children.

"Medical colleges can keep cadavers around for donkey's years," he said, turning back to me, "but they don't look very appealing, I'm afraid."

He was a miracle. "I can't believe you're not in medical school."

"Yeah, well."

"Seriously, why aren't you studying to be a doctor?"

"My dad's dead keen on that," he said, shaking the hair back from his glorious face and looking up at the ceiling. "He would love me to be a doctor like him. Go into practice with him. Father and son." He gave a little laugh.

"So why don't you?"

"Oh, I don't know," he said, blowing a breath out. "Truth is, I've got a photographic memory." He delivered this extraordinary talent like it was a freckle on his arm.

"Wow."

"Yeah. Bloody fuckin' wow. Here, I'll show you. Find me something to read." He handed one of the medical books over.

"Okay," I said, and started paging through Syndromes— Hurler, Prune Belly, Sirenomelia (lower legs disconcertingly fused at birth)—I stopped at Cri du Chat syndrome because the name was catchy and the text long-winded.

"Try this one," I said, folding my arms and leaning back against the headboard to watch.

George read silently. When he was finished he got up and paced around the room for a while, excused himself to go to the bathroom, returned, and then, standing in front of his bureau, he recited the page and a half worth of *deletion of the short arm of chromosome 5*, verbatim. It was unreal.

"It's all very well to know the stuff," he said. "I could pass the exams; that's not the issue. Anyway, I've pretty much fried my brain on psychotropics. Nothing like a steady diet of acid, opium, and mushrooms."

I wanted to say, *That's okay, I intend to love you forever—even if you're a completely brainless tape recorder. But couldn't you please just kiss me?*

"Hey, you want to see a book on ophthalmic surgery?" said George.

With that, all the seduc flooded out of the seductress.

"Could I, um, take a rain check?"

We descended through the silent house, and he and the beagle ferried me back across the water. George helped me out politely, but when I turned to thank him for a lovely evening, he had already climbed back into the dinghy and was languidly feathering his way home, lighting a fresh cigarette off the butt of the old and searching up at the sky.

My mother was sitting at the table in the kitchen. She was wearing a hideous terry-cloth robe. The hood was pulled up over her head and she had on her glasses instead of her contact lenses. This was always a sign of trouble; the only time my mother was not clad for coition was when the Lord and Master was away buying hardware in Beirut, or she was having a very bad day.

The rum bottle was at her elbow, and the roast beef pan from dinner, with its congealed drippings, in front of her. She was alternating spoonfuls of beef fat with slugs from her 7UP can. The diet notes on the fridge shivered as I entered. I steeled myself for a scathing comment on my outfit, or maybe my shutout with George, which I knew she could smell on me. However, it wasn't *my* sex life that was on her mind.

"The shin of Shodom is upon us," she said by way of greeting. She squinted down at the grease-caked pan. "The shin of Shodom is upon thish house."

It appeared she was in a ruminative mood.

"Whatever you say," I said, leaning against the fridge to cover the notes. It was the least I could do to help her.

My mother took a pull on her drink and fixed her Coke bottle lenses upon me. "Here'sh a word for you," she said. "Analingush."

Here we go again.

I sat down beside her. She did look terrible. "Hey, guess what famous psychiatrist was embalmed at Harrods." Anything Harrods usually cheered her up.

She shook her head and spooned up some more fat.

"Algolagnia," she said.

"I'll give you a hint—his first name is Sigmund."

She sucked at the soda can, tilting her head so far back the hood fell to her shoulders with a *thwop*. "I'm gonna shell my ITT and my Guf 'n Western shtock and buy a place of my own."

"That's right," I said, patting her hand. "Freud."

"An my Kodak too." She shook my hand off, and took another hit of suet.

"I'll bet you didn't know you could buy a baby elephant at Harrods." It killed me to see her beaten down like this. We certainly had our issues, but when the shit hit the fan my mother was there for me. On a recent overnight school trip, I had stayed innocently out past curfew, but the school had responded with a barrage of letters to my mother about my very American disregard for authority. My mother, in turn, had launched a campaign against the teacher who'd outed me, one that only the daughter of a colonel steeped in Revolutionary history could wage. She was brilliant. I just had to learn how to be there for her too. It sure wasn't easy.

My mother belched, and then fixed me with a surprisingly sober stare. "No, I did not—and frankly, Tootsh, all I care ish that I can get my hair colored on the fifth floor, buy a toplessh bathing shuit on the fourth, and a shix-pack of Tab on my way outta the door." She sloshed a few more fingers of Bacardi into her 7UP can.

"You are so fucking selfish!"

"Up yours," said my mother through a mouthful of rum and beef fat.

I took that as a good night.

⚮

Lucky I'm an optimist. I rationalized that George was shy, that he was the type that waited until the fourth or fifth date to get physical. Hey, I could wait, I had all summer. All my life in fact.

But this power thing, the notion of control through one's sexuality, I was starting to figure it out. I had power over the butcher boys with the raising of my hemline. I had power over my brothers, because they were dyslexic, Type B non-survivors. My stepfather had tyrannical and financial power over my mother, but she was able to manipulate him with what she wore, or whether she put out, and whether she even stayed with him. And with my father, she may have wielded the ultimate power— if the rumors spread by my father's shattered parents were to be believed.

A couple of weeks later I was at my usual position, at the window on the second-floor landing, with a high-powered telescope trained on George's window. My transistor radio was tuned to Radio Luxembourg, the volume so low you could barely hear the bleat of the American disc jockeys. Stakeout provisions included two packets of salt-and-vinegar crisps, a Mars bar, and a copy of *Candy*, the filthiest book I had ever come across. Every three pages or so, I checked the window. Evening was coming on, and out of the goodness of her heart, Candy was having sex with her father's brother when suddenly the lights flicked on in George's bedroom.

I palpitated when I saw a figure enter behind him. I relaxed when I saw it was a guy. Must be one of his mates, I thought. But then the mate put his hands on George's shoulders. And then the mate pulled George's shirt over his head. And then he pulled off his own Led Zeppelin T-shirt. (That's how good that telescope was.) George just stood there, arms and hands at his sides. That's when the little shit leaned forward and put his lips on my George's tender smoky mouth. And that's when I went berserk and must have screamed, because my stepfather came running up the stairs, *Herald Tribune* still in hand. He snatched the binoculars from me. "Ha *ha!*" he snorted. "You are in luff with a pansy!" Shaking his head, he sauntered back to his armchair in the living room.

I got a bead on George's window again. They were still standing. That was good news. But now the interloper was leaning down to unfasten the buttons on George's Levi's. He knelt to do it. That was very bad news. His head dipped below the sash of the window, so it was hard to rate his performance, or pick up tips for future reference. George remained upright, arms by his sides, like he hadn't asked for this, but as long as it was happening and he didn't have to contribute, it was bloody all right with him.

My mother suddenly appeared and pushed me aside. She watched for a moment in silence. "Well that's just ducky," she said. Straightening up, she patted me awkwardly on my drooping shoulders. I let down my guard and clung to her for a good three seconds. After my sobbing had subsided, she detached herself and began to dismantle the telescope, clucking sympathetically, and telling me how many handsome men were in my future, and how George wasn't good enough for me, although she had rather liked the beagle.

Being young and resilient, I immediately transferred my affections to the reptile keeper at the zoo where I had a summer job.

⧸⧹

A week before school started up again, I was road testing a new pair of Zeiss eight-by-sixty field glasses. I trained them on

George's window, sort of for old time's sake. Lo and behold if he wasn't in pretty much the same spot I'd left him: arms by his sides, gazing at whatever—only this time the hands unbuckling his belt and the mouth addressing his southern hemisphere belonged to a girl.

It didn't take me too many years past puberty to figure out that it had been nothing personal; I'd just been too slow on the uptake.

I never saw George after that summer. His parents moved away and a professional race car driver and his bouncy-breasted girlfriend bought the house. I did hear from him once, though. A flimsy envelope the same color as his damn faded Levi's arrived in the post a year or so later. It was the sort of old-fashioned airmail stationery that makes you think of the time when overnight transatlantic flights were full of adventure and promise. The stamp and postmark were from somewhere that echoed that notion. Anyway, he'd forgotten to put the letter inside, so that was that.

Maine Revisited

WE SHOULD HAVE anticipated a sea change when our mother insisted all three of her children accompany her on a pilgrimage to Plymouth Rock. Taking time out from our fun-filled tour of boarding schools, my mother, Edward, and I met up with Will in Boston and drove south *en famille* in a rented Plymouth Valiant—the irony of which was lost on our mother.

"It's time you three started appreciating the other side of your family," she lectured, hands on the wheel at precisely ten and two as she barreled along down Route 3. Edward and I quarreled in the backseat while Will, who at sixteen was in the throes of silent adolescence, glowered out the window. "All those servants waiting on you hand and foot in Burdenland must have your Colonial ancestors rolling in their graves!"

"It's not our fault our grandparents are so rich," I said.

"*It's not our fault our grandparents are so rich . . .* ," she mimicked back. "Well d'you think it's their fault they didn't pass some of your father's money along to help me pay the goddamn bills? They cut me out of the bloody will, for Christ sake!"

We had all heard this story many, many times. Will turned to give her a mutinous look, and I was about to jump in when we were saved by the vision of Plymouth Harbor.

"Look! There it is—" said my mother in campy reverence,

and her eyes actually welled up. It was maybe the third time I'd ever seen her cry.

Later, when I caught her whipping out a chisel and mallet from under her yellow and black cape, I tried to stop her, citing the words written on the "Do Not Touch!" signs everywhere, but she only said, "Oh, don't have a cow. I have a right to some of this. My great-great-great-great . . . great . . . oh, whatever he was, my uncle Myles Standish was one of the first men to land on Plymouth Rock. Besides, they used to sell pieces of this thing as paperweights. My father even has cuff links and a watch fob out of it." Shouldering me away, she found a foothold for the chisel. "I'm just taking a little souvenir for the Beast House," she muttered, and with the muted *chink* of the professional, she clipped off an eight-inch piece from the seaward side of the iconic landmark.

The Beast House, that stunted, eighteenth-century Chinese chest of drawers that housed the artifacts of my mother's forebears, now stood in a place of honor beside the large fireplace of the very small cottage my mother had recently purchased. We'd all questioned her motives when she'd cashed in her blue chip stocks six months before, but she must have known she would be needing a safe house. The cottage sat directly behind a hedge next to a busy road that led out to the causeway between the Old Town harbor and the ocean—and it had no view. It was the kind of beach house that owners never bother to winterize—a funky, sandy-floored, rundown thing with a kitchen too small to eat in, a bathroom with a rusty metal shower stall, and a well-rotted porch. And this was after the contractor had supposedly been working on it.

❧

Six months later we were in our second semesters at boarding school—seven-year-old Edward at North Country School in upstate New York and fourteen-year-old me at National Cathedral in Washington, D.C. Our mother was back in her English prison. A telephone call came on a spring evening just as the lady of the house, wearing nothing but Saran Wrap (another of their favorite outfits), was serving the Lord and Master his dinner. He got up to answer the phone (*Beer here*) and remained for some time in the hallway, listening intently as a woman on the other end of the overseas line delivered a death sentence.

Ten minutes later the plastic-wrapped Accused, even as she soaped the Dutch oven, was handed a twenty-four-hour eviction notice. My mother hightailed it out of there faster than you can say Tab, leaving everything behind except the dog. I still wonder what became of the contents of my room: all my hippie clothes, childhood books, LPs, posters, letters, and drawings—all my precious, identifying junk.

My mother's two-timing came as no surprise to me; her appetite was bound to singe a hole through that marriage sooner or later.

That August, before the wronged wife's call, my mother had been acting disturbingly unlike herself: soft, gooey, and transcendental. I'd seen that look on Maria Schneider's face in *Last Tango in Paris*, when my roommate and I had used our fake IDs to see it.

"I've made a wonderful new friend," my mother kept saying every time I passed through the kitchen.

"That's great! How many legs does it have?" I kept saying in return.

"Don't you want to know who it is?" she'd simper as I rummaged through the fridge.

"Friendships are so fun when they're kept secret." How stupid did she think I was? My mother didn't have friends.

One Sunday morning she couldn't hold back any longer. When I came into the kitchen to make toast, she was waiting to ambush me. I busied myself with the kettle, keeping my back pointedly toward her, but she continued from where she'd left off the night before, as if we were actually having a conversation about this. "He lives in Marblehead—"

She might as well have said: *Okay, so I've been screwing the contractor I hired to fix some stuff on that beach house I bought back in the States, and I forgot what it's like to be all infatuated and horny for someone, and so what if he's married, only now I'm back over here in this miserable little house with that sodomizing S.O.B. and I'm all moony over the contractor, and I really want to tell someone about it, but since I don't have any friends, I'm going to unload it on YOU, Toots.*

When I was young and nosy, and all I wanted were answers, I couldn't get anything out of her. Now that I was older and didn't want to know *anything*, I couldn't get her to shut up.

A British Airways flight from Heathrow to Logan brought the Accused back to the land of her forebears; more specifically, the New England town of Marblehead, where her grandfather had summered, and where the *Spirit of '76*, that emblematic portrait of young America, hangs in the town hall. My mother moved into her tiny one-bedroom beach house. When news spread that the ex-pat home wrecker had moved to Marblehead, the contractor's wife kicked him out, and he and his Labrador, Mac, moved in with my mother. For all of her trouble, the wife then got cancer and died.

My mother threw herself into the role of wicked adulteress. She streaked her hair platinum and didn't get out of a bikini all summer. She sold off Kodak stock and bought herself a red Fiat convertible and drove around town with the top down, plying her fake English accent on anyone who would listen, like the checkout girl at Schube's liquor store. In the beginning the contractor, whose name was Gil, tried to get us to like him. And we were prepared to—anything would be better than Hitler's littermate—but we just couldn't. For one thing, he was *old*. He had gray hair and a gray beard, and he was barrel-chested and bowlegged and tubby, and had the kind of hands that only look comfortable holding a can of beer or a hammer. He tried the Dad thing by palling around with Edward, who wasn't having anything to do with tossing a football back and forth or building a shoe box, and he tried to be cool bumming cigarettes and mixing Will and me drinks and trying to smoke pot, but he wasn't cool because he was still *old*. The first time I went to visit (armed with three girlfriends for moral support), my mother and the ancient boy toy gave us the bedroom, and they slept in a tent in the scraggly backyard. You could hear them doing it all night, what with the tent bouncing around like its stakes were going to pop out of the ground every time one of them climaxed.

"You do know that Gil went to Williams," my mother kept saying, whenever she thought we were brushing him off.

"Uh huh," I'd answer, thinking, *So fucking what.*

"And he's a member of the Eastern Yacht Club, which is very snooty."

"Wow."

"So I really don't understand why you can't treat him with a little more respect!"

"Well, he is a contractor," I'd fake-joke, like that was the real reason, and I was just the worst snob ever.

Going "home" became a necessarily brief, annual event. And with the three of us spread up and down the Eastern Seaboard in boarding schools, we were able to keep it that way.

❧

Through the miracle of Island Divorce (and it will come as no surprise that the island was Haiti), my mother and the contractor became man and wife. They moved from the one-bedroom beach house into a one-and-a-half-bedroom beach house next door. The new house had even more of a transient feel to it than the old, despite their proud makeover of the bathroom, which boasted a plastic all-in-one tub-shower-and-tile unit that looked like it was pressed out by a Mattel Vac-U-Form. The living room had my mother's signature hard couch, and a couple of small, square armchairs that were as comfy as bleachers, and all the furniture was covered with old sheets to protect it from the dogs. The rear of the house had two enormous sliding glass doors that led onto a deck and provided, at last, a wide view over the marsh to the sea.

Now my mother requisitioned the boxes she had stored when we'd moved to England. In a when-in-Rome celebration of her Colonial roots, she savored her trove of ancestral leavings: the Federal candlesticks, the tarnished sterling Queen Anne tea set, the various pewter soup tureens and chargers, the blue and white creamware, and mismatched plates by Spode, and Copeland, and Wedgwood. There must have been fifty christening mugs alone, many of them dating back to the early 1600s and passed down so many times the 1900 babies had to have their names inscribed in a jumble on the bottom. Out of their shallow wooden graves came portraits of long-dead Pilgrims—huge oils of large-eyed men and women in oddly modern, stark gold frames, and miniatures of their mothers and sisters and children. A long brown paper box revealed the wedding shawl of one Mary Lane of Bedford, Massachusetts, a kinsman known for a habit of picking off Indians with a shotgun from her upstairs bedroom window. There were enough domestic artifacts to start a museum, what with all the tortoiseshell hair combs, needle-pointed purses, cross-stitched patriotic slogans, golden thimbles, buttonhole scissors, pillowcases packed with yards of hundred-year-old lace, and frayed linen envelopes containing scraps of clothing purportedly belonging to everyone from the aforementioned Myles Standish to Bonnie Prince Charlie. On the mantel my mother proudly placed her favorite relic of all: the hallmarked family silver mug made by Paul Revere. (Which, of course, the Chosen One would get when she died.)

After they were settled in to the new house, my mother and the contractor settled themselves into a pattern of drinking and arguing, and fawning over their out-of-control Rhodesian ridgebacks—huge, insane dogs that took up every inch of space in that tiny house. You see local stories on TV about the raiding of the homes of weirdos harboring hundreds of animals living in a sea of their own feces. Visiting my mother's house was beginning to feel dangerously close to this. It might only be a matter of months before the floors became carpeted with a two-inch-thick layer of dog stool. There would be no money to heat the house, but the larder would be stocked with Iams and booze. My mother would be forced to pawn her leather outfits, and would trail around in winter wearing layers of filthy, hooded, zip-up terry-cloth robes. When summer came, the single raggedy bikini she was down to would expose a body covered with bruises from the happy, beating tails of her dogs.

❧

When you leave home, you instinctually modify the passage of time so that you, the child, develop at a normal rate, while your parents, and in my case my grandparents, age at about ten times that. I had seen little of my grandparents over the last few years and was unprepared for their sudden decline. Either that or I was able to see them for the first time with a modicum of objectivity. Between my grandmother's Dubonnet and Percocet-coated perception of reality and my grandfather's diminishing control over his limbs, and increase in drinking, they were a mess.

When they were courting, my grandmother, who had been ingrained with a love of art by her parents, was surprised at how little my grandfather knew or even cared about painting or sculpture. She set about educating him and took him to her father's studio, and the Metropolitan Museum, and the Frick. My grandfather took it upon himself to tutor his future bride in his area of expertise—the art of drinking—and every night they went to parties and speakeasies to increase her knowledge of wine and other libations. Who knows whether she would have found her way to alcoholism without his guidance, but she was as much an expert as he was now.

For as long as I could remember, my grandfather always began his day's drinking well before noon. Wherever he was— Hobe Sound, Mount Kisco, Northeast Harbor, New York—he would abruptly launch himself, like a wet rag fired from a slingshot, and make his way to one of the cabinet bars located throughout his homes and his office. Selecting a Baccarat highball glass, he would fill it to the brim with Wild Turkey and drink it off in one go while standing there. Then he would replace the glass exactly where it had been and return to his seat. This routine was so, well, routine, you only took notice when he was staggering.

Oddly enough, alcoholism suited him. My grandfather was a part of that urbane, if self-impressed, counterestablishment that never stopped thinking, or drinking. He was also from a long, proud line of drinkers. In the same way the royal French Bourbon nose was said to denote enormous sexual appetite, the VanderBurden nose, less protuberant and infinitely more refined, prophesies an insatiable appetite for drink. Alcoholism never suited my grandmother, though. Whereas her husband, when over-served, would simply pass out in situ, my grandmother would dance among the goldfish or crash to the floor in a maelstrom of Dior, pearls, and poodles. In the morning she would explain her bruises by saying she had stumbled over an eye mask on her way to the bathroom.

My transatlantic homecoming had not been an entirely welcome one to my grandfather. Alas, he got to see a lot of me, because when I wasn't in a dorm room, I was in Burdenland. We muddled through, mostly by adhering to a strict regime of ignoring each other. And if things like my grandparents' decision to attend my brother's high school graduation and not mine hurt my feelings, I'd take them to the grave rather than admit it.

Nineteen seventy-four was the annus horribillis. In June, my uncle Bob was killed while making a U-turn in his rented green AMC Gremlin. He was forty years old and had never been married. There was talk of suicide, but it was never confirmed. For my grandmother, the gloves were now off; she began drinking in earnest. Uncle Bob had been her favorite.

My grandfather was diagnosed with Parkinson's disease, and he did not take it well. The pharmacological effect of the experimental drug he began taking, L-dopa, combined with his daily fifth of bourbon, two to three bottles of Bordeaux, and a handful of sedatives was a disastrous one. Despite her grief over another son's death, my grandmother continued to wear her usual armor of denial, but around her husband, she was walking on eggshells. She was desperate to help him, but he was making himself inaccessible with his misery.

That mid-summer before I started college, I drove up to Maine, arriving late in the afternoon after a ten-hour drive in my windfall Porsche 911 T, a car that had adventitiously found its way to me after yet another suicide. The year before, my maternal grandfather, the Colonel, had shot himself when his doctor informed him he had cancer. Thankful to have made it without the cantankerous engine erupting on I-95, I pulled up to the small parking area behind the bomb shelter, only to find it entirely taken up by my uncle Ordway's Greyhound bus. A police car of indistinct origin was parked beside it. Fearful of flying, and unable to drive himself (due to alcohol and drug dependencies plus an acute case of agoraphobia which had, at one point, prevented him from leaving his apartment in New York for an entire year), Uncle Ordway transported his entourage from Point A to Point B in his very own tour bus and satellite squad car.

Of the youngest of our father's brothers, Uncle Ordway had at one point been enigmatic to my brothers and me. When he was in his prime, and girlishly handsome, he had gone through a series of pretty women and hip cars that falsely foretold success. Now thirty, Ordway was bloated and gray-skinned, and a recent hair transplant (that appeared to have been harvested from his pelvic area) had left his head looking like that of a cheap doll, with plug marks marching in regimental rows across his scalp. He should have stuck with the toupees.

At least I didn't have to worry about running into him; I knew he was holed up in the third cabin, up near the dock, and would stay there, maybe even through dinner if I was lucky. I parked the Porsche under the sappy pines near my own cabin and made my grand entrance into the main house at what was traditionally teatime, only to find my grandmother with a half-empty glass of Dubonnet instead of the usual four o'clock cup of Constant Comment.

"Hello, dearie," she said in greeting, not rising from her chair. One poodle was on her lap, and the other was feebly trying to scale its way into it. I kissed my grandmother's soft, squooshy cheek and breathed in the usual aroma of Joy and hair spray and face powder.

"No tea?" I said.

"Oh—well, uh, Popsie and I have already had ours, but I'll ring for some right away, won't we, girls?" *Brfffftt.* My grandmother grappled with the buzzer, which turned out to be the TV remote. Phil Donahue came booming onto the Sony embedded in the bookcase.

"Don't worry, I'll go ask for some," I told her, replacing the remote on the table beside her. I bumped smack into Uncle Ham–Uncle Ham slipping out of the pantry with a six-pack of Coke. "Oh, hullo! Hullo!" he tooted, eyes on the floor, and flew past me to the powder room.

Note to self: don't go in there for a while. And take a deep, deep breath: seems the whole family would be together for a few days. Out the big picture window I could see my little brother,

Edward, burning something gratuitously nasty on the rocky beach. I decided to skip tea and went out to join him.

❦

"*Man*, what a weird night," I said to Will the next morning. "Have the GPs lost it or what?" By the time we'd all sat down to my welcome home lobster dinner, my grandfather had soiled himself, and my grandmother had five stitches and a bag of frozen peas taped across her swollen left temple. We had tried to play a game of Hearts after dinner, but in the middle of the second hand, a Gremlin commercial had come on and my grandmother had burst into tears and sloshed her drink all over the cards. Turning on her husband, she had demanded that he call CBS at once *and tell them to stop running those godforsaken ads.* Then she excused herself, headed for the bar in the hallway, refilled her glass, and retired for the night.

Will and I were lying on the long built-in sofa in the living room, listening to Todd Rundgren. After a brief stint at Hampshire College, Will had given up any further attempts at higher education and was now living full-time in one of the cabins and having a go at sculpture. He had made the classic WASP mistake of remaining in a summer place after Labor Day, and, faster than you can say substance abuse, he had joined forces with the ranks of Maine's full-time drug abusers and alcoholics. Unless I was in Maine, I hardly saw him anymore because he never went off-island. I only saw my younger brother in Maine too, it seemed.

"I guess," grunted my brother. He was critically hungover. His hair was as thick and unruly as a hay field, and his glasses needed some serious updating.

"Don't you think we should do something? I don't give a shit about Granddaddy, but Gaga's going to break her neck."

"They'll be fine," said Will, closing his eyes.

The new butler, who was disconcertingly young, good-looking, and Basque, abruptly materialized with a silver tray. He set it down between us on the sofa and, after asking our permission, poured out thick black coffee into two perfectly white Limoges cups. Assured there was nothing more required, he left as quietly as he'd come in.

"Anyway," Will said, through a mouthful of English muffin, "they'll be going in the hospital after Labor Day, as usual. Pass me the marmalade."

Before there was the Betty Ford Center or Promises, there was good old New York Hospital. That's where my grandparents went once a year to dry out. They took a room together and lay in their beds with private nurses bustling around them and IV drips in their arms as if they were afflicted with an entirely different disease. They planned their detox around the chef's vacation and had all their meals catered by their favorite restaurants—La Caravelle, Le Cygne, the Four Seasons, and La Grenouille. When they got out of the hospital, clear-eyed and healthy, they took up right where they had left off the week before.

My grandmother seemed resigned to her general deterioration. She stayed in bed longer in the mornings, watching television, munching on her All-Bran, sipping from her thermos of coffee, an old pink bed jacket around her shoulders and a fire crackling away. Instead of who would be her doubles' partner, her greatest concern now was who would be attending which meal.

"Will you be in for lunch?" she'd ask, when we popped our heads in to say good morning.

"How many for dinner?" she'd call out anxiously as we ran through the living room later in the day.

A lifetime spent monitoring the comings and goings of family and friends, household and staff, and this was what it had come down to.

I voiced my concern after stopping in to see her one picture-perfect morning when the sky was sapphire and the breeze fresh. She seemed genuinely taken aback.

"But, dearie, I'm always up and out for my ladies' game by nine!"

"Then you're an hour late," I pointed out.

"Ah. Well, that's because I'm having my hair done this afternoon." She nibbled on the end of her pencil and went back to studying the *Ellsworth American* crossword puzzle. "I simply cannot get twenty-three across—*Bennie and the* blank. Four letters, ends in S."

"Jets."

"The jets?"

"It's a song. Would you like to come for a little hike with me?"

"Well aren't you clever!" Ignoring my question, she penciled in the answer.

After she'd asked me what meals my brothers and I would be in for, I left her sipping the last of her coffee with a small frown on her face.

Half an hour later, I heard the soles of her Belgian flats come squeaking down the hall. She was humming one of her favorite hymns of fortitude: *And it holds, my anchor holds: Blow your wildest, then, O gale* . . . The kitchen door swung open, and there stood my grandmother, battle-ready in yellow linen slacks and her favorite black cardigan with the yellow velvet piping and the appliquéd bumblebees around the neckline. She had her face on and her hair pinned together as best she could.

"Good morning, all!" she said. Then, clearing her throat, my grandmother announced that she wanted to make dinner.

The chef ran his knife straight through the squab he was disjointing; Selma let go of a pitcher of orange juice and it exploded as it hit the pantry floor; Juan, the new butler, audibly sucked in a breath. Madame only appeared to comment on the success of dinner or to forage for a nightcap.

I happened to be in there. My favorite spot was still up on the counter with my heels banging, bugging Michel, the chef, and stealing bacon from the pile on the shelf over the stove. Captain Closson leaned beside the screen door, drinking Sanka while he waited for Selma to finish packing up a wicker picnic basket he would then carry down for lunch on the boat. It was taking Selma forever, because now she really was about a hundred.

After an awkward moment, everyone started saying good morning back, and nodding, and shuffling their feet, unsure of what to do next.

"You want to do *what*?" I said in disbelief.

"Well, dearie, I thought I might try cooking Popsie's dinner one night when the help are off."

My grandmother could not even boil water. I'd seen her make a cup of tea—just once—using tap water. The idea of her operating the twelve-burner Garland was enough to jolt Michel out of his stupor. "*Oui*, Madame!" he blurted. "Yes, of course. You have something particular in mind?"

"I would like you to teach me how to make Steak Tartare," said my grandmother, visibly brightening.

There was a collective sigh of relief. Steak Tartare is served raw.

News travels fast in an overstaffed household. Suddenly the kitchen was filled with all kinds of people busily intent on doing next to nothing. My grandmother accepted a fresh apron from Michel and tied it over her bee ensemble. Then, while he nervously minced an onion, she stood eyeballing the mound of hamburger meat someone had placed on the table before her.

"You're supposed to squeeze it around like Play-Doh," I told her.

"Right-o—like this?" Marshaling her courage, she picked some up and patted it with her hands. This wasn't so bad. Emboldened, she picked up another bright red handful. "Oh!" she cried, surprised by the squelchy sound of it going through her fingers. Everyone laughed, and my grandmother giggled a little herself. Before long her manicure was smeared with fat and tissue, and her big diamond flashed through the globs as she squished and squeezed and hummed and mooshed the meat around like a two-year-old making gory mud pies. As Michel instructed her, she added the onions, capers, Worcestershire sauce, parsley, some mustard, and an egg, and then smoothed it all into the shape of a loaf before etching decorative crosses over the top with a butter knife.

"There!" She beamed. (And farted the tiniest of tinies in her pleasure.) She smiled at everyone around the room, and everyone smiled back at her. We knew she would as soon repeat this exercise on her own as she would apply for a job at Dairy Queen.

On the evening of August 8, my brothers and I sat with our grandparents in the big, curved living room and watched Nixon give his resignation speech. Tears streamed down my grandfather's face as he slumped in his yellow Saarinen chair, a dark Rorschach stain spreading across his lap. It was as if the entire carpet of his world had been pulled out from under him. Nixon had been my grandfather's last ticket to diplomatic fruition. Through favors and donations, my grandfather had long been greasing the conduit to what he wanted most in the world: the ambassadorship to France.

A couple of weeks later there was a cocktail party at Nelson Rockefeller's place in Seal Harbor. My grandfather and Nelson were good friends. Both were from wealthy families, and both had the ambition to govern. They shared other passions: France, art, food and wine, and (surprise) the Republican Party. Their summer houses had been designed by Wallace Harrison, the architect of Rockefeller Center and the United Nations. Each was a past president of the Museum of Modern Art (Nelson's mother had founded it), and philanthropy was of paramount importance to both. The difference was, Nelson was the real thing; he was not only substantially richer, he was far better at being rich. He was from one of the contemporary world's wealthiest families, whereas the financial glory days of the Burdens and the Vanderbilts was his-tor-ee. Career-wise, Nelson had it going on too. He was a professional politician who won elections (even if his campaigns were heavily self-funded), not a diplomat who had to win appointments. Now, to cap off a perfectly ghastly summer, President Ford had nominated Nelson for the vice presidency.

My grandmother was desperate to make her husband feel better. She figured it was high time she made Popsie that cozy dinner, or at least pretended she had. The morning of the Rockefeller party, she resolutely reentered the kitchen. This time Selma slopped onto the floor only a little of the gazpacho she was ferrying.

"Now, I want you all to take the night off, and Mr. Burden and I will eat Steak Tartare when we return from cocktails at the Rockefellers' this evening."

"*Oui*, Madame," said Michel.

"Oh, and, Michel," said my grandmother with an embarrassed little *brrfffttt*, "would you mind dreadfully if we told Mr. Burden that I made the meal?"

Michel smiled and bowed.

Turning to me, she said, "Why don't you come too? I'm sure there'll be lots of nice young there." I knew what "young" meant—anyone in the *Social Register* between the ages of ten and fifty. I said I'd go. I could tell she wanted to show me off, not because I was so great, but because that's what summer people do with their progeny. Uncle Ham–Uncle Ham would have given half of his Hitler memorabilia to go, but my grandfather wasn't having any of that. He never allowed himself to be seen in public with his third son; it was too humiliating.

And out she went, leaving the staff flummoxed and preparations started for the various things that would have to accompany her masterpiece (including the masterpiece itself): a butter lettuce salad, some French bread, cheese, a crème caramel. The wine needed to be selected, the butter curled, the linens chosen, and the finger bowls set on trays with a leaf of verbena in each. Someone would have to serve the meal, then clear and wash up, and get the Mr. and Mrs. up the three little stairs and into their bedroom and draw their baths and make sure they didn't drown in them and help them brush their teeth and get them in their pj's and finally into bed. Night off, indeed.

The three of us were dressed and ready to go at six. My grandfather could barely walk, but that didn't stop him from driving. He shoved aside my urgent petition and, with a struggle that had me wondering how we were going to pry him out at the other end, managed to get himself behind the wheel of his 6.3-liter 300 SEL Mercedes—a car so powerful it was forever leaving coats of paint in its wake.

The road to Seal Harbor is a twisty one that follows the curves of the shoreline. It was Mr. Toad's Wild Ride over, but we made it, with my grandmother only shrieking, "Mercy! Bill, you'll kill us!" twenty-six times. We missed the entrance to the Rockefeller estate because my grandfather was going about ninety, but he remedied that by executing a U-turn into oncoming traffic. (*Shades of Uncle Bob!* I screamed to myself.) As we were thundering up the long gravel driveway, I spotted the Secret Service checkpoint and told my grandfather to slow down, as in "Oh my God! Stop! Stop!" A long table had been placed across the driveway, making it impossible to continue on to the house without verification. Dark-suited agents were looking into all the cars and checking the occupants against a guest list.

My grandfather wasn't going for it. "Goddamn it!" he raged, spit flying. "This is outrageous, Peggy! Don't they know who I am?" And he floored it.

"Bi-illl—" my grandmother wailed, covering her eyes with one hand and with the other clawing a long tear in the leather upholstery.

The agents realized what was happening. Quickly, they mobilized themselves in front of the table and withdrew their guns. One of them grabbed a bullhorn and bellowed at us to "HALT!"

My grandfather didn't hesitate for one second. We flew through the center of the table, smashing it to pieces and sending papers and operatives flying. I could have sworn I heard a couple of shots zing past us, and I started to pray. *Oh God, please don't let me die from a bullet defending a man who isn't even vice president yet. I'll miss orientation week at Cornell, and I'm sorry, Lord, but that's when I'm intending to lose my virginity. You wouldn't want me to die a virgin, now would you?*

The madman remained unfazed. He peeled around the corner, up a little hill and past a planting of ferns, and finally ground to a halt in a shower of pine needles and chipmunk body parts in front of the house, whereupon he lurched out of the car, and up the steps, and into a bear hug with the future vice president of the United States.

We'll Always Have Paris

THERE WERE ACTUAL occasions when my grandfather made an attempt to honor me, like the impromptu lunch party he threw for my sixteenth birthday in the jungle-like humidity of the indoor pool in the country, where the menu featured Beluga, lobster, and Dom Perignon, and the guest list consisted of my best friend, the butler, and four of my teenaged cousins. Then there was the dinner dance at the New York apartment for my eighteenth, when my grandfather stood up to toast me and forgot my name.

Another time, he magnanimously offered to bulletproof my car. Seeing as how it was a convertible, there didn't seem much point, but my grandfather was seriously into bulletproofing. The windows and skylights of the rooms he personally frequented were installed with impenetrable metal blinds that went up and down and across at the touch of a switch. These provided hours of entertainment when we were little, and when we were older they became the ultimate party trick that no one, other than a Rockefeller, suspected. People would start screaming and diving under the Bertoia chairs when the shutters came rumbling down.

When my grandfather's behavior toward me turned philanthropic, I got nervous. Invariably it began with a call from Miss Pou. At some point my grandfather would interrupt from the extension where he'd been listening and bark out something like, *Ever been to Tahiti?* I'd say no, and he'd say, *Well you're going!* and I'd say, *Wow, really? When?* And he'd say, *Today.* Then I'd tell him I had school or work or something and couldn't possibly, and he'd say take it or leave it, and hang up the phone. He offered Hong Kong and an African safari with no forewarning, and always when he knew it was impossible for me to accept.

The invitation to Paris was issued on a bone-chilling, overcast day in March. I was in my sophomore year at Cornell and hating every minute of Ithaca's so-called spring. The phone was ringing when I walked into the cramped one-bedroom apartment I shared with my pre-law roommate.

"Hi, darlin'," Miss Pou said. "Your grandfather would like to know if you would like to go to—"

"I'll take it."

❧

By the time he died, my grandfather had visited Paris ninety-eight times. It was my grandparents' favorite city. I was there with them once before, when I was seventeen and doing my gap year at a gonzo finishing school in Florence, Italy, an institution that featured style over education. They had come over to see the spring fashion shows and were staying at the Ritz, where my grandfather retained an entire home-away-from-home wardrobe. My roommate and I were crashing with her sister, a California hippie who ran an American restaurant called Mother Earth's Lost and Found, a sort of flower power subterranean café that specialized in oversized hamburgers and tabbouleh. I think I had maybe one shower the whole week we were there.

We met up at the Givenchy show, where my grandparents had been justifiably horrified at my reinvention as a Californian free spirit, with frizzed-out hair, frayed bell-bottom jeans, batik coat, and platform boots that had me hitting the six-foot mark. By intermission I had to acknowledge my lapse in fashion judgment, and pledged to henceforth re-reinvent myself as a *jeunesse dorée* and wear navy cashmere cardigans over my shoulders, pale pink lipstick, and Hermès scarves. That idea lasted the twenty-four hours until I left Paris.

❧

When I told my mother that I was going to fly to Paris on the Concorde and get to stay at the American embassy, she was characteristically delighted for me.

"Bitch," she hissed, and hung up the phone.

She called back a day later:

"Well, I suppose it's their choice if your decrepit grandparents want to spoil the bejesus out of you and waste thousands taking you to Paris." I could hear the ice cubes tinkling in her glass. My mother hadn't been anywhere other than downtown Boston since she'd thrown in her lot with the contractor.

"I'll bring you back a Chanel suit," I lied.

"Huh!" she said, and hung up the phone.

❧

Luckily my fear of flying did not extend itself to supersonic travel.

The best thing about taking the Boomer, aside from the head rush you got traveling at Mach 2, was that you never saw anyone but your fellow high rollers. No screaming babies or obese golfers on vacation. You went directly from the ultra-exclusive Concorde lounge, down a private escalator, and *alors* right onto the plane. No one even looked at your passport. It might as well have been Air Force One for all the attention they gave you, not to mention the free gifts, like sterling silver letter openers, Porthault hand towels, and pen sets.

There were four of us: my grandparents, *moi-même*, and Juan, the handsome, if still inscrutable, Basque butler. I was a late reservation, so I was seated apart, next to a red-haired woman who ignored me as soon as she discovered I was neither famous nor French. Paul Newman was sitting two rows behind me, practically on my right shoulder, and without even trying I could see the hairs in Halston's nose one row in front.

The flight to Paris left early in the morning, so I was unprepared for the three-hour alcohol soak. As soon as the plane leveled off in outer space, flight attendants began serving aperitifs, and those jellied little truffle-decorated bateaus of this and that the French so love. Next came caviar, accompanied by champagne and iced vodka. I chose vodka, a wise decision at ten in the morning only if you intend to accost Paul Newman and not be embarrassed by your actions. Whenever Paul got up to use the head, I got up too, forcing him to squeeze past me with a full frontal rub. After the third time (I think he had prostate trouble) old Joanne was on to me, but I didn't care. We'd progressed to the fish course and drinking white Burgundy, and I was gabbing away to my seatmate, who turned out to be an impresario named Regine. A Bordeaux followed with a filet de boeuf, and then petits fours, coffee, and Armagnac. By the time we landed in Paris, I was a lifetime member of the conglomerate of Regine's nightclubs, even the one in Rio, and on the guest list at a bunch of weekend parties which, sadly, I would discover were all at Jimmy's, a club that catered to lecherous old men, where they sized you up through a peephole even if your name was on the list, and then welcomed you in crocodile-style if you were remotely young and female, and had most of your teeth.

The fact that my grandfather had brought me along at all should have apprised me of his internal state of affairs. Likewise that in lieu of the Ritz, he had chosen for us to stay at the American embassy residence, which is a privilege granted to all former ambassadors, and without a doubt the most masochistic thing my grandfather could have done since all he had ever wanted, and worked for, and *paid* for, was to be the US ambassador to France. For decades he had headed up the French-American

Council. He was an authority on French art, French aviation, French defense, and French wine and food. He had honed his language skills to the point of fluency. He had been bitterly disappointed when he did not receive the nod after his ambassadorship to Belgium, which he felt had been merely the groundwork for the real thing, France. Oh, to have joined the illustrious ranks of Benjamin Franklin and Thomas Jefferson and Douglas Dillon. My grandfather had recently been offered Japan, but he'd petulantly turned it down; he continued to believe that France was his diplomatic destiny. A president would have to have been mad to appoint a man who was as mentally and physically competent as a bug on Raid to represent the country.

The embassy residence in Paris is the former Hotel Pontalba, a nineteenth-century mansion built for a New Orleans heiress. It is located on the Rue du Faubourg Saint-Honoré, on a beautiful courtyard set back from the busy street behind the original Visconti gatehouse. The graceful arched windows and formal gardens, Baccarat chandeliers and gold-leaf embellishments, inlaid marble floors and unrestrained ceilings, opulent reception rooms, the extraordinary art collection, even the Krug in the bedroom mini-fridge were nothing compared to the white-gloved marines who lined the sweeping stairways twenty-four seven. The ambassador's wife had to have vetted them; they were like Chippendale dancers vogueing in military costume. Going up and down the stairs gave me serious palpitations.

As we stepped into the small elevator to go up to our rooms, I saw my grandfather wince with envy at the luminous Milton Avery landscape hanging on one of its walls. It wasn't for the actual painting; he already owned several Averys. It aroused a rare wave of sympathy in me. It was easy to forget that he had once been a cultural icon in the restricted world of his contemporaries. The Museum of Modern Art, the Air and Space Museum, those had been his pet projects and brainchildren. He had overseen much of MoMA's expansion during the fifties and sixties, and remained a trustee after several terms as president. And he had been the one to convince Nixon to build the new Air and Space Museum to open on the nation's bicentennial. Once the ultimate twentieth-century man, my grandfather had become outmoded on this, the cusp of the next. He'd had a great run, from the edge of the Edwardian era, to the Atomic, but he was no longer a viable source of energy. The boards he still sat on didn't have the heart to throw him off.

Saddest of all, there was no one to hand the hard-fought reins to.

His four sons had disappointed him cruelly. My father's suicide would be something he could never make his peace with. The warmth and the intellectual bond between them were evident from the letters they'd written back and forth to each other about cars and motors and more cars, and foreign policy, and the children and the newspaper and upcoming holidays, and all the normal stuff that fathers and sons confer on.

His second-born, also dead, had disillusioned him differently. Robert had made a beeline for as radically different a life from his father's as he could have. The army, a simple teacher's existence, closeted homosexuality; and then to get whacked by a truck that he could have seen coming from a mile away?

Hamilton was a perpetual thorn in his side, and if he acknowledged him at all, it was as the author of a book my grandfather had contracted someone to ghostwrite for him during the late sixties.

Ordway had initially made his father proud. But after attending Harvard, and then the business school, he had continued his obsession with the police, and established a foundation that gave money to the families of officers killed in the line of duty. This laudable act provided him with a tax deduction and a steady flow of plaques and medals and certificates, with which he covered the walls of his apartment. This in turn led to an obsessive, countrywide pursuit of honorary sheriff appointments that became so prolific, Ordway had to purchase the apartment next door just to get more wall space for his shrine. He rarely left his two apartments now. A prostitute visited him once a week, and the rest of the time he sat around in a manic-depressive cocoon, consuming prescription drugs and watching the porn movies he had his secretary or bodyguard go out and rent.

Total washout.

⁂

The Madness of King William began in earnest the morning after we arrived. My grandfather placed a call to New York as soon as he awoke. "Miss Pou!" he said excitedly. "I've just seen the new Mercedes W124 and it's superb, absolutely first-rate! Order four for the houses, and I want one delivered to the embassy residence by noon. Of course I mean today! I intend to use it while I'm in Paris. Edward can have it afterwards. Nonsense. Of course you can get a license at thirteen! Have Heidi take the next plane to Stuttgart, and pick one up and deliver it to the embassy by lunchtime. I want to go to Versailles. Hire a driver as well." He paused. "Oh, very well, then have her get it here in time to take us to dinner. And while you're at it, order one for yourself. And for Heidi. That will be all." (Transatlantic click.)

So there we were, on our way to Versailles for an ultra-exclusive private tour to be conducted by a strange woman who had lived her entire life in the palace and claimed to have been born ninety-something years prior, almost to the day, on the floor of the Passage du Midi. And yes, we were in our gleaming new Mercedes, which poor Heidi, Miss Pou's co-secretary, had managed to drive in record time, and without incident, from the factory showroom in Stuttgart, into Paris, arriving during Friday evening rush hour, the experience of which actually cracked her famous Swiss composure and nearly gave her a nervous breakdown. I was sitting up front with the driver, which was far worse than riding shotgun with George the Nazi, because this guy maybe got through one bar of soap a decade. He kept flicking his mustard-colored eyes over my legs.

The tour was not what I would call a complete success. Certainly we gained access to all manner of off-limit salons and *chambres de lits*, and there's no place on earth as magnificent as Versailles, but I can never again think of the Sun King's Hall of Mirrors any way other than in terms of how long it takes a person with Parkinson's to travel down it. Likewise, the Opéra, though exquisite, will forever remind me of my grandmother's sustained, if melodious, passing of air during the climax of our tour guide's reenactment of a scene from Molière's *Malade Imaginaire*.

At least the sorest loser in the history of international diplomacy was enjoying his psychotropic drugs. My grandfather scoured Paris for available Monet water lily paintings and ordered the embassy staff around as if he were Sinatra. In public he was the archetypal crass American tourist he so despised, snapping his fingers and shouting at waiters: "On-core doo van!! Je voo-ray luh captain im meed eee at uh man!" Both my grandparents were fluent in French, but they might as well have been speaking the dialect of Dixie for all the trouble they took with their pronunciation.

Ambassador Hartman was very busy. Either that or he was avoiding us. He finally agreed to squeeze in the briefest of cocktails before fleeing for a state dinner elsewhere. My grandfather utilized the five minutes we sat together in the gilded Louis IV salon to rake the poor man over the coals, criticizing him, his chef, the residence staff, the diplomatic corps, and the entire Carter administration. I could see the pity on the faces of the marines standing guard outside the salon, and inwardly I curled up like a slug hit with salt. Voices were raised as the two men got into an argument, which was quickly resolved when the ambassador leapt to his feet and sprinted to the door, with the briefest of nods to my grandmother and me.

I wanted to tell the ambassador that it wasn't my grandfather's fault, that it was the drugs and the alcohol and—wasn't it obvious—because *he* wanted to be the ambassador so badly. Wanting to protect my grandmother, I followed Ambassador Hartman to the entrance and began to stammer out excuses, but he cut me short, telling me not to worry. "The old man's reputation precedes him," Hartman said with a dry laugh. "Everyone in the Foreign Service knows he did the same to Churchill when they met during the war."

Further shamed, I returned to the salon. My grandfather was blithering on about the insufferable pardoning of Vietnam draft evaders, and my grandmother was ripping farts and spackling on Cherries in the Snow like a transvestite. The look on her face made me bite back any number of things I was going to say. I resolved to swipe my grandfather's American Express card and go on a serious shopping expedition with it—until I remembered my grandfather never carried a wallet.

(My grandfather was like the queen. He never carried cash, or even identification. When he had fallen in the street one day after lunch at the "21" Club, blotto and looking like a Bowery bum, he had managed to convince a policeman to escort him to the office. There, Miss Pou had identified him as indeed the man whose name was on the elegant entryway of William A. M. Burden and Company.)

By morning I had grown an anxiety zit the size and color of a pomegranate. I needn't have worried about my grandmother; she was humming along, happily enjoying the buoyant pleasures a double dosage of Miltown can bring. Juan was the most resourceful—he came down with the flu and took to his bed for the duration of the trip.

On our final evening in Paris we went to an obscure restaurant on the outskirts of Clichy, the favorite auberge of the truly cognizant cognoscenti. On a dark street a single lamppost illuminated what looked like a set from a hard luck scene in an animated Disney movie. Inside, the place was virtually empty; there was nary a gastronome to be found. A labyrinthine staircase led to a simply furnished dining room. Given my grandfather's physical condition, not to mention my grandmother's pharmacological one, it took us an hour to reach our table.

The meal was everything whatever panel of experts Miss Pou had been directed to consult had foretold. It was sublime, like eating orgasms. As I was scraping the last molecule of manna from the Sèvres, trying not to actually lick the plate, I noticed my grandfather searching through his jacket pockets.

"Are you looking for matches, Granddaddy?" I said. "There are some right in front of you in the ash—"

"Checkbook," he grunted. "See here, Peggy, you wouldn't have any checks in your pocketbook, would you?"

Brffft, said my grandmother, shaking her head. *Checkbook? What was that?*

Her husband continued to dig around, nearly falling under the table in his slurry efforts. I had no idea what he was up to. The bill had been taken care of in advance by Miss Pou. As a last resort he looked at me, and I could see the lightbulb go on over his head.

"Checkbook," he demanded.

Whatever he was after, I was certain the hundred and two dollars in my Citibank account was not going to cover it.

My grandfather began snapping the fingers of the hand that still worked. "Gar-sone—I say, Gar-sone!" The waiter approached fearfully; it had been a trying three hours. "Luh proprietor silverplay," my grandfather said to him loftily.

"*Oui,* Excellency."

The owner came trotting up the stairs from the kitchen, rubbing his hands anxiously. "Yes, Your Excellency? Is everything to your satisfaction? Shall I tell the driver you are ready to leave?"

"Everything is marvelous, *marvelous*," my grandfather said, waving his hand. "And the Bordeaux was superb, first-rate. There is a problem, however."

"Excellency?"

"It's damned inconvenient to climb the stairs. You must have an elevator."

The owner laughed and spread his hands. "Unfortunately that is not possible."

"Nonsense, my good man." Turning to me, he said, "Write a check for two hundred thousand dollars. Miss Pou will wire the funds to your account to cover it."

To stave off his having a stroke, I did it. He snatched the check from me and presented it to the proprietor, saying, "When I return in the fall, I expect to ride in an elevator instead of taking those infernal stairs." And with that, he grappled to his feet, and we made our way at a majestic snail's pace down the affronting staircase and out to the waiting Mercedes. The owner, now joined by his wife and staff, stood in the doorway bowing and scraping and touching their forelocks.

On the way back to New York, I got Jacques Cousteau. He must have been a Concorde regular, because he knew the names of all the flight attendants. JC was way too important to even acknowledge me—until they brought out the caviar. Then he downed three shots of Absolut in as many minutes and came on like a barracuda. After seconds on the caviar, and fifths on the vodka, he began expounding on his theory about the cosmos, which was somehow wrapped up in the linking of constituent universes, love, and transpersonal psychology. Then he took my hand. This gesture gave me the hint that old JC was not talking about a mystical kind of love. I tried not to laugh, and it worked for a while because his Rolex, which was the size of a sea turtle, was slicing into my wrist in a decidedly un-funny way.

The Coulibiac of Salmon was served, and JC still had my hand, only now it was clamped to his thigh and he was asking me to "give in and feel the Power." Jesus Christ, the guy was maybe eighty. I started to giggle.

The effect on JC was catastrophic. It was as if I had murdered a pod of dolphins on the pull-out tray in front of him. He squinted his eyes and shook his blade of a head in disbelief at my amusement. He returned my suddenly offensive hand and picked up some papers he had been reading.

"God, I didn't know you took it that seriously. I mean I thought you were sort of kidding."

"Do not even speak. Poor girl, you are ignorant, that is for certain."

We landed twenty minutes later and I had to go to my "History and Theory of American Illustration" class with a mother of a developing hangover.

⌒⌒

Unfortunately for the proprietor of the auberge, Miss Pou stopped payment on the check as soon as we returned to New York. She also stopped the orders on five Mercedes, and a couple of *nympheas* paintings by Claude Monet, my grandfather having insisted the single water lily masterpiece he owned was not enough. Then there was that verbal promise to Fauchon for part ownership, in order to ensure that company's continued production of his favorite Lapsang souchong tea.

Everyone thought I was making it up about Jacques Cousteau except my mother. Knowing she had watched every single episode of *Undersea World*, I rang her a couple of days after my return. Forgetting my self-imposed rule of never calling past five, I caught her at a bad moment. She was drunk, and crying— something she was beginning to do with disconcerting regularity. One thing for sure made my mother cry: the death of an animal. One of the dogs had been run over in the driveway by the liquor store delivery van. "Thank God it was over quickly," my mother sniveled. "He didn't have time to feel much pain." I could hear the clink of ice as she picked up her drink.

"Oh well," she said, resuming her chronic practicality, "next one will be a female. I have the litter already picked out."

"Hey, guess who I sat next to on the plane back from Paris."

"I couldn't care less, Toots," said my mother. *Clink! Clink! Clink!*

"Jacques Cousteau."

"Cunt."

"You would have liked him." I laughed. "He was a total horndog."

"Mmmm." The ice cubes tinkled even more excitedly. "I'll bet he has a huge cock."

"*Stop.*"

"Oh well," my mother said, "I'd better go give the beast a proper funeral," and she hung up.

Go Fish

After Paris, things in Burdenland spiraled downward faster than you can say amphetamine psychosis. Turns out my grandfather had been going to four different doctors for his L-dopa. The adverse reactions of a single dose alone would have explained his recent behavior. Hallucinations: check. Thought disorder: check. Wild mood swings: check. Megalomania unseen since the Roman Empire: check. It would also explain his purchase of a hundred ant farms from FAO Schwarz, and his attempts to channel Howard Hughes, insisting Miss Pou wear white gloves when typing all correspondence.

It's amazing how resourceful an addict can be. In the midst of all this self-medicated madness, my grandfather invented and patented the Tippler's Bathroom. Fed up with broken bones and telltale bruises, he designed a john that was entirely padded. The prototype was installed beside his dressing room in the country house in Mount Kisco. Everything in it—the floor, the walls, the ceiling, the shower, the toilet, the toilet handle, the toilet paper holder, the towel racks, the tub, the sink, the faucets on the tub and the sink, the lights around the mirror, and the light switches on the wall—*everything* was covered with a two-inch-thick layer of spray-on foam and twenty coats of Benjamin Moore Chalk White enamel. With no discernible edges and everything a glossy, arctic whiteout, it looked like something from the Futurama exhibit at the 1964 World's Fair. You could bounce around dead drunk in the shower and never hurt yourself, and if you chose to bathe instead, there were ropes with big knots in them hanging above the edge of the tub so you could haul your Lafite-soaked hiney out of the water without having to call for assistance.

It was a sign of my grandfather's self-absorption that he didn't have one constructed for my grandmother, who bravely and consistently wore the black and blue (and green, and yellow) badge of Dubonnet and withstood all four of her slippery, sharp-angled bathrooms like the Christian she was. She might as well have just kept herself packed in ice. Modernism is such an inhospitable décor scheme for drinkers; there's a reason the classic English drawing room has remained soft and downy throughout the ages.

As my grandfather's drinking worsened, his brain rewarded him by undergoing a series of strokes that deprived him of his two favorite diversions: speech and taste. He continued to consume food and wine as if his senses were unaltered, but dining with him was a different experience. One could now voice an opinion—on anything: thermonuclear war, the amount of coke being done in the Studio 54 bathroom, genital mutilation, mixed marriages, civil libertarianism, Super Tampax versus Regular. The only word he could get out was a relatively harmless "phooey." Except one time, when we were discussing my cousin Connie's upcoming nuptials to a man named Rosengarten, he began to splutter and thrash around in his wheelchair, and finally managed to choke out, "J . . . J . . . J . . . JEW! JEW! JEW-WWWW!!!" He continued to call the word out throughout the rest of the meal, and was put to bed still repeating it. Luckily, by the next morning he was back to good old "phooey."

It was a dark day in Burdenland when Miss Pou was forced to sign on round-the-clock nurses. This event coincided with my little brother's horizontal consideration of suicide. Poor Edward, he had been to so many schools by now that no one was completely sure what grade he was in. I rarely saw him, and when I did I had to get a recap on his history as if he were a long lost roommate who had moved to the West Coast. Recently, Edward and his grandfather had latched on to each other in what could have been called destiny, but more likely was a last-ditch effort for the patriarch to locate a successor among the family rubble. The upshot was that Edward, like his father, was sent to Milton Academy—where he was now an immensely unhappy ninth grader. One beautiful Indian summer day in October he decided he wouldn't get out of his dorm room bunk bed and that he would lie there until he died. Nobody would have paid much attention to this, indeed they would have hauled his ass out of bed and thrown him in a cold shower, but for the fact that at the same age, and in the same school, our father had tried to kill himself.

It was around this time that Edward began to suspect he was the reincarnation of our father. Since that made my brother my father, my brother his own father, and—creepiest of all—my brother our mother's husband, I found, and still find, the whole thing extremely unsettling. (Edward maintains I will come to accept it in time.)

For some reason it was me who got pulled out of school and dispatched northward to deal with the situation. I guess I was as close to my brother as anyone was, which wasn't saying much. I talked to Edward for a while as he lay there in bed. I don't remember much of what I said, maybe lame platitudes like *You have a wonderful future ahead of you* and *Think of the pain and anguish you would cause everyone*, but probably I said something like *Why don't you put suicide on hold because the pharmaceutical companies are making incredible inroads with new antidepressants.* Edward just grunted catatonically back at me, so after a while I gave up trying to reason with him. What did I know about depression? I was a girl. I didn't get stuck with our family's male strand of

DNA. Recalling that there's nothing better than underage drinking to set things right, I suggested we go out for a beer, whereupon my brother got dressed and we went to a cheesy lunch spot in town and had burgers and Heinekens. The latter made us both feel better, and when I dropped him off at his dorm a couple of hours later, he seemed like he was going to be okay. That's what I told his dorm master anyway.

I continued around Route 128 and up to Marblehead to give a progress report to my mother. She was convinced that Edward was predestined to kill himself and that there was nothing anybody could do, and so she was washing her hands of the whole thing. I knew she was just saying that; she was as worried about him as the school was. She had been dating my father in the ninth grade.

"Those fucking Burdens," she ranted. "I swear, they've spoiled all of you rotten, and when you have to deal with something even vaguely unpleasant, like getting up in the goddamn morning, you fall apart! Edward should have never been sent to Milton. He doesn't fit in there. He's not athletic, and he's . . . well, I don't think he's equipped to deal with the academics because of his dyslexia and all, and . . . and—" She fizzled there, but took a breath, and a gulp of her diet iced tea, and picked up the thread of her tirade. "And your good-for-nothing brother Will is so goddamned coddled, he's living off the fat of Burdenland and drinking the wine cellar in Maine dry! No one is keeping an eye on him, I mean I'm all the way down here, and frankly I'm worried that he's going to do something birdbrained too, like—"

Zinggg!!! The egg timer buzzed, and my mother leapt up from the kitchen table to pluck a suspicious loaf from the oven.

"That's not your famous Velveeta Cheese Bread, is it?" I knew I'd smelled bad nostalgia when I walked in the door.

"I thought I'd make you something," said my mother. "You used to gobble this down like a little piggy." She wafted a porcupine-shaped pot holder over a pan that contained what looked like a steaming, squashed basketball. Inside, as I well knew, were hidden globs of molten orange cheese food. Glancing at the clock on the stove, she said, "I figured if I make my rotten children food they like, maybe they'll come visit more. Is it drink time yet?"

One of the many reasons I rarely went to visit my mother was because she spent most of the time complaining that I never came to visit. She would go on about how it wasn't her fault that she didn't have houses and servants like my grandparents, which would inevitably lead to a diatribe on how they had taken everything away from her when my father died, leaving her virtually penniless, and then tried to get custody of her children—*her* children, *hers*—and on and on. It was enough to make me hanker for the good old days when she pretended she was childless.

Slouched in a high-backed Hitchcock chair at the drop-leaf kitchen table, I was watching more than listening. My mother's figure had taken on that melting candle wax effect women get in their fifties, when the soft parts begin oozing downward. She had given up her extreme dietary vigilance when she'd married a man that could drink with her. The calories of undisguised boozing, and a more sedentary lifestyle, had taken their toll. Unbelievably, she now had a stomach that no amount of sucking in could invert. I would have been overjoyed to witness the decay of her famous physique if it hadn't brought so much fallout on me. Ever the competitor, it drove her crazy that I was young and that my skin still had elasticity.

"Have some," she said, putting the bread down on the counter. "You can work it off with all that sex I'm sure you're enjoying." She moved closer. (Warning signal.) "Goodness, Toots. I never had wrinkles like that at your age."

We were saved by the entry of the contractor. "Sun's over the yardarm," he said, reaching for the scotch.

❧

My mother was right about the perks of Burdenland. They were pretty great.

On the second of January each year, my grandparents headed south to Hobe Sound. Over Presidents' Weekend, I opted to take a break from New York's kick-ass winter and flew down for a visit. I had issues with the Jupiter Island Club, starting with the dress code. All that Lilly Pulitzer, plus the frogs and whales and Nantucket red pants and kelly green everything, the Sperry Top-Siders and the Pappagallo shoes, the bleeding madras jackets and upturned Lacoste collars—they all made me queasy. It also bothered me that nothing bad could happen to you there (other than alcohol poisoning), and that the speed limit was ten miles an hour, and that if you exceeded it, one of the invisible policemen patrolling the tiny enclave would spring from the sea grape bushes, pull you over, and ask you whose house you were staying at. Then they'd let you go, even if you were doing ninety. I hated it that the worst thing you could do was to write *penis* in a sand trap on the golf course, or swim in the ocean when the red flag was up, or not attend the tea dances. And I loved it that when you were being snubbed, you received a black sweater on your doorstep. Try as I might, I could never get one.

In spite of all that, the island was lovely, as untainted and lush and picturesque as a collective billion dollars could make it. My grandparents' house was built on two acres of the most overcultivated land this side of England. The house faced west over the Intracoastal Waterway with a view of spectacular sunsets that became positively trippy after a couple of Juan's famous daiquiris. Everywhere orchids cascaded from the trees, and near the pool an aviary housed my grandmother's hyacinth macaws and leadbeater cockatoos. (They tried flamingos one year, but they kept flying away.) The house was large and vaguely tropical, with lots of French doors and louvered windows. There was a courtyard on the west side, with a tree topiaried to look like a giant aspirin tablet, and a pool and guesthouse on the east. The lawn that ran down to the Intracoastal had towering, root-strung mangrove trees that made my macabre heart go pit-a-pat when I saw them in the moonlight.

Mr. Opie, the caretaker, picked me up from the West Palm Beach airport in my grandfather's 6.3, which was surprisingly intact. Mr. Opie was eighty-nine, and a dwarf, which made him more suited to piloting a roller skate. He had to drive with the front seat all the way forward and extenders on the pedals. Mr. Opie never stopped talking. He lived in a cottage on the property with his four-hundred-pound wife, several macaws, and an organ, which husband and wife both loved to play, often in the middle of the night. It didn't take a genius to figure out who belonged to the tiny shadow lurking in the potted gardenias and kumquat bushes whenever anyone went skinny-dipping in the pool at night.

Dan Rather was hosting the cocktail hour when I arrived, and I expressed gratitude for it as, gin and tonic in hand, I surveyed the situation in the light of the *CBS Evening News*. My grandmother was sitting in a bright yellow armchair. She was dressed in a hostess skirt that mimicked the Matisse cutouts on the walls, and her arm was in a sling fashioned from a matching scarf. She had recently taken one of her late night spills during a rendezvous with a bottle of grenadine in the pantry. An algae-colored bruise was yellowing over her left temple, and she had made an attempt to camouflage it with a heavy dusting of powder. Her head was coiffed, but it was lolling a bit as she munched on Finn Crisps and Brie that could have been riper. Poodle A was alternately clawing its way up and then slipping off her lap; Poodle B lay curled like a fossil at her feet.

My grandfather, who had recently suffered another stroke, was seated an arm's length away, on a large pillow in his Harvard

"University" chair. He was dressed in adult diapers and a pair of blue Turnbull and Asser pajamas.

Jesus, I thought, *has the cypress paneling always been that screaming-loud turquoise? And what's with all the Matisse paper collages?* There must have been a dozen of them struggling for exhibition space amid the jumble of aeronautic prints and autographed headshots of Gemini and Apollo mission astronauts. Potted orchids arced from every horizontal surface, lending the place an air of inconceivable sexuality.

"Will you be in for lunch, dearie?" my grandmother asked.

"Uh, sure," I answered automatically.

"And will you be in for dinner?"

"I don't know yet, Gaga, could I let you know in the morning?"

"Yes, of course. Just let me know if you'll be in for lunch, dearie."

"Yes, I will be. I said I'd be in for lunch, and that I would let you know about dinner."

"Right-o, then it will be the four of us for dinner."

"Phoo-ey," my grandfather corrected.

But his wife had turned her attention back to the television. "She died of what? What's this amahexia? Why would that poor thing starve herself?"

To banish the television image of an emaciated fashion model, my grandmother helped herself to some more cheese from the hors d'oeuvres tray. In the process she dropped the gooey bamboo-handled knife, and the dead poodle shot after it like the tongue of a frog.

"Anorexia nervosa," I said. "It's an eating disorder where you think you're fat when you're not."

"Phooey!" my grandfather scoffed, and doused himself with Wild Turkey as he tried to get the glass to his lips.

More often than not now, dinner was served on trays in front of the television, and tonight was no exception. Juan and Selma brought in the first course, a cream of sorrel soup. My grandfather gave Juan a meaningful stare and pointed at his wineglass. He needed it now, not after the main course was served. Juan dipped his head in recognition and quickly returned with a bottle of Meursault. He poured a half inch into the glass for my grandfather to taste.

"Phoo-ey!" demanded my grandfather, tapping the top of his wineglass. Juan complied and filled 'er up. My grandfather could hardly grip anything with his half-frozen hand, but he managed to get the glass to his dry lips, and drank it off in one long guzzle before signaling for a refill. Juan complied, and then used the remote to switch to *The MacNeil/Lehrer Report*.

My grandmother overshot her mark and spooned green soup down her front. She dabbed at it absently, eyes on the television. She got the next one into her mouth. My grandfather wasn't faring much better, but at least Juan had taken the usual precaution of tucking a jib-sized napkin in at his throat. I watched him eating and wondered how he could stand having no sense of taste. They say 50 percent of it is from stockpiled memory, which would explain why he didn't seem affected by his lack of buds, as long as he kept to his favorite diet of haute cuisine and alcohol. A month before, I'd seen his insular cortex light up like Las Vegas when a waiter put a dish of flaming woodcock in front of him.

The soup bowls were cleared, a second bottle of wine was started, and now Juan approached Madame with a large platter draped in halibut. Oh God. I closed my eyes. Disassembling a large fish is tricky enough when one is sober. After several attempts to pick up the serving utensils, and then a few more to snag some of the fish, she succeeded in getting a piece in the clutches of the fork and spoon. Juan stood unflinchingly, as he had been trained. Whoops—she dropped it. There was another tussle, and my grandmother finally had a sizeable chunk and was half scraping, half lifting it off the platter when, instead of getting the fish onto her plate, she succeeded in depositing it right down—as in all the way down—the considerable depths of her bosom. Smiling, my grandmother replaced the serving fork and spoon carefully on the platter, mission accomplished.

My grandfather signaled for more wine, and my grandmother began stabbing at her empty plate. I gaped at Juan. A bead of sweat stood out on his imperturbable brow. After a few seconds, he took off for the kitchen and returned with a tea towel. Hands in front, as if he were approaching a wild animal, he attempted to remove the fish with the towel, but only succeeded in driving it further between my grandmother's sizeable breasts. Juan stood back and for once looked utterly helpless.

"Delishosh fish," pronounced my grandmother, and sucked at her empty glass.

"*Phooey!*" cried my grandfather.

"I'll get the nurse!" I cried back, and bolted for the kitchen. The situation called for a professional.

I returned with the nurse, a heavily built and heavily mustachioed Florida temp with about as much command of language as her patient. "Well, well, well," she said in a bass voice. My grandmother rolled her head backwards and beamed at her. The nurse plunged her hand so far down my grandmother's front she could have wiped her, and scraped out the fish.

"Phooey! Phooey! Phooey!" Bits of food flew out of my grandfather's mouth. One of them landed on a nearby sea urchin arrangement. Another struck a poodle in the eye.

I drained my own glass.

My grandmother was borne away by the capable arms of the nurse, and my grandfather and I, in our first and last act of unity, watched *Dynasty* in a dazed silence.

The next morning was as bright and shiny as a gardening staff and their hoses can make it. When I came over from the guesthouse to get breakfast, the evening's events had been washed as clean as the grounds and patio. My grandmother crept into the living room, where I was having a cursory look at the obits. She eased herself into a chair next to the sofa, where I was stretched out amid the papers.

"Good morning," I said, trying to be cool. "Feeling okay?"

She managed a rueful smile and handed me an envelope. She had written my name on the front in a very shaky hand. Then she struggled to her feet and made her way out to the pool to go talk to her crazy birds.

It was hard to read my grandmother's sorry note because it was as legible as Sanskrit. The gist of it was that she was appalled at her behavior and deeply embarrassed. She promised, swore even, that it would <u>never</u> happen again. She was vowing off drink for good.

My grandmother had been raised a Christian Scientist. It was ingrained in her to disregard in life whatever she found too distressing to handle. Thus, she maintained that Popsie didn't smoke despite his two-pack-a-day habit; that her eldest son hadn't shot himself—it had been an accident; and that her sweet grandsons, young Will and little Edward, never touched even an aspirin, much less pot and hard drugs. Her note to me was a bombshell. I knew she had a problem, and I knew she knew I knew, but to admit it was so bleakly out of character, I wanted to vaporize. What the hell was happening to everyone? My grandfather was in diapers and couldn't speak, my grandmother was becoming a caricature of a drunk, my mother was getting fat and trying to please me, Will was holed up in an un-winterized cabin in Maine and drinking himself stupid, and Edward was stealing the Percodans and Darvon and Valium from his grandparents' medicine cabinets and making a fortune selling them at his new school.

My grandmother stuck to her guns all day, but by evening she couldn't hold out any longer and was at it again, accepting her six o'clock cocktail from Juan and sneaking from the bottles she kept hidden all over the house. I was out of there by the time she woke up the next morning.

Checkout Time

SURPRISINGLY, NO ONE in the family died that year, not that they didn't try. Will dove headfirst into the empty indoor pool in Maine one night, and it was a big fat wake-up call. As in, time to get sober. At the Eastern Maine Medical Center in Bangor, my brother bunked down with the kind of die-hard alcoholics and addicts that only a state with Siberian winters could produce. I drove up for the requisite family confessional-slash-shaming session near the end, where those who were wronged get to publicly voice off at the recovering patient, who is now deemed strong enough to take it. It was the first time I'd been Downeast in the winter, and I really got a feel for why Maine has the highest rate of alcoholism and child pornography in the country. At the hospital, my mother and younger brother and I sat with a bunch of raggle-taggle, very local families, in an increasingly odorous room that had speckled blue industrial carpeting and bulletproof plastic seating lined along its perimeters. In the center of the room a single chair faced a small row of others. Each patient took a turn in it and was confronted by his or her family, who blasted the patient with their declarations of pain. How the guilty ones (now costing the state thousands of dollars to eat four meals a day, sleep in clean sheets, and spend the bulk of their time doing what others merely dreamed of—talking about themselves endlessly to professional listeners) had hurt them with their drug-ery, or thievery, or drunken fits of rage. The stories revealed in that circle, told by people dressed in an assortment of stretchy clothes and lumber jackets, had a harsh, native reality that contrasted sharply with my brother's entitled misdemeanors. A seventeen-year-old mother told her husband that she could forgive him for not coming home every night, or even for beating her up, but when he got drunk and set fire to their trailer, well that was bad because now they didn't have any place to sleep. But what really pissed her off was that he had traded the food stamps for drugs and now there was no money to feed the two babies.

When it was our turn, our nervous little group took our seats across from my brother, who bowed his head and seemed to excitedly await abuse as a monk awaits flagellation. There was an awkward silence, because no one could come even close to respectably matching the previous litanies. After a long interval, during which several of the audience members hawked and spat, I managed to timidly say, "Well I guess it was sort of irresponsible that you left your BMW where it could get stolen, and that you spent the insurance money on cocaine . . . um"—I looked around at the slack jaws of the audience, and, even though I knew I sounded like the worst spoiled princess on the planet, I forged ahead anyway—"and you *really* scared us when you dove into the indoor pool!" Mouths were dropping. "Yeah. And I can't *believe* you slept with your girlfriend in front of the living room fireplace last summer, and that the butler walked in on you doing it."

There might have been a round of very sarcastic applause but I couldn't swear to it.

The following year Will was at the Johnson Institute, trading Hallmark cards and crying buckets and hugging big black football players and anorexic girls, and I did *not* go to family weekend; nor did I go to the one at Sierra Tucson. Or was that Hazelden? Maybe that was Edward—Lord knows he has a few treatment programs under his belt too. But I'm getting ahead of myself. Anyway, throughout his long, but ultimately successful, recovery process, Will found God—in the form of an Indian guru with a 501(c)(3) nonprofit corporation—and married his four-hundred-pound therapist.

Edward scraped through a series of high schools, at one point living in a foster situation in Boston and, when that didn't work out, in Marblehead with my mother and the contractor (nightmare), and eventually coming to rest at the apartment on Fifth Avenue and living with our grandparents, where he was pretty much—no, make that absolutely—left to his own devices. Those included an unlocked wine cellar and a readily available supply of heavy-duty prescription drugs.

Edward had been smoking pot for years, but in New York he was turned on to coke, and then heroin. He claimed he didn't have a habit because he snorted his drugs instead of mainlining them. His VanderBurden nose was perpetually scarlet and his hair was greasy and he hung out with people much older than he was. He was particularly close to a family that had a house near us in Maine. So close, in fact, that he was sleeping with the chatelaine, a wonderfully effusive and insouciant fifty-something-year-old free spirit who claimed to be a white witch. When I found out about it, it absolutely enraged me, and I felt guilty that I hadn't been looking out for my very wayward baby brother. It was summer, and I was in Maine, so I marched next door to lambaste the cradle-robbing, pot-dealing sex maniac; but within five minutes, she got me to forget what I was there for. She had me drinking white wine with her (which her adorable husband brought us) and laughing cozily away in her hippie, crystal-strung bedroom that looked out past pine trees and flapping Tibetan prayer flags to the brilliantly blue ocean, and I swear if I had it in me to do it with women, I would have slept with her too. I was glad in a perverse way that my little brother had found someone to mother him, even if it wasn't the generally accepted notion of mothering. In fact, I was jealous.

As for the real mother, she got fatter, and more into her Greek coins, and was asked to lecture at Harvard, which she never let us forget.

Me, I transferred from freezing cold Cornell, to Parsons School for Design in the city. Instead of drunken frat boys everywhere, boys in dresses were now the norm in my classrooms. I graduated, and started looking for a job. What I wanted more than anything was to work at *Mad* magazine. (*CREEPY* was long gone.) Flattered by my adulation for Alfred E. Neuman, the editor took pity and put me on the wait list, but it was like trying to get into the River Club; someone had to die first. I gave up and went to work at *National Lampoon*, though I considered it sloppy seconds. I was given the scarred desk belonging to the previous year's art department grunt, who bequeathed me her gallon of Duco rubber cement.

My job basically consisted of gluing copy and photostats of photographs onto Bristol boards, hand-lettering the Foto Funnies and comics, and getting chased around the art director's desk, which didn't bother me in the slightest because sexual harassment was fun back then.

All of the articles in the once cool *Lampoon* dribbled with campy satire. Almost all of them were about sex—sex from a guy's point of view, that is. The editor, then P. J. O'Rourke, would climb on top of his desk and yell, "I need big tits! Somebody find me some BIG TITS!" I couldn't figure out if he needed them for personal use, or for business.

The most important thing I learned at *National Lampoon*, other than perfect block letter penmanship, was how to snort cocaine. I say important, because the eighties were only a sniff away. On Friday afternoons someone would go around the various departments collecting money in a hat. At five we'd assemble in the editor's office to drink beer and snorkel up the thirty or so chalky white lines laid out on his desk. Then we'd go back to work, wonderfully invigorated. Sometimes we'd use all that energy to pose for stupid pictures. As in no, that's not really Jon Voight on page fifty-six of the October 1978 issue; it's me.

It was fun for a while, but fun for minimum wage gets old fast, and besides, I don't particularly enjoy drugs.

It figures I'd end up working in the porn industry.

At that time it didn't matter where you got your design experience—*Soldier of Fortune, Crochet!* magazine, *News of the World*—only that you got it. A friend of mine was working at a downtown head-shop publication called the *Daily Dope*, and they needed a design assistant. I gratefully left the boy's club of soft porn and anatomical jokes, only to discover more of the same at my new job. Except now all the naked, large-breasted women were having real sex, often with aliens.

I'd been working there for about a month when it came to my attention that the publisher of *Daily Dope* needed an art director for a new magazine, one that would be devoted to the review of adult films being put out in the nascent format of video. I wanted to be an art director. Porn didn't bother me; hey, I'd seen sex before. I'd been around it pretty much all my life, in fact. As an observer, I was an expert—which made me perfect for the job.

Within three months I was fired for being too tasteful. Luckily, I had come into some of my trust fund, enough to buy a loft in Soho, and a lot of Stephen Sprouse and Azzedine Alaïa clothing, and enough to become a bona fide downtown painter. More importantly, I got myself a dog, an English bull terrier I named Pearl, and in her I found the true meaning of family.

And as for my grandparents, they continued to erode, and so did Burdenland.

In spite of its perfect address and immense square footage, the Fifth Avenue apartment now appeared dingy. In the forty years since they had bought it, the place had remained virtually unchanged from its original Philip Johnson reformation. Just about every piece of furniture in each of the twenty-one rooms remained in the exact spot where it had been photographed by *Vogue* during the fifties.

In Maine the sea still wore diamonds in the morning sunlight, and there was the childhood-familiar crush of the raked bluestone gravel under your feet when you walked the long path up to the dock. The house still smelled of roses and pine and woodsmoke and mold, but now you could catch a whiff of dirty adult diapers. Handrails had been installed at strategic points, and the yellow Saarinen womb chair had been replaced with a dung-colored Barcalounger. There were wheelchair ramps and potty chairs and the television was always on. I knew things were wrapping up when I noticed, on a routine snoop through the bomb shelter, that nobody was bothering to restock the Campbell's. (Unable to keep up with the demand, Miss Pou had long since ceased to replenish the morphine, Seconal, and opium capsules in the medical kit.)

The estate in Mount Kisco saw a succession of scurrilous gardeners and live-in Portuguese couples who named their children after things they saw on television. The liberty my grandfather had exulted in when cocooned in his Tippler's Bathroom eventually paled. Neither he nor his lifelong mixed doubles partner could even make it to the second floor, let alone down to the indoor or outdoor tennis courts. They still made the winter pilgrimage to Hobe Sound, and the summer one to Maine, but after a while my grandparents stopped going out to Mount Kisco, because it was just too much effort—for everyone.

It was hard not to take advantage of my grandparents. I started having weekend parties out in Mount Kisco, playing house big-time and cooking up huge meals with all the tomatoes and squash, and carrots and beans and peas, and herbs, and strawberries and beautiful flowers from the garden, because honestly, no one else was using them. My grandparents didn't entertain anymore, they ate next to nothing, and the vast gardens were planted each spring as if they were still supplying their hospitality of the past. Everyone ran naked around the indoor pool, and swung like monkeys on the ropes in the Tippler's Bathroom, and downed cases of Petrus and Cheval Blanc and Margaux and Yquem like they were bottled water. The staff of yesteryear would have tanned my hide, but no one was left at the helm. Chef Michel was long gone, and in his place was an Irish cook named Nora. Her assistant was a Honduran woman who had been promoted to the position from laundress. The chauffeur was an Irish boozer, and the gardeners were all American. Juan was hanging on by the barest of threads, and a sense of Basque loyalty. Captain Closson had been injured while working on the boat in dry dock and was consequently let go. For a while, Will and I would drive over to the other side of the island and take him out to breakfast, but he spoke of his enforced retirement with such bitterness, we were always relieved when we left him. Finally, on a summer afternoon, he went into the workshop behind his little house in Southwest Harbor, took down the shotgun he used to hunt bears on the mainland in winter, and killed himself.

That same year, Ann Rose didn't show up for my grandparents' forty-something annual New Year's Day party, where her presence was even more acutely required, due to the faltering condition of the host and hostess. (The regulars may have been dropping like flies, but that show would go on until the final exit.) When Miss Pou failed to rouse Ann Rose on the telephone, she went over to her apartment. She found Ann Rose dead on her sofa, drowned in an ocean of her own regurgitated blood.

And as for the poodles, one dried up completely and was borne off to heaven on an updraft, and the other fell into the pool and was drowned.

No one wanted to take responsibility. My grandparents' two remaining sons were non compos mentis: Uncle Ham–Uncle Ham was only allowed to visit the apartment once a week, when he came to take tea with his mother on Wednesday afternoons; Uncle Ordway was finding it impossible to be even quasi-normal. When he wasn't enwombed in his honorary sheriff ciborium watching porn, or *The Blue Lagoon* (he was still fixated on Brooke Shields), he lay in bed surrounded by newspapers and periodicals, reading and underlining and clipping articles written about the ills of inherited wealth and the sorrows of the incapacitated children of the rich, which he had his secretary send to everyone.

My brothers were also helpless: Will was focusing on himself, floating along the path of sober, vegan spirituality up in Maine, examining his navel through multiple courses and workshops to see where things went wrong. Poor Edward was trying to be the son his grandfather wanted him to be, wearing Huntsman suits and feigning an interest in the world of finance, but he was still just a teenager. Plus he was so doped up and wasted all the time, he was incapable of being anything to anybody. I'm surprised he still has all the parts of his body.

I wasn't any more accommodating; when they were in the city, I'd see my grandparents maybe a couple of times a month, and I always spent part of the summer with them up in Maine, but selfishly I had zero interest in becoming involved with the minutiae of their deteriorating lives. I was way too busy. It was the 1980s, and I was a Soho party girl having a blast in New York. As much as I loved my grandparents, I consciously adopted my grandmother's Christian Science frame of mind toward the situation.

Miss Pou was up to her eyeballs. My grandfather was getting as crazy as a coot, and he kept firing everyone, including Miss Pou when she wouldn't do things like book the Chinese polo club to fly over for a match on the (nonexistent) polo field in Mount Kisco, and Miss Pou kept rehiring everyone, with raises in salary and concessions all over the place.

It was becoming the reign of the nurses. You'd walk into the living room at night and they'd be lounging there, thumbing through magazines and reading the mail. My grandmother, once so vital and idiosyncratic, was now allowing her functions to be monitored alongside those of her genuinely ailing husband. Everything was meticulously recorded: time and body temperature, time and blood pressure, intake of fluids (legitimate ones), output of urine, intake of solids, number of poops. With nobody to deny them, the nurses soon took to making wardrobe decisions, and my grandparents were presented in clothing so radically different from their usual style that if it had been somebody else's relations, it would have been hilarious. Like tracksuits—navy with white piping for him and pink for her. The only pink I'd ever seen my grandmother wear, besides her Playtex girdle, was her quilted velvet bed jacket. The Mainbocher luncheon suits, the Dior dresses, the chic Balenciaga jackets with three-quarter sleeves, the cashmere appliquéd sweaters from Belgium, the Givenchy evening gowns were all shoved to the back of the closet. The nurses took my grandmother shopping at Macy's and gave her a makeover in pale, suburban old lady trouser suits, lace-trimmed polyester dresses in pastel colors, and Reebok sneakers, all of which my grandmother was too puzzled by to refuse. The flag over Revlon's headquarters flew at half-mast when the stockpiled Cherries in the Snow and Love That Red were replaced with Maybelline peach-toned lipstick.

My mother's wardrobe was faring just as poorly. She had migrated from leather minis and over-the-knee boots to terrycloth bikinis and cheap Indian caftans she got from a store near the Harvard Square MBTA stop. With her amulets of ceramic, rock, bead, and bone, and the hand-beaten jewelry she'd begun to create, she was starting to look like a walking museum gift shop.

In time my little brother's drug addiction became so obvious that even a family like ours had to acknowledge it—if only because there was no Krug left in the wine cellar. I got involved with a couple of the interventions, where we had him secured in a psychiatric holding tank, but Edward always freed himself after the mandatory seventy-two hours were up. He eventually ended up as a long-term patient at the White Plains Psychiatric Hospital. I didn't visit him there very often because the inmates creeped me out.

"See that girl there?" my brother would say, indicating a normal enough looking brunette with a cast on her arm.

"Yeah?" I would reply.

"They had to put her in the Quiet Room for a while, and she smashed her hand through the window and swung it around all the jagged parts. Almost got to bleed to death. See that guy?"

"Yeah?"

"He got so fucked up one night, he tried freebasing someone's stick deodorant. See that other guy?"

Technically, Edward had been admitted for his heroin problem, but after a year in the hospital he confessed he was staying on because it was as good a place to live as anywhere. Plus, he really enjoyed all the therapy.

While Edward was in his second year, an art school friend and I decided he should get to have sex with someone since he'd basically only experienced it with a mother figure in her fifties. We fixed him up with her studio assistant. Norah was from New Jersey and had big hair, a big ass, and humongous breasts. We figured on the strength of those features alone, she should be the one to sleep with my brother. That she resembled him in both coloring and physique—they had the same pinky-blond hair and soft, gel-filled bodies—made it seem a little like incest, but when you live at the funny farm you can't be too choosy.

A few months later, Edward gave up hospital life and moved in with her. Then he began looking around for something to do. He tried a few semesters of college at SUNY, but college life wasn't able to hold his attention. Managing the assets of his grandparents seemed a good alternative—and he wouldn't need a degree. In seemingly next to no time, my brother became a partner in William A. M. Burden and Company and went to work all dressed up in Huntsman pinstripe suits and John Lobb shoes. He proved to have an astute and creative financial mind. He became a trustee of his grandmother, and then of Uncle Ham–Uncle Ham, earning a salary for the positions. He oversaw the trembly signing of papers, and he became involved with managing the household staff, and the nurses. Both would scatter like mice when he walked into the room. He seemed like he was in control of himself as well, but he wasn't. He relapsed, and started back in on heroin, and on painkillers. He had a devil camped full-time on one shoulder, and an angel only part-time on the other.

My grandfather was now in and out of the hospital on a regular basis. Each time he was admitted he made sure he had two things with him: his favorite flashlight (the one packed with miniature airline bottles of hooch) and a copy of his autobiography, *Peggy and I.*

It had taken my grandfather years to dictate his memoirs, and many hired professionals to put it into something resembling a narrative. The book had been privately published, and my grandfather had ordered a first printing of ten thousand copies. He was certain he had a blockbuster on his hands. Not wishing to insult him, Miss Pou had asked what she should do with the remaining nine thousand after she'd sent the book to everyone my grandfather had ever known, and to the few bookstores that would accept a couple.

"Why, Miss Pou," he had said, "I want you to send a copy to every library, every university, and every college in every city in every state in the United States!" In spite of a full-page ad in *The New York Times Book Review*, maybe three copies were sold.

My grandfather had Miss Pou come to the hospital every day to read to him from his autobiography. He particularly liked to hear the beginning chapters—those extolling his heritage and the past opulence of Florham. He was probably the only one left now who still viewed the Vanderbilt name as one aligned with God, not apocalyptic genetics. He had been born into a societal position that had been ripe with opportunity. Anything, especially for a man with privilege, brains, and money, had been possible. The world had been his Oyster Rockefeller, New York City the epicenter of cool, twentieth-century America.

His life, at once so gilded and so scarred, now had the unpredicted denouement of no worthy successor or dynasty.

Given my grandfather's limited vocabulary, conversation with him tended to be one-sided. Luckily, Miss Pou had learned to speak Phooey.

"Certainly, Mr. Burden. I'll schedule the architect to come to the hospital and meet with you. May I ask what for?"

Phooeys, hand gestures, nods, grunts, and more phooeys.

"A swimming pool. But, Mr. Burden, you already have five of them."

Meaningful eye rolling, hand gestures, and multiple phooeys.

"A swimming pool in your hospital room. I see. Well, Mr. Burden, I don't think it matters if you are a trustee, and that you did give that bank of elevators; I can't imagine—"

"Phooey! Phooey, phooey, phooey, *Phooey!!!*"

"No, I don't want you to fire me, Mr. Burden, but if—"

Agitated gestures with pointed frozen fingers, and so forth and so on.

Eventually my grandfather checked into New York Hospital for what would be his final visit. In his mind, he had always been immortal, but just in case he wasn't, Miss Pou had been updating his obituary on a regular basis for years. Certainly he had no discernible religion, other than old French vines, the mandate of the mid-sixties Republican Party, and the internal combustion engine. Even though he was terrified of dying, my grandfather begged Miss Pou to help him do it each time she came to see him. The hospital nurses were tired of his craziness and his arrogance. He was tired of the indignity and the painful tests. Necessity had enabled him to add two words to his vocabulary: *no more.* He repeated them over and over.

One day when Miss Pou went to visit, she found my grandfather alone, sitting in his wheelchair, naked from the waist down, covered in his own shit. It was caked all over him, the chair, and the floor. The bank of elevators with his name on it was only twenty feet away.

I went to see him the day before he died. I stood toward the rear of the room, as far away as I could get while still managing to convey a sense of compassion. My grandfather was as shriveled as a freeze-dried apple, and his glasses were enormous on his face. A feeding tube was stuck in the side of his neck, and he had lines and wires traversing his body like an old-fashioned switchboard. He saw me flinching uncontrollably, and it embarrassed both of us.

A nurse was standing by the bed, holding on to my grandfather's exposed foot with the intimate familiarity of a woman holding on to her lover's cock. To think it had come down to this—my arch nemesis, lying wretchedly in a hospital bed, his bare foot being fondled by a Filipino immigrant who had no clue of who he had once been; and could not have cared less if she had.

Talk about feeling conflicted. Standing in that room of imminent death, I was still mad at him for something that had happened years earlier, before he had lost his speech. My grandfather had just returned to the apartment after one of his first stays in the hospital. When he had been settled by the nurses, I had gone into my grandparents' bedroom and welcomed him home. He had looked at me coldly and said, "It's *my* home. Not yours."

I thought of my favorite picture of my grandparents, a black-and-white press photo taken when they were newly married.

They're walking down Fifth Avenue in front of St. Thomas Church in the Easter Parade. He's in a top hat and spats and is looking at the photographer with an expression of mingled surprise, both at having his picture taken and at his extraordinary good fortune. She's in a gray fox coat with padded shoulders and a huge corsage. They are young and vibrant, cultured and entitled. He is rich and she is beautiful, and they are the envy of the city.

I thought of the packet of love letters and telegrams I had found deep in an old Vuitton trunk in the Mount Kisco barn. They had been sent from my grandfather to my grandmother during the summer of 1930, when they were at the peak of their courtship. My grandfather had been abroad, and the envelopes bore the postmarks of far-off places like the Panama Canal and Brazil. The scribe referred to his sweetheart as Goldilocks, and himself as Big Bear, and the pages were covered with funny little drawings of a bear doing silly things, and missing his Goldilocks, and getting up to no good, and even though it was a little dopey, it was achingly cute. There was also a stapled sheaf of telegrams (the Twitter of yore), sent from a couple of lovelorn weeks aboard the SS *Bremen*. My grandfather, so remote, so parsimonious, declared his adoration for my grandmother with obtuse, pasted-on dispatches like *True Blue Love* and *Phone interruption frightful at sea but connection perfect in forest*. I remember watching my grandparents unfold as people I'd never imagined, as, like a compassionate spy, I read my way through their summer.

❧

That night, as he had done for a week, Edward maintained a solemn vigil, lying on the floor beside our grandfather's bed. He had insisted that the nurses wake him if he fell asleep, because he did not want to miss the exact moment when his grandfather reunited with Eisenhower and Pompidou. (Whereas I am merely morbid, Edward likes to witness the crossing.)

The old man kicked the bucket in the night, and his grandson slumbered on. The nurses sniggered behind their latex gloves as they stepped soundlessly over him, unhooking catheters and monitors, and quietly removing the body. Like grandfather, like son. They were tired of being ordered around by the rich.

Edward was inconsolable.

As we filed out of St. Thomas Church, a light rain had begun to fall. I stood at the top of the steps, looking down on Fifth Avenue. My mother stood beside me, looking like the cat that ate the canary. There was the hearse, a long lineup of dark limousines, and a police motorcade. Nixon came out of the church and scanned the cortege for his vehicle, while a Secret Service man struggled to open a massive golf umbrella.

Seeing me standing there, Nixon smiled and said, "Your grandfather and I had something very important in common."

I smiled back, but didn't say anything.

"Matthew," he said.

"Matthew?"

"Our barber." He sighed fondly. "Now *there* was a great man."

Leaning on the arm of the agent, he limped down the puddled steps, past the mildly interested passersby, to his waiting car.

❧

Edward would be smarter the next time; when our grandmother tottered on the brink, he pretty much moved in with her and waited for her to die. Nobody was going to take this one from him.

Deposition

OKAY, SO MAYBE I didn't know where the ten-thousand-dollar Russian bribe money was hidden in the bomb shelter, but I knew where just about everything else was in Burdenland. Like how many English shooting bags were in the basement cupboards in the country (five), or how many pairs of Sperry tennis shoes were in the dressing rooms of the indoor tennis court (twenty-one—thirteen men's and eight ladies'). I knew that at any given time there were between four and six Indian nickels in the tray on my grandmother's vanity in New York City, and that in the third drawer down in the fifth file cabinet to the left of the door on the second floor of the garage in Maine were twenty-three copperplate-signed checks from Grandpa Twombly to McKim, Mead and White Architects.

From near-infancy I'd been the cataloger of all things inanimate, be they moldering luxury items, office supplies, or creatures newly dead. Snooping gave tangible substance to the lack of structure that surrounded me. I was good at it. The *best*. I thought nobody could out-snoop me. Wrong. I was completely outclassed by my baby brother, because he had discovered the metaphorical key to the locked drawers of the desk formerly belonging to the recently deceased gatekeeper, Ann Rose.

Usually, we bartered, but now, unasked, Edward presented me with what I continue to imagine had been hidden for years in the depths of that rectangular metal vault: a twenty-six-page carbon copy of the statement taken from our grandfather two days after our father's funeral. Half expecting it to self-ignite, I quickly stuffed the thing in my handbag. Then, out of habit, I told Edward something like when he was two he used to eat his own feces for fun. When I got home I glanced at the document, decided I couldn't deal with it, stuck it in a drawer, and consciously forgot about it. It wasn't until a few years after my grandfather's death that I finally read it.

It was one of those days when your family just can't haunt you enough. The phone had rung shortly after nine: "Hey," began a friend of mine, "isn't that your uncle on the front page of the *Observer*?"

"Oh God, what?"

"Yeah, Ordway Burden. Great story."

"I didn't know . . ." I said, and signed off as economically as I could.

It used to be that everyone read *The New York Observer* (I for one liked the pink pages), so the wires were burning up all morning. The sensationalism of Uncle Ordway's escapades inspired me to unearth some more family adventures. Of course I knew exactly where I'd hidden that sheaf of damning, onionskin pages way back when.

Armed with a Coke and a pack of Marlboro Lights, I settled myself on the couch in front of the windows overlooking noisy Prince Street. Pearl lay on the floor beside me, crunching on her soup bone like an industrial log splitter. I started in on the deposition my grandfather had given at the apex of his grief.

March 2nd, 1962

My son, Bill, was a very brilliant boy; graduated valedictorian of his class from Milton, cum laude from Harvard, and has al-

ways been extremely brilliant, yet he had some psychological
problems . . . there was talk of a suicide attempt when he was
fifteen, but the doctors agreed it was merely a childish thing . . .

My grandfather went on to tell how my parents had met in high school and married while they were both at Harvard. He said they'd been happy and interested in each other's pursuits. Following an initial reporting job at the *Blade Tribune* in Riverside, California, my father moved on to *The Washington Post*, where he was a cub on the night police beat, covering homicides, suicides, and car crashes, and was "extremely brilliant." Being a perfectionist, he couldn't take the pressure of deadlines. He had to get every word right. So he quit, and took a job at the Foreign Policy Research Institute, where he studied the effect of modern weapons on international policy. Again, my grandfather described his son's efforts as "enormously brilliant." There must have been a hundred of those adulatory modifiers throughout the deposition. In my head I heard my grandfather articulating them in eulogy, and I felt his anguish at the loss of so much potential, even as I imagined my father's suffocation from the expectation.

The marriage grew troubled after Will and I were born. There was a miscarriage, and my mother started behaving erratically, and became increasingly unpleasant toward her husband. She took to drinking in the morning—cranberry juice with rum. She threw plates. She began to "compulsively sunburn her body" and to seek the physical attention of every man in her path. My father started seeing a psychiatrist, on the pretense of having to deal with his wife's emotional problems over her miscarriage. The psychiatrist decided my mother was far more disturbed than my father. He convinced her to come in for a couple of sessions. During the second one, my mother revealed that she hated her father, she hated her husband, and, as a matter of fact, she hated *all* men, thank you. The psychiatrist concluded that my mother was suffering from an acute castration complex.

My mother then took off for Haiti, and she stayed away for several weeks. It was no secret to my father that his wife was having an affair with an attaché at the American embassy, a man named Charles Thomas, but he believed that she had been tricked into it.

"Oh my God!" I said aloud. Why it was none other than the glorified daddy figure of yesteryear. Thanks to my youth, and my own self-centered bubble, I had completely forgotten about Charles. I put the deposition down and called my mother.

I didn't tell her what I was in the middle of; I just casually said, "Hey, for some reason I got to thinking about that guy you used to date before Pete. What was his name—Frank? No, maybe Chauncey?" (What a lame liar.)

"Charles," said my mother with suspicion. Or maybe it was apprehension. She was in the kitchen and I could hear her walking over to the shelf above the washer and dryer where she kept the gallon bottle of Bacardi.

"Yeah, Charles!"

"What about him?"

"Oh, uh, I was just wondering whatever happened to him. I mean he seemed like such a great guy and everything. Do you ever talk to him?"

Plink! went the ice cubes into the glass.

"You want to know about Charles?" my mother said. "Charles hung himself after your father decided to quit life. That's what happened to *Charles.*"

I didn't know what to say. I felt achingly sorry for her, but mostly because I couldn't imagine having two dead men under my belt.

❧

The following day I gingerly picked up where the testimonial action had left off. When urged by his parents to seek a divorce, my father refused, saying he had seen too many examples of children being destroyed by split homes and he couldn't do it to his son and daughter.

My mother returned on Sunday, February 25. Monday morning, my father telephoned his psychiatrist and told him he was very depressed. The psychiatrist prescribed some "energizing pills," as well as some Seconal, and made an appointment to see my father the next day. My father picked up the prescriptions, and then drove home and went to his desk on the third floor, where he typed out his obituary. This he placed in an envelope he marked "Press." He then handwrote eight other letters, including one to the police, to which he paper-clipped the receipt for a .357 Magnum he had purchased the previous week.

The following day, my father did not keep his appointment with the psychiatrist. He went to work as usual, but left around 1:00 P.M., saying he would be back at 3:00. He drove home. No one was around except Obadiah, the basset hound. My father went upstairs to retrieve the letters and the gun. Then he drove to the DC city morgue, parked in front, and blew his brains out all over the backseat of the family car.

Things did not go according to plan. For one, the obituary that ran in *The New York Times* and *The Washington Post* was not the modest, forthright one he had written. Imagine his disappointment; the reason he had quit his job at the *Post* was that he couldn't stand people messing with his copy—he would drive down there at two in the morning just to make sure the rewrite men didn't change his words. For another, contrary to my father's explicit instructions not to blame his wife, boy did my grandparents ever.

Things got worse: At the funeral parlor my mother displayed no sentiment. At the service, she was equally composed and was even seen smiling at several young men. On the train up to New York for the burial at Woodlawn Cemetery, she asked everyone why her in-laws were treating her so coldly. Following the burial, my grandfather showed my mother the suicide note, in which my father admitted that a major part of his decision to end his life was my mother's affair with Charles Thomas. My grandfather then told her that he had incontrovertible evidence of her affairs with several other men.

"Is that true?" he demanded.

"Yes it is," my mother replied, "but I have been advised to do so by my psychiatrist for my gratification."

"You know that's a lie!"

"Okay, by my gynecologist then."

Here was the part I had the most trouble with, even though I knew it was in the violently predisposed voice of my grandfather:

> *She showed no emotion, did not even say that she was sorry for us at the loss of our son, and gave no indication that she had any sorrow whatever about Bill's death. The three main points that she made in this discussion were: 1) It was very unfortunate that Bill had committed suicide at this particular time because she had a girlfriend from Haiti with her and had been hoping for ten days of pleasant vacation; 2) that it was very thoughtless of Bill to commit suicide without making a will because this meant "that his checks would bounce." Her third point was that it was very thoughtless of Bill to have committed suicide in such an obvious way as shooting himself whereas it would have been easy to drive his car off a bridge or take an overdose of sleeping pills.*

Not until I'd have children of my own would Miss Pou divulge how profoundly my grandparents had despised my mother. At the funeral, they broadcast details of her past and present lovers—the diplomat in Haiti, the beatnik sculptor in Maine, the arms dealer in Washington, who happened to be her husband's best friend. In a circular to the "girls of the office," in a transparent attempt to absolve herself, my grandmother declared her son would never have killed himself had he only received the love and support he needed at home.

Of course, manic depression had *nothing* to do with it.

The man who had delivered the eulogy at the funeral kept referring to my father's deep strain of morbidity and the "chasm between the humor and the deep melancholia that was to make life intolerable for him." Everyone knew about my father's bipolar disorder, even though the medical community had yet to call it that and Prozac was still a twinkle in some future billionaire's eye.

The deposition was a road map backwards. For years I had wondered why, beyond the obvious reasons, my grandparents had been so god-awful to my mother. I put the document down on the sofa and rubbed my eyes. *Nymphomaniac* was now permanently tattooed on the inside of my eyelids. I'd heard about my mother's conduct at the funeral, even when I was young, but I assumed everyone had just read her wrong. She was an undemonstrative woman. I don't remember her ever kissing us goodbye, or touching us even, except for the times when we clung to her back as she walked us around the swimming pool. But she wasn't a killer. She wasn't cruel; she was only mean.

When pressed, my mother liked to rationalize her husband's suicide by saying that he'd been in love with death. She made no bones about the fact that they had grown apart, and would have eventually divorced, and when she was really into the Bacardi, sometimes she would rail on about how sexless he had been. If my mother felt herself at all culpable, she never showed it. She had disassociated herself with a survivalist practicality you see only in the insect world. And if my father's suicide had been intended as the ultimate fuck-you, it was a wasted effort. She was over that one in the time it takes for self-tanner to work.

Nobody dislikes confrontation more than me; I mean unless it's a matter of life and death, why bother—it only gets everyone all riled up. But this really was a matter of death. To my mother's guardedly concealed joy, I called to say I would be coming up for the weekend. It was time to ask her a thing or two before she got condemned to the legendary boiling ocean of excrement.

At my mother's house in Marblehead, after she and the contractor had weaved off to bed, I pulled out the frayed photograph albums from my parents' marriage and lay down on the floor with the dogs to look through them.

The albums tell the story through the transformation of my mother's appearance alone. In the earliest photos she comes across as almost tender; she is very young, and a little plump, and her shoulder-length hair is mouse-colored, and her glasses thick, with clear, scholarly frames. There is a lot of studying going on, and open books are everywhere. There are pictures of a party at my uncle Shirley's house in Beverly Hills, and my mother is dressed up, but still sweetly dumpy and unsophisticated. You can see Fred Astaire in the background, which is probably why she has removed her glasses. Her bare arms press tightly against the satin bodice of her cocktail dress, and she's gripping the stem of a martini glass like it's a lifeline.

There are pages and pages of friends and family, and everyone seems pretty darn happy. My brother gets born, and now there are a zillion pictures of him, and he's adorable, the cutest baby you ever saw, on the potty, under the Christmas tree, sitting on the laps of his doting grandparents, and my mother is looking somewhat confused and still dorky, but you can tell it's okay, and that as parents they're getting the hang of things. There are no pictures of my father because he's the one taking them.

Then I come along, and I am just about the ugliest thing anyone ever pinned a diaper around, but I'm a girl, so they dress me up in frills and start taking a zillion pictures of me and my brother doing cute things together, and my mother's in there, orchestrating things. Her hair is getting blonder, and she's thinner, and starting to wear dresses with wide, brass-buckled, cinched-in belts. Her glasses are gone, traded in for those revolutionary new contact lenses. There are birthday parties, with the candles—three, and then four, and then five of them, being blown out on cakes crowded with so many cowboys and Indians and fairies and ponies that you can't see the icing. There are fewer friends in the photos. Then, within a couple of pages, there are none of them.

Somewhere between the second potty chair and the Christmas in New York where Will gets the four-lane slot car racetrack, the bookish young wife and mother has transformed into a full-fledged man-eater. In snapshots taken by the sea in Maine, she now lazes, legs apart, in a strapless one-piece. Her hair is lemon blond and her sunglasses dark and slanted, like those of a movie star. And she just gets hotter and hotter; one summer and a couple of pages later, she is on the bow of my grandparents' boat, and the one-piece has been replaced by a bikini. Her hair is swept back by the wind, and her deep tan is the stuff Bain de Soleil executives dream of. If a camera can pay grimly wistful homage, my father's Leica was doing just that.

The third photo album contains our one and only family trip to Disneyland, and the focus is decidedly on my mother. There she is—carefree in the twirling teacups, circling the air on Dumbo, and giggling in a hovercraft bumper car as she tries to catch up with my brother and me. She is breathtakingly beautiful in a man's untucked white shirt, black capri pants, and pointy black flats, her hair down and loose. Next to her, Will and I look like prairie children from the Dust Bowl.

And that's it. The remaining soft black pages are empty.

The following afternoon I sat across from my mother at the kitchen table. I was prepared for anything. Kitchens are meant to be the heart of a house, and the beating one at that, but I couldn't help thinking that this one was a reflection of my mother's: the cupboards were a nondescript prefab wood, and the floor was a brick linoleum that could only be described as inventive, but the counters were beautifully fitted, custom maple and cherry butcher-block. The stove was Kenmore green and obsessively clean, and the textured fridge door had diet notes stuck all over it with animal magnets, only now they were intended for my mother's husband instead of her. Superstition about the year she was going to die, along with breast cancer, had enabled her to finally let herself go.

She was poring over a dog-eared, fan-shaped diagram of hand-lettered names: a genealogical map of five generations of Hamiltons. My mother had discovered genealogy, not religion, in her waning years. There were enough ancestral registers and charts—dozens of them, all recorded in tight cursive by her own bored, sickly mother—to keep her busy throughout the several courses of chemotherapy she would endure. The comings and goings of people with names like Sarah and Fanny, and Ephraim and Nathaniel and Phineas, had become the object of her academic curiosity—men who were born in log cabins but went to Harvard, if only to become shoemakers and bricklayers before eventually getting murdered by Indians. (It was something of a family tradition—excellent education, unambitious choice of career, and untimely death.)

❧

Anyway, there we were. I was going over in my head how I was going to get her to come clean about the death of my father, when she beat me to it—only it wasn't exactly the information I'd been after. It was about how my sister had died in the toilet.

The fact that I'd had a sister at all was a revelation to me. All I'd ever wanted was a sister. Someone to haggle over the Balenciagas and the Schlumberger with. Ally, co-conspirator, or worthy opponent, we would have been tighter than ticks. I would have been able to call her, page her, text her, e-mail her—and say, *You get this?* And she would have gotten it.

My sister had been born at seven months, when my mother

thought she was evacuating her bowels, not the contents of her uterus.

"All of a sudden, there was a tiny arm hanging out of me," my mother said, weaving her head at the memory. She reached to gather a few of the ever present Greek coins that lived on the table, and her fingers clicked nervously over them as she spoke of the botched delivery and subsequent trip to the hospital.

"But I don't understand! Why couldn't they save her?" I cried. "They save preemies at four months!"

"They didn't back then, Toots."

"I don't believe it," I said flatly. "Somebody must have screwed up at the hospital or something." I persisted, as if this were happening in real time.

"Nothing could be done. They did all they could. End of story."

I folded up my arms and glared at her. I hated myself for thinking she hadn't tried hard enough, but I just *knew* she hadn't.

"The worst part," my mother said, and then she paused. "The worst part was leaving the maternity ward with empty arms."

I looked at her, sitting there in her hideous caftan, all bloated and cancer-riddled, with her Greek coins and her Diet 7UP and rum—and my heart broke in pieces. My poor, pathetic mother. Once again, I couldn't imagine that kind of sorrow. We sat there on opposite ends of the table, and like the enigma she was, my mother wept as she said that all she had ever wanted was a houseful of babies.

"A house full of babies. Go fucking figure," I repeated in the car driving home.

Epilogue

EDWARD MANAGED TO miss out on his grandmother's demise, as well. Even though he had set up a vigil, Will was the one who was with her when she died at home, and the inebriated chauffeur was the one who got to call everyone.

Edward was beside himself. In the months, and the years that followed, he developed a New Age theory involving a parallel spiritual world to help him make sense of the one in which he had been doled such wildly uneven shares. He became more convinced that our father had come back as him. He even took to calling people up and apologizing for killing himself. He tried to unravel the mysteries of his muddled life with knowledge gleaned from his fledgling faith. And from instructional Web sites like Healpastlives.com . . .

Are You Being Affected by Your Past Lives?
Heal Your Life NOW By Healing Your Past Lives!

When I allowed myself to consider Edward's theology, I found the similarity to my other brother's chosen Eastern path oddly reassuring.

❧

When our mother's breast cancer eventually meandered its way down to her liver (which, aside from the tumors, was surprisingly intact), she summoned Will, Edward, and me to her final Christmas. In Nantucket.

Nantucket? we all marveled. There's got to be a mistake. She must have told the booking agent the wrong island. She meant Nassau. Or Nevis. *Nantucket?* Who the hell would rent a house in the North Atlantic for Christmas? An alcoholic Yankee on chemo, that's who.

My brothers and I agreed to stagger our visits, so that no one would have to suffer unduly. A couple of days before Christmas I drove from Manhattan to the Woods Hole terminal in a whiteout blizzard, and spent the three-hour ferry trip cowering belowdecks in my car as we pitched across the stormy sound. It was after midnight when I rang what I hoped was the right doorbell. (Locating one out of a thousand historically correct clapboard houses is challenging when, out of mortal fear, you've been imbibing the special edition Stolichnaya originally intended to go under the tree.) In a flash, like she'd been waiting there all night, my mother threw open the door. She glared at me under the light of the reproduction gas lamp.

"Wha took you sho long?" she snarled.

"And merry Christmas to you too!" I said. The vodka coerced me into kissing her chemo-orange cheek.

At the end of the dim hallway, I could see her husband. He was seated at a table in a scrimshaw-decorated kitchen, his grizzled head in his carpenter hands. The girth of his waist had enabled the frogs on his belt to stretch back into tadpoles. Edward was sitting quietly beside him, and he gave me a brotherly *Thank the Universe you're here!* look. My mother remained where she was in the entry, searching my face. I thought she was going to embrace me—I mean God knows she should have after the crossing I'd endured to get there—and I dropped my bags in order to receive her, but instead, she spat out, "Wrinkulsh *and* acne at your age?" and marched into the kitchen to refill her drink.

Two dirgelike days later, I crept up the narrow staircase to say good-bye. My mother was asleep with her two Rhodesian ridgebacks curled up like parentheses on either side of her. She looked like her tribesmen had already laid her out for burial; her flat, brutally scarred chest was ablaze with amulets of gold and silver, and ceramic and rock, and bead and bone. Bracelets and bangles lined her dehydrated arms, and a bit of bluish scalp peeped from under her embroidered emerald green skullcap. I didn't wake her; I just stared at her for a long time. I wasn't crying or anything, but I'm sure my face was an obliging flush of red.

The inevitable predawn phone call came in February. No way was Edward going to miss this one; he had stuck by our mother's side (helping himself to her morphine patches) until one night the hospice nurse had cranked up the drip and she'd slept so well that she'd died.

According to my brother, the nurse was in hysterics. It had been her first death.

❧

Out of curiosity, I recently Googled Charles Thomas, the glorified daddy figure of yesteryear. I'd seen his full name in my grandfather's deposition, so it wasn't hard to find him. There wasn't a lot of info; turns out all along he'd been a CIA spook. The last entry I could find on him was a stint posing as a foreign service officer in Lisbon in the late 1970s.

There was no death date on any of the entries.

· ACKNOWLEDGMENTS ·

I would like to thank:

My family for the material, especially Will and Edward, my
   two weird but much adored brothers
Charles Addams
Kim Witherspoon, my agent
Lauren Marino, my editor
Julia Gilroy, who whipped things into shape
Cathy and Stephen Graham for the *world*
Brian Siberell for his good looks and his enthusiasm
Grant Manheim for the title. And everything else.
Jay Presson Allen and Wendy Wasserstein
Readers and supporters: Nancy Palmer, Prudence and Teddy
   Ragsdale, Tracy and Dan Oseran, Patricia Bradbury, Ivan
   Gold, Ann Leary, and Gus Van Sant
Amy Dickinson for her timely counsel
Brianne Mulligan, Julie Schilder
The Lake Oswego Library for free office space, and the staff
   at the LO Peet's for caffeine

❧

And Charlotte and Celeste, my two gifted and beautiful daughters. Here's the definitive answer to your childhood question
about the strange lady with the tinkly ice in her glass.